SECOND CHANCE

FOR YOUR MONEY, YOUR LIFE AND OUR WORLD

BY ROBERT T. KIYOSAKI

SECOND CHANCE

FOR YOUR MONEY, YOUR LIFE AND OUR WORLD

By Robert T. Kiyosaki

PLATA®
PUBLISHING

Published by Plata Publishing, LLC

CASHFLOW, Rich Dad, B-I Triangle, and CASHFLOW Quadrant are registered trademarks of CASHFLOW Technologies, Inc.

are registered trademarks of

CASHFLOW Technologies, Inc.

Plata Publishing, LLC
4330 N. Civic Center Plaza
Suite 100
Scottsdale, AZ 85251
(480) 998-6971

Visit our websites: PlataPublishing.com and RichDad.com
Printed in the United States of America

012015

First Edition: January 2015
ISBN: 978-1-61268-046-0

Best-selling Books
by Robert T. Kiyosaki

Rich Dad Poor Dad
What the Rich Teach Their Kids About Money –
That the Poor and Middle Class Do Not

Rich Dad's CASHFLOW Quadrant
Guide to Financial Freedom

Rich Dad's Guide to Investing
What the Rich Invest in That the Poor and Middle Class Do Not

Rich Dad's Rich Kid Smart Kid
Give Your Child a Financial Head Start

Rich Dad's Retire Young Retire Rich
How to Get Rich and Stay Rich

Rich Dad's Prophecy
Why the Biggest Stock Market Crash in History Is Still Coming…
And How You Can Prepare Yourself and Profit from It!

Rich Dad's Success Stories
Real-Life Success Stories from Real-Life People
Who Followed the Rich Dad Lessons

Rich Dad's Guide to Becoming Rich
Without Cutting Up Your Credit Cards
Turn Bad Debt into Good Debt

Rich Dad's Who Took My Money?
Why Slow Investors Lose and Fast Money Wins!

Rich Dad Poor Dad for Teens
The Secrets About Money – That You Don't Learn In School!

Escape the Rat Race
Learn How Money Works and Become a Rich Kid

Rich Dad's Before You Quit Your Job
Ten Real-Life Lessons Every Entrepreneur Should Know
About Building a Multimillion-Dollar Business

Rich Dad's Increase Your Financial IQ
Get Smarter with Your Money

Robert Kiyosaki's Conspiracy of the Rich
The 8 New Rules of Money

Unfair Advantage
The Power of Financial Education

Why "A" Students Work for "C" Students
Rich Dad's Guide to Financial Education for Parents

Dedication

This book is dedicated to Dr. Richard Buckminster Fuller, 1895-1983.

Dr. Fuller is a man who is almost impossible to describe or put into a category. He is referred to as a futurist, an inventor, a teacher, a philosopher, and an architect. Twice he was admitted to Harvard University and twice he was asked to leave.

He has numerous doctorate degrees, U.S. patents, awards and honors, including the Gold Medal from the American Institute of Architects and the Presidential Medal of Freedom from President Ronald Reagan.

Bucky Fuller is most recognized for his work on the Geodesic Dome, a structure used today all around the world. Disney World's Epcot Center features one of Fuller's domes. He has been called the first futurist, a man who turned predicting the future into a science. Many of his predictions have come true, and many are coming true today.

Most loved for his humanity, Dr. Fuller is often called "The Planet's Friendly Genius" and "Grandfather of the Future." In 1982 John Denver wrote and recorded the song *What One Man Can Do,* a dedication to Dr. Fuller.

Pictured above is Fuller's geodesic dome, the U.S. Pavilion at the 1967 World's Fair—Expo 67—in Montreal, Canada.

This book, *Second Chance*, begins with my trip to Expo 67. I hitchhiked from New York to Montreal to see Fuller's dome... and to see the future.

In Appreciation

A heartfelt thank you to Mike Sullivan, CEO of The Rich Dad Company, and Shane Caniglia, President of The Rich Dad Company, for cleaning up the past and taking Rich Dad into the future.

And for giving The Rich Dad Company its Second Chance.

A special "thank you" to the team at Rich Dad for supporting Mike and Shane through times that tested our souls.

The Rich Dad Team

Kathy Grady	2000	David Leong	2009
Mona Gambetta	2001	Rhonda Hitchcock	2009
Bob Turner	2002	Idalia Fuentes	2010
Christina Ingemansdotter	2004	Darrin Moore	2010
Greg Arthur	2006	Jack Koch	2011
Mike Allen	2007	Zeke Contreras	2011
Brett Bottesch	2008	David Adams	2012
Ryan Nalepinski	2008	Derek Harju	2012
Mike Sullivan	2009	Matthew Stein	2012
Shane Caniglia	2009	Tony Femino	2012
Robert Boorman	2009	Melissa Marler	2012
Robb LeCount	2009	Josh Nesa	2014
Brad Kendall	2009	Matt Quirk	2014

Shane Caniglia, President   Mike Sullivan, CEO

In Appreciation

 Special thanks to Mona Gambetta. Without Mona, this book and most Rich Dad books would not exist. Mona is like the Eveready Energizer Bunny, consistently going far beyond the call of duty, 24/7. If Rich Dad was a military organization, Mona would be awarded the Silver Star for valor and courage under fire.

I know Mona joins me in acknowledging and thanking the Plata Publishing team as well as everyone at The Rich Dad Company. Each of them, in some way, has contributed to and supported this book project. Special thanks to Rhonda Hitchcock, Steve King, Greg Arthur, Dave Leong, Jake Johnson, Kellie Coppola, Garrett Sutton, and Darrin Moore.

To my sweetheart Kim, for being a rich woman in love, brains, and beauty… and for being the quiet power at the heart of The Rich Dad Company.

And of course, to the millions of people like you, from all over the world, who read the Rich Dad books and play and teach our games. Thank you for being the engine of Rich Dad and for being a part of our global mission:

To Elevate the Financial Well-being of Humanity

In Appreciation

Thank you to the Rich Dad Advisors for sharing their uncommon wisdom.

Blair Singer
Rich Dad Advisor
since 1981 on

Sales and
Team Building

Ken McElroy
Rich Dad Advisor
since 1999 on

Real Estate, Debt,
and Raising Capital

Garrett Sutton, Esq.
Rich Dad Advisor
since 2001 on

Asset Protection and
Business Plans

Darren Weeks
Rich Dad Advisor
since 2001 on

Entrepreneurship
and Education

Tom Wheelwright, CPA
Rich Dad Advisor
since 2006 on

Tax and Wealth
Strategies

Andy Tanner
Rich Dad Advisor
since 2006 on

Paper Assets

Josh and Lisa Lannon
Rich Dad Advisors
since 2008 on

Social Entrepreneurship and
Behavioral Changes

Author's Notes

Although this book references government and politics,
it does not have a political agenda. The author is not a Republican
or a Democrat. If anything, he is an Independent.

This book mentions god and spirit. This is not a religious book.
It has no religious agenda. The author believes in the freedom
of religion, the freedom to believe—or not believe—in god.

*"We are called to be architects of the future,
not its victims."*

– R. Buckminster Fuller

CONTENTS

CONTENTS

INTRODUCTION

Once Upon a Time...
America was the richest creditor nation in the world.

Once Upon a Time...
The U.S. dollar was backed by gold.

Once Upon a Time...
Printing money was a crime known as *counterfeiting*.

Once Upon a Time...
A person went to school, got a job, retired young, and lived happily ever after.

Once Upon a Time...
All you had to do was buy a house, and when your house went up in value you were rich.

Once Upon a Time...
All you had to do was invest in the stock market, and when the stock market went up you were rich.

Once Upon a Time...
A college degree meant higher pay.

Once Upon a Time...
Age was an asset.

Once Upon a Time...
A retired person could count on Social Security and Medicare to take care of them.

Unfortunately, **Once Upon a Time is *over***. The fairy tale has ended. The world has changed and continues to change.

Q: *So what does a person do now?*

A: That's what this book is about. This book is about a second chance for you, your money, and your life.

This book has three parts: the Past, the Present, and the Future.

The Past... examines *the real causes* of the financial crisis we're facing.

The Present... analyzes where *you* are today.

The Future... explores your second chance for your money and your life and how you can use the opportunities that are found in crisis and adversity to create the life you want.

The most important word today is crisis. Remember that there are two parts, two sides, to the word crisis: *danger* and *opportunity*.

Your second chance requires that you avoid the *dangers* that lie ahead and be prepared for the *opportunities* that exist in a *growing, global financial crisis.*

Part One
The Past

Old School

Go to school, get a job, work hard, save money, buy a house, get out of debt, and invest for the long term in the stock market.

Part One: The Past

INTRODUCTION

I was in a Starbucks the other day and ran into a friend I had not seen in years. Although happy to see him, I was surprised to find him working behind the counter.

"How long have you worked here?" I asked.

"About five months," he replied as he took my order.

"What happened?" I asked.

"Well, after the market crashed in 2007, I lost my job. I found another one, but that job soon disappeared, too. Finally, after burning through our retirement and savings, we lost our house. We just couldn't hang on." He continued: "Don't worry. We've been working. We're not unemployed. We both have jobs, but we're not making much money. So I work here, at Starbucks, to make a few bucks. Get it, I work for *bucks* at Starbucks?" He said, laughing out loud.

Stepping aside so the customers behind me could place their orders, I asked, "So what are you doing for your future?"

"I'm back in school. I'm getting another Masters degree. It's kind of fun being in school again. I even take a few classes with my son. He's earning his first Masters degree."

"Paid for with student loans?" I asked.

"Yeah. What else can we do? I know they're terrible loans. I know I'll be working for the rest of my life, just to pay off *my* loan. My son has more time to pay off his. But we all need more education if we want high-paying jobs. We have to make money. We need to earn a living. So we're in school."

I paid for my coffee and was handed a steaming cup. When I offered him a tip, he refused… and I know why he refused. So I wished him luck, and walked out the door.

Part One of this book is about the past. More specifically, how we got into this global financial crisis.

As George Orwell wrote in his book 1984,

"In a time of universal deceit, telling the truth is a revolutionary act."

Chapter One

WHY THE RICH DON'T WORK FOR MONEY

"They're playing games with money...
Our wealth is stolen via the money we work for."
— R. Buckminster Fuller

Rich Dad Poor Dad was self-published in 1997. It had to be a self-published book because every major publisher we pitched it to turned it down. A few publishers commented, "You don't know what you are talking about."

Some of the points they objected to were my rich dad's statements such as:

1. Your house is not an asset.

2. Savers are losers.

3. The rich don't work for money.

Ten years later, in 2007, the subprime mortgage crisis hit and millions of homeowners found out—first hand—that their house is not an asset.

In 2008, the U.S. government and Federal Reserve Bank began printing trillions of dollars, causing millions of savers to be losers via the loss of purchasing power due to inflation, higher taxes, and low interest rates on their savings.

Rich Dad's Lesson One in *Rich Dad Poor Dad* is The Rich Don't Work for Money... and it was the least criticized of rich dad's three teachings on money. In this chapter, you will learn why this comment is the most important of my rich dad's lessons, and why it is important to understand before you consider your opportunities for a second chance, a fresh start for both your money and your life.

What You Need to Know About Money

The subject of money can be complicated and intimidating. But if you start with the basics and use them as building blocks you can gain the knowledge you need to understand money and investing and how to make your money work for you.

The most basic thing you need to know about money is that it is a subject that you *can* become smarter about, a subject that can give you the confidence to make informed and educated decisions.

Q: *Who needs a second chance?*

A: We all do.

Q: *Why?*

A: Because money—as we know it—has changed and continues to change.

Q: *Why is that important?*

A: Because the poor will become poorer, the middle class will shrink, and the rich will get richer.

Q: *I think we all know that. What is different about the rich getting richer and everyone else becoming poorer?*

A: Many people who are rich today will be among the new poor.

Q: *Why will the rich become the new poor?*

A: There are many reasons. One reason is because many rich people measure their wealth in money.

Q: *What's wrong with that?*

A: The fact that money is no longer money.

Q: *If money is no longer money, then what is money?*

A: Knowledge is the new money.

Q: *So if money is knowledge, you're saying that many who are poor and middle class today, have the opportunity to become the new rich of tomorrow?*

A: Exactly. In the past, the rich were those who controlled land and resources such as oil, weapons, or giant corporations. Today things are different. Today we live in the Information Age—and information is abundant and often free.

Q: *So why isn't everyone rich?*

A: It takes education to process information into knowledge. Without financial education, people cannot process information into personal wealth.

Q: *But America spends billions on education. Why are there more poor people than rich people?*

A: Hundreds of billions of dollars *are* spent on education, but almost nothing is spent on *financial* education.

Q: *Why isn't financial education taught in schools?*

A: I have been asking that question for years, ever since I was nine years old.

Q: *And what did you find out?*

A: I learned that knowledge is power. If you want to control people's lives, limit their knowledge. That is why, throughout history, despots have burned books and exiled (and even killed) those with knowledge who threatened their power. Before the Civil War in America, it was against the law in many states to teach slaves to read and write. Knowledge is the most powerful force on earth. That is why the control of knowledge is essential to the control of power.

The formula is:

Information x Education = Knowledge

Knowledge is power—and lack of knowledge is weakness.

My poor dad was a highly educated man with a PhD, but he had almost no financial education. He had authority within the school system, but little power in the real world.

My rich dad never finished school, but he was highly educated in the world of money. Although less formally educated than my poor dad, he had more power in the real world than my poor dad.

Q: *So those in power maintain control of that power through the school system... through what's taught—and what isn't taught. That's why there is no financial education in schools?*

A: I believe that's true. Today financial knowledge is more powerful than a gun or the whips and shackles of slavery. The lack of financial education enslaves billions of people in all parts of the world.

Q: *What has replaced the whips and shackles and guns?*

A: The monetary system.

Q: *The monetary system? Our money? How does the monetary system control people?*

A: The money system is designed to keep people poor, not to make them rich. The monetary system is designed to keep people working hard for money. Money enslaves those who are uneducated financially. Those who are financially uneducated become slaves to a paycheck.

And our wealth is stolen through money, through the very thing most people work for all their lives. That is why the people who work the hardest for money, often called the "working poor," continue to grow poorer, not richer, no matter how hard they work.

Q: *How is our wealth stolen via our money?*

A: There are many ways. You may already know some of them. They are:

1. **Taxes**
   The value of your labor is stolen via taxes.

2. **Inflation**
   Prices rise when governments print money. As prices rise, people work harder, only to pay more in taxes and inflation.

3. **Savings**
   The banks steal savers' wealth via a banking process known as the fractional reserve system. Let's use a fractional reserve of 10, as an example. A saver puts $1 into his or her savings account. The bank is allowed to lend $10, against that $1, to borrowers. This is another form of "printing money" which is not only inflationary but reduces the purchasing power of a saver's money. This is one of a number of reasons why rich dad often said, "Savers are losers."

Later in this book I will explain other ways in which your money is stolen from you. As I've said: The monetary system was designed to make people poorer, not richer.

Q: *Can you prove that?*

A: I will show you a graph. As the saying goes, 'A picture is worth a thousand words.' The graph is not proof, but it does tell a story about the growth of people needing government assistance.

The War on Poverty

In 1964, President Lyndon Johnson declared a war on poverty. Many believe we won that war. Others do not. The chart below shows the numbers of people who use "food stamps," today called SNAP: Supplemental Nutrition Assistance Program. Although many believe we won the war on poverty, the increasing reliance on food stamps tells a different story.

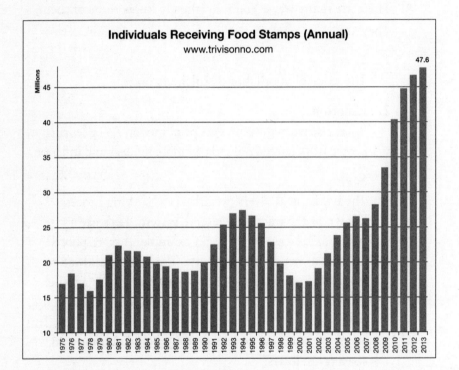

The chart of individuals receiving food stamps shows that, in 1975, approximately 17 million people received food stamps. By 2013, the number had increased to approximately 47 million people and continues to increase.

Q: *If the number of poor people is increasing, where are they coming from?*

A: The middle class. Many of today's poor were doing well as middle-class Americans a few years ago.

The War on the Middle Class

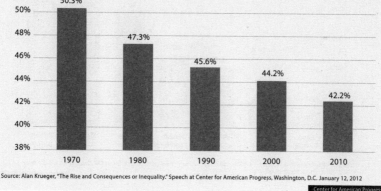

Fewer households are earning middle-class incomes

Not only have middle-class incomes stagnated, but the share of households that are earning middle-class income has also been in decline since the 1970s. The share of American households earning between 50 and 150 percent of the median income was 42.2 percent in 2010, down from 50.3 percent in 1970.

Percent of households with annual incomes within 50 percent of the median

Year	Percent
1970	50.3%
1980	47.3%
1990	45.6%
2000	44.2%
2010	42.2%

Source: Alan Krueger, "The Rise and Consequences or Inequality." Speech at Center for American Progress, Washington, D.C. January 12, 2012

Center for American Progress

The chart above shows what's happening to the middle class.

A few years ago, TV journalist Lou Dobbs wrote a book on this middle class decline, *The War on the Middle Class: How the Government, Big Business, and Special Interest Groups Are Waging War on the American Dream and How to Fight Back.* His point: If the middle class is in decline, the United States is in decline, since the middle class is the engine of the U.S. economy.

During the 2012 Presidential campaign, both candidates Barack Obama and Mitt Romney promised to save the middle class. An inquiring mind might ask, "Why does the middle class need saving?" As most of us know, if the government is promising to save you, you have already lost.

Inflation Steals Wealth

The monetary system steals our wealth through inflation. The chart below explains why the poor and middle class are struggling, regardless of how hard they work.

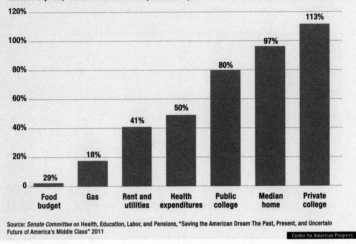

The cost of important middle-class goods and services have grown rapidly

While incomes for the middle-class have stagnated, the cost of important middle-class goods and services have increased significantly. If these purchases were luxuries, then the large price increase wouldn't be much of a concern. But gas, health care, a college education, and home ownership are not luxuries. They are all key features of joining or being in the middle-class, and the cost of all increased significantly faster than inflation.

Growth in price, net of overall inflation (1970- 2009)

Source: *Senate Committee* on Health, Education, Labor, and Pensions, "Saving the American Dream The Past, Present, and Uncertain Future of America's Middle Class" 2011

Center for American Progress

Q: *How does the monetary system cause inflation?*

A: The primary cause of inflation is the printing of money. When money is printed—by banks or governments—two things happen: inflation kicks in and taxes goes up. When prices and taxes go up, people struggle financially.

Q: *How do people survive when prices go up?*

A: When prices go up, people use their credit cards to survive. Many are forced to cut expenses… like healthier food or dental care. Many become slaves to debt. And many more become little more than indentured servants, or slaves to their paychecks.

Debt Slaves

As middle-class income declined, and taxes and prices went up, many turned to their credit cards to survive, becoming slaves to debt. The chart below tells that story.

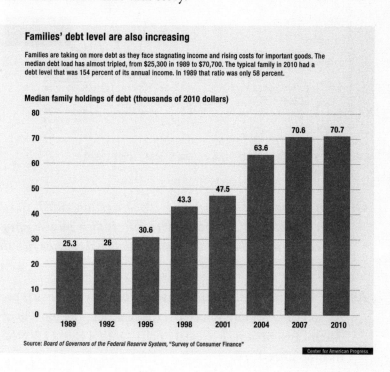

Families' debt level are also increasing

Families are taking on more debt as they face stagnating income and rising costs for important goods. The median debt load has almost tripled, from $25,300 in 1989 to $70,700. The typical family in 2010 had a debt level that was 154 percent of its annual income. In 1989 that ratio was only 58 percent.

Median family holdings of debt (thousands of 2010 dollars)

1989	1992	1995	1998	2001	2004	2007	2010
25.3	26	30.6	43.3	47.5	63.6	70.6	70.7

Source: *Board of Governors of the Federal Reserve System, "Survey of Consumer Finance"*

Center for American Progress

Today, taxes, debt, and inflation are the iron shackles that bind modern-day slaves.

Two Types of Rich

Q: *How are the rich getting richer, if the poor and middle class are growing poorer?*

A: There are two types of rich people. One type of rich is the truly rich. They are getting richer. The other type of rich is getting poorer. The chart on the next page tells that story.

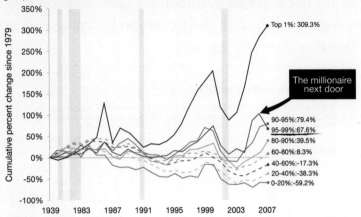

Figure 2U Cumulative change in real annual household capital income, by income group, 1979-2007

Q: *I can see that the rich, the upper 1%, are getting richer. But what is happening to the 90-95%? Why is their income going down? Are those the rich that you're talking about, the rich that are growing poorer?*

A: Yes. This chart tells a tale of two different types of rich people. As you can see from the chart, the real rich, the top 1% of all Americans, became extremely rich—with a gain of 309% in income since 1979.

Yet, the top 95-99% are losing ground. Their income is not growing.

Q: *Is this why you said earlier about some of the rich becoming the new poor?*

A: Yes. Notice the chart we just looked at only takes us to 2007. That was the year the Great Recession began. After 2007, many millionaires were wiped out in the subprime mortgage fiasco and the stock market crash.

Q: *So this chart would look worse today?*

A: Yes. The upper 1% of Americans has gotten richer. Many of the others, the other type of rich I've described, are now poorer. Many slid from rich to poor in less than a year. Many were wiped out when they lost their high-paying jobs, their homes, and their wealth as stock portfolios collapsed.

Of the rich who survived the crash and remain in the upper 20%, many (thanks to inflation) are becoming poorer. Some have already slid into the middle class.

Q: *Tell me again... what's the difference between the two types of rich?*

A: One type of rich is people with high-paying jobs, such as corporate executives, professional people such as doctors and lawyers, athletes, and movie stars. They are high-income rich.

The other type of rich is the person who does not need a job to be rich. Most of these people are asset-rich.

The Millionaire Next Door

In 1996, *The Millionaire Next Door* was published. It was a great book for its time. Written by Thomas J. Stanley and William D. Danko, the book described how ordinary, middle-class citizens had become millionaires. They did it without being Donald Trump, Steve Jobs, or Gordon Gekko from the movie *Wall Street*. They were not millionaire movie stars, rock stars, or professional athletes. They had become middle-class millionaires by having a good education, living in a modest home in an upscale neighborhood, driving sensible cars, saving money, and investing steadily in the stock market.

Many were "net-worth millionaires," people who had become rich as a result of the rising value on their homes and retirement portfolios. They had become middle-class millionaires through inflation, by being part of the rising U.S. economy. They were living proof of the American Dream.

The September 11, 2001 terrorist attacks signaled the start of the new millennium and end of the American Dream.

The chart below shows that, since 9/11, life for the millionaire-next-door has not been easy.

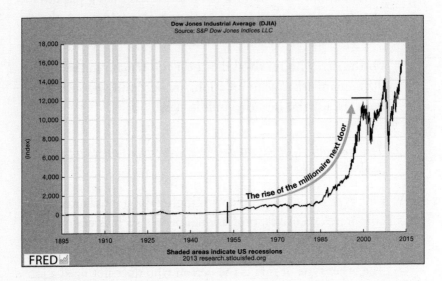

In 2000, the NASDAQ or dot-com crash triggered a series of booms and busts, shaking many millionaires-next-door out of the millionaire category.

The Foreclosure Next Door

In 2007, when the subprime-mortgage bubble burst, many millionaires-next-door became the foreclosure-next-door.

Figure 4: U.S. Homes Foreclosed
June 2012

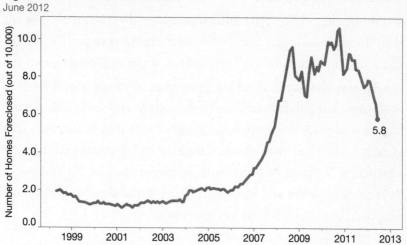

Prior to 2007, housing prices had been rising steadily for years. As home prices rose, millions of homeowners began taking out "home-equity loans," which many used to pay off credit card debt or go on vacation. Using their homes as ATMs... they learned the hard way—when they were upside down—that their "house is not an asset."

When housing prices crashed, credit card use went down. When homeowners stopped using their credit cards, the economy slowed because the economy depends upon consumer spending and use of their credit cards. When consumers slowed their spending, retailers began to suffer, and when retailers suffer the world economy suffers.

Today, in 2014, there are approximately 115 million households in the United States. Of those 115 million households, 43 million are renters and 25 million are households or families who own their homes free and clear. Of the approximately 50 million households with mortgages, it's estimated that over 24 million are "underwater," which means they owe more on their home than their home is worth.

As long as homeowners feel poor, the economy will suffer.

The Lost Generation

When the middle-class millionaires-next-door lost their jobs and their homes, and began using retirement accounts to pay the bills, there was another casualty: The children of the millionaire-next-door.

All over the world, there is a generation of young people known as the new lost generation. They're the college and trade school and high school grads who cannot find jobs or jobs that utilize their level of education. More than income, they are losing crucial real-life work experience. Without real-life work experience in their 20s and 30s, their earning power and income in later years will suffer, which is why they're often called the lost generation.

Young, Educated, and in Debt

Many of these highly educated people graduate saddled with student-loan debt, quite possibly the worst of all possible debt. Unlike a car loan, home loan, or business loan, student loan debt is rarely forgiven. A student cannot declare bankruptcy and expect to be released from the loan. Student loan debt is an albatross around the neck of a student for life, accruing interest for life. Many will have problems buying a car, home, or investing for their future until their student loan debt is paid off. The current overhaul of the student loan programs may address these issues and challenges.

Many of these young people are boomerang kids, kids who leave home, only to return to live with mom and dad. This makes many moms and dads, the sandwich generation, people who are now caring for their kids *and* their parents, often with three generations living under one roof.

Other countries offer free higher education. In America, we create debt slaves out of our students.

Q: *Is this why you say everyone needs a second chance? Because some of the rich are becoming poor, the middle class is shrinking, poverty is increasing, and our students are highly educated, underemployed, and deep in debt?*

A: Yes. The world is changing and money is changing. Those who are operating in the past, with the old-world rules of money, are being wiped out in the present.

We live in the Information Age. There is an abundance of information, and much of it's free. But without financial education, a person cannot convert that information into knowledge.

Q: *And if knowledge is power, then millions are highly educated but without much power. Is that why millions of people need a second chance… to get their power back?*

A: Yes.

Q: The Millionaire Next Door *was published in 1996.* Rich Dad Poor Dad *was published in 1997. What was the difference between the two books?*

A: *The Millionaire Next Door* was about *net-worth millionaires.* Rich Dad Poor Dad was about *cash-flow millionaires.*

Q: *There's a difference?*

A: A very big differences. Many net worth millionaires were counting their *liabilities,* such as their home and their car, as *assets.* When the real estate and stock markets crashed, many *net-worth millionaires* were wiped out as the value of their liabilities crashed.

Many *cash-flow millionaires,* millionaires who receive their income from real assets, got richer. They got richer buying the liabilities of the net-worth millionaires at bargain-basement prices.

Q: *So without financial education, millions do not understand the difference between the different types of rich people?*

A: That is correct. There are many different ways a person can achieve great wealth. For example, a person can inherit wealth or marry into wealth. As Warren Buffett often says, "There are many ways of getting into financial heaven."

Since my poor dad was poor, a man without assets, I had no wealth to inherit. Nor did I want to marry for money. At an early age, I decided I would gain my wealth my rich dad's way—via financial education and acquiring assets.

Q: *So... without financial education, most people don't know the difference between assets and liabilities. So their wealth is stolen via a lack of financial education. Is that what you're saying?*

A: Yes. If a person knew the simple definitions of basic financial words, their wealth would increase. The good news is that words are free.

Past, Present, and Future

Q: *And that is why millions of educated, hard-working people are losing their wealth? They have become educated slaves to money, much like the uneducated slaves before the Civil War. Is that what you are saying?*

A: Yes. Education—or the lack of education—is one of the keys on the key ring of those in power.

Q: *What is happening to those in power?*

A: The Information Age is causing those in power to lose power. That's why your personal financial education is more important today than at any other time in history. Desperate people in power are doing desperate things to hold on to their illusion of power.

Q: *What do you see in the future?*

A: Once again, pictures are more powerful than words. I will show you a few pictures, add a few words, and let you decide what the future holds.

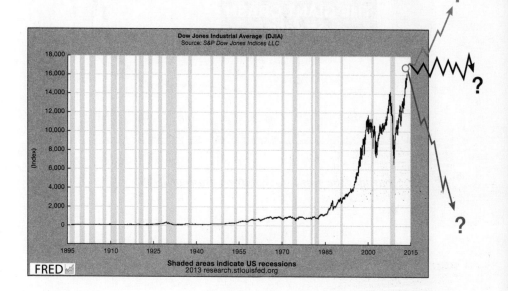

On this one chart, you are looking at the past, present, and future of the Dow Jones Industrial Average. It is not a measure of the whole economy, but it *is* a snapshot of what has been going on in one part of a complex economy.

Q: *So there are three choices for the future: up, down, or sideways?*

A: Yes. The choices are always the same.

Q: *What do you see for the future?*

A: The best way to see the future is to look at the past. In the chart we just looked at you can see the past and an event known as the Great Depression, an event marked by the stock-market crash of 1929.

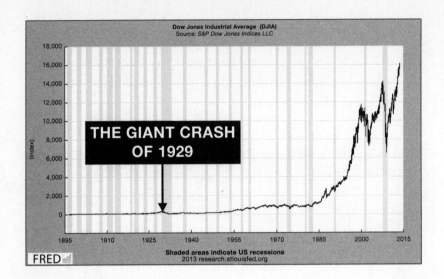

Q: *That was the giant stock market crash of 1929?*

A: Yes.

Q: *Could a next crash be bigger?*

A: Yes.

Q: *What would happen if the next crash were bigger?*

A: Look at the Great Depression.

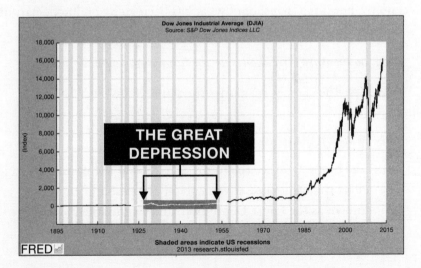

The Great Depression, when measured against the Dow, lasted 25 years, from 1929 to 1954. In 1929, the Dow hit an all-time high of 381. It took 25 years for it to reach 381 again. This is an alternative point of view, as there are those who believe it ended in 1939.

Q: *Could we be entering a New Depression?*

A: Yes. Many people already are in their own New Depression. That's why food stamp use is up, the middle class is shrinking, students who are loaded with student-loan debt can't find jobs, and many of yesterday's millionaires-next-door are broke. On top of this we have the first of approximately 76 million American baby boomers retiring. Many, if not most, of these aging baby boomers don't have enough money to retire. Advances in healthcare and medicine may mean these baby boomers will live longer, while the cost of healthcare is likely to continue increasing, as is the cost of food, fuel, and housing.

So-So Security

Take a look at the chart below on the condition of the United States Social Security Fund.

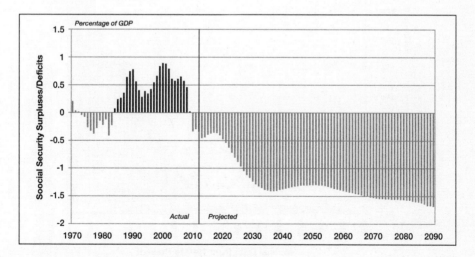

Q: *What does this chart mean?*

A: It means different things to different people. If you are young, it means you'd better not count on the government to take care of you. If you are a baby boomer, it means the money you paid into the Social Security fund is gone. If you are of the World War II generation, your timing was good.

Another interesting chart is this one on the National Debt. It tells another story.

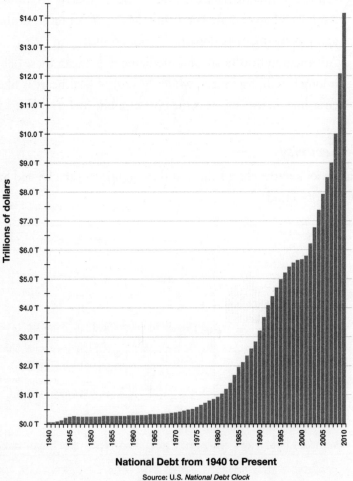

National Debt from 1940 to Present

Source: U.S. *National Debt Clock*
www.brillig.com/debt_clock/

Q: *What story does this chart tell?*

A: Again, it depends upon who you ask. For most people, and the average American, it means nothing. Without financial education, most Americans are clueless. This chart has very little meaning to them.

Today the national debt tops $17 trillion. To some people it means the end is near. And to a few, it points to the opportunity of a lifetime.

Q: *What does it mean to you?*

A: While I empathize with the first two groups, I am in the third group. Although I'm a bit fearful and very concerned for those who will be hurt, I view the future with excitement, excited to be a witness to the biggest power shift and transfer of wealth in the history of the world. It is the dawn of a new age. If the change is managed well, many of humanity's shackles will be thrown off and we will enter an age of sustainable prosperity for all. If things do not go well, and those in power today win using violence to retain control of their power, we may enter a New Dark Age.

Q: *What will make the difference?*

A: Many things will play a role... such as technology and the rise of China as a world power. Yet the big shift must come in education, not only in what we teach and but how we teach.

Q: *What do you think the chances are? Do you think education will change?*

A: No. Not in the near future. A case could be made to support the position that those who control the monetary system also control the educational system. That is why I became an educational entrepreneur back in 1984. That is why I write my books and create financial education games outside the school system. Today I am a hybrid, an entrepreneur like my rich dad and an educator like my poor dad.

As you may know, I believe in personal responsibility. I believe in changing the things we have the ability to change and control. Each of us has the power to change ourselves. And the easiest—and often most powerful—change we can make is through education.

Q: *What do you see in the future?*

A: To see the future you must study the past. As the saying goes, "Those who do not learn from the past are condemned to repeat it."

In the past, there were two different types of Depressions:

1. The American Depression (1929 to 1954)

2. The German Hyper-Inflation (1918 to 1924)

Q: *What was the difference?*

A: In very simple terms, Americans did not print money and the Germans printed money.

Pictured on the next page is what happened when Germany began printing money.

A millionaire in 1923 was broke five years later.

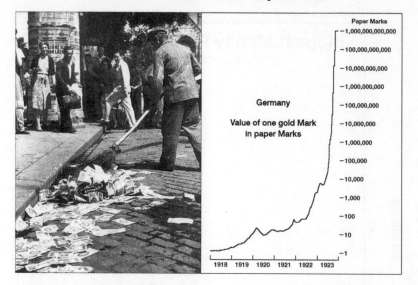

The picture above shows what happens when a central bank and a government print money to pay their bills.

In 1918, a German citizen could be a "millionaire" by having millions of German Reischmarks in savings. In less than five years, that same German millionaire was poor.

Q: *Is the same thing happening in the United States today?*

A: Yes.

The following is a chart on QE, Quantitative Easing.

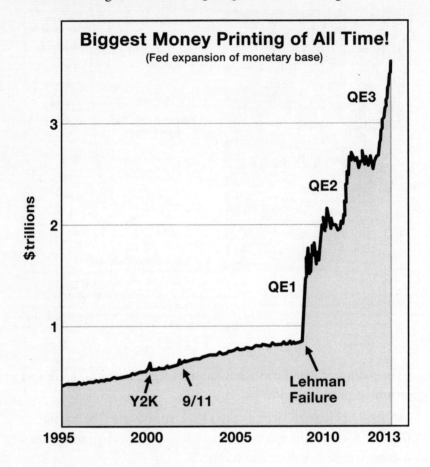

Biggest Money Printing of All Time!
(Fed expansion of monetary base)

Q: *What does this mean?*

A: It means the United States is following the German model from the last Depression. America is attempting to "print" its way out of financial crisis.

Q: *What does this mean to me?*

A: It means exactly what I stated earlier in this chapter. It means your wealth is being stolen via the money you work so hard for. As I said, the monetary system was not designed to make you rich. Money was designed as a means to steal your wealth.

Look at the chart below. It shows what has happened to the purchasing power of your money.

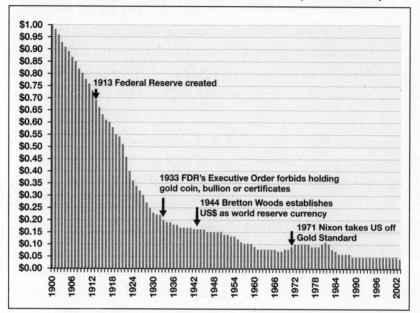

Purchasing Power of the US Dollar (1900-2003)

© 2003 Mary Puplava, Financial Sensa. Data Source http://eh.net/hmitppowerusd/

It has taken about 100 years for the dollar to lose 95% of its purchasing power. I doubt it will take another 100 years to lose the last 5%.

Q: *Are you saying the dollar will go to zero?*

A: If the United States keeps printing money, it might.

Q: *But it can't happen in America, can it?*

A: It has happened a number of times.

Q: *When?*

A: During the Revolutionary War, President George Washington and the Congress of the United States began printing a currency known as the Continental to pay for the war. The British helped destroy the Continental by printing bogus Continentals. Soon the Continental was worth less than the paper it was printed on. During the Revolutionary War, "Not worth a Continental" was the slogan of the war.

The same thing happened to the Confederate dollar. The Confederacy printed money to pay its bills and buy weapons. In many ways, the Civil War was lost because of "bad money."

The U.S. government printed the "greenback" to pay for the Civil War. If the North had lost, the "greenback" would have followed the Confederate dollar into the trash can.

Today, if the U.S. government keeps printing today's "greenbacks," they, too, may be as worthless as the Continental and Confederate dollars.

Q: *What happens if the dollar goes to zero?*

A: It means savers will be the biggest losers and those who work for money will have lost the battle. Their wealth will be gone. I always remind myself that a German person could be a millionaire in 1918 and wiped out by 1923.

And that's why Lesson One in *Rich Dad Poor Dad* is The Rich Don't Work for Money.

Q: *If the rich don't work for money, what do the rich work for?*

A: That is what this book—and most of my books and games— are. Many people need a second chance to rethink about what they work for.

Q: *What do I need to learn?*

A: We will start with the past.

Q: *Why the past?*

A: Because it's from the past that we can see the future. From the past, you will learn how the rich and powerful steal our wealth via our money.

   In the following chapters, you will learn how the rich and powerful have ripped us off via a Cash Heist. If you understand how the Cash Heist works, you will have a better chance to make smarter choices in the *present* for a more prosperous and secure *future.*

Q: *Will everyone have a prosperous and secure future?*

A: No, unfortunately. I'm afraid not.

Q: *Why?*

A: Because most people are still in the past. If they are stuck in the past, they will not understand Rich Dad's Lesson One... The Rich Don't Work for Money.

   Today, most people are too busy working for money, working hard to pay bills and save enough for the future. They will not understand Lesson One unless they are willing to take the time to first understand the past.

   A second chance will do little good for people stuck in the past. As the saying goes, *"The definition of insanity is doing the same thing over and over and expecting different results."* When it comes to money, many people are insane.

   Since we must start with the past to see the future, are you ready to move into the past? If your answer was "Yes" please read on.

Q: *One last question: If money was designed to make people poor, to steal their wealth, then whom does money make rich?*

A: The rich... the rich who do not work for money... the rich who control the game of money.

Q: *How long has the game been going on?*

A: The game of money has been going on for as long as humans have walked the earth. Humans have always wanted to enslave others or take what others have. It's not a new game. The rich have been playing the game for a very long time.

If it is your turn to learn the game of money, the game the rich play, then this is your second chance.

Chapter Two

THE MAN WHO COULD SEE THE FUTURE

"Most of my advances were by mistake.
You uncover what is when you get rid of what isn't."
— R. Buckminster Fuller

In the summer of 1967, a classmate and I hitchhiked from New York City to Montreal, Canada. At the time, Andy Andreasen and I were both 20-year-old students attending the U.S. Merchant Marine Academy at Kings Point, New York. We were hitchhiking to Montreal to see the future.

Montreal was the site for Expo 67, the World's Fair dedicated to the future. The centerpiece of the World's Fair was the U.S. pavilion, a massive geodesic dome that could be seen for miles. The creator of the dome was Dr. R. Buckminster Fuller, considered to be one of the greatest geniuses of our time.

Dr. Fuller had a reputation as a futurist and was often called "Grandfather of the Future." It seemed appropriate that the U.S. government had chosen Dr. Fuller's dome, a structure that *represented* the future, to be the U.S. Pavilion.

Dr. Fuller, or "Bucky" as many called him, was an enigma; he was someone who could not be defined. Harvard University claims him as one of their more prominent alums, yet Bucky did not graduate from Harvard. Although Fuller never graduated from college, he was awarded 47 honorary degrees over his lifetime.

The AIA, the American Institute of Architects, consider him to be one of the world's leading architects. Bucky was not an architect by training, yet his buildings are found all over the world. In the lobby of the AIA headquarters, a bust of Fuller is prominently displayed.

He is considered one of the most accomplished Americans in history, having more than 2,000 patents after his name.

Fuller authored many books ranging from science and philosophy to poetry. President Ronald Reagan awarded Bucky the Presidential Freedom Medal in 1982, and he was once considered for the Nobel Prize.

Although extremely accomplished, Bucky often referred to himself as a "just a little guy."

Poor Dad and Bucky

It was my father, the person I refer to as my "poor dad," who first introduced me to Dr. Fuller. In the late 1950s, while I was still in elementary school, my dad and I would sit for hours building

Bucky's models out of glue and sticks. We created the tetrahedrons, octahedrons, and icosahedrons that Fuller said were "the building blocks of the Universe." My poor dad and Bucky had a lot in common. Both were extremely bright men who thrived in the world of academics, especially math, science, and design. Both men were committed to a better world, a world that worked for everyone. Both men dedicated their lives to serving humanity and world peace.

In 1964, when Dr. Fuller made the cover of *Time* magazine, my dad was ecstatic.

Standing in the Future

In 1967, Andy and I, both Bucky devotees, could not wait to visit the U.S. Pavilion and stand inside Fuller's massive dome. The feeling inside the dome was magical, a surreal environment of peace and possibilities. I never dreamed that one day I would actually study with the "Grandfather of the Future."

In 1981, I was invited to spend a week studying with Dr. Fuller at a lodge outside of Lake Tahoe, California. The title of the conference was "The Future of Business." It was a week that forever changed the direction of my life.

I wish I could say I attended the lecture series to learn more about world peace, math, science, design, generalized principles, or philosophy. I can't. My primary reason for attending the conference was to learn how Fuller could predict the future. I was motivated by pure greed, not world peace. I wanted to learn how to predict the future so I could use that knowledge to make more money.

On the last day of the event something happened to me. I wish I could explain it, but my limited vocabulary makes it hard for me to describe the experience.

I was standing behind the video camera and tripod, working as a volunteer and taping the entire event. I volunteered to stand behind the camera because I was falling asleep as a participant in the audience. Fuller was not an especially dynamic speaker. In fact, I would say he was boring—he mumbled and used words I didn't understand.

Just as the event was coming to a close, I looked up from the eyepiece of the camera, directly at Bucky, and a gentle a wave of energy went through me. I could feel my heart open and I began to cry. They weren't tears of sadness or pain, but tears of gratitude for this man's courage to do what he had been doing for years: guiding and teaching and looking into the future.

John Denver wrote and recorded a song dedicated to Dr. Fuller, after Bucky touched and inspired John's life. The title of the song is "What One Man Can Do."

John Denver's tribute to Bucky Fuller in that song does a far better job of describing the experience I had that day with Bucky than I can do with words in this book.

The words in John Denver's song that have always moved me are these:

It's hard to tell the truth
When no one wants to listen
When no one really cares
What's going on
And it's hard to stand alone
When you need someone beside you
Your spirit and your faith
They must be strong

Followed by the refrain...

What one man can do is dream
What one man can do is love
What one man can do is change the world
And make it young again
Here you see what one man can do

Since this book is about second chances, I describe that event with Bucky Fuller because it was one of the many second chances I have had in my life. I returned to Honolulu a changed person.

At that time, in 1981, I had factories in Taiwan, Korea, and Hawaii that manufactured licensed products for the rock and roll industry. My company was producing products for the rock bands Pink Floyd, Duran Duran, Judas Priest, Van Halen, Boy George, Ted Nugent, REO Speedwagon, and The Police. I loved the business. My factories rolled out hats, wallets, and bags with faces and logos of the bands silk-screened on the products. On the weekends I would be at concerts watching my products being scooped up by raving, happy fans. It was a great business. I was single, living on the beach in Waikiki with neighbors like Tom Selleck, and making a lot of money... which used to make me happy.

The problem was that Fuller had touched my heart and I knew, in *my* heart, that my days of sex, drugs, rock and roll, and money were coming to an end. I kept asking myself, "What can I do to make the world a better place?" And "What am I doing with my life?"

In 1981, I was 34 years old. I now had three professions. I had gone to the U.S. Merchant Marine Academy in New York, received my Bachelor of Science Degree, and a third mate's license to sail on oil tankers. I had gone to U.S. Navy Flight School and learned how to fly professionally. I briefly considered flying for the airlines, but when I returned from Vietnam, I knew that, although I loved flying, my days as a pilot were over. I was now an entrepreneur with a global manufacturing and distribution business. My rock and roll products were in national chains like JCPenney, Tower Records, and Spencer's gift stores, at concerts with the bands, and offered by retailers in countries around the world through worldwide distributors.

My problem was I had met Bucky Fuller. And when I returned to my factory in Honolulu, my mind would drift back to what I had experienced in Montreal. As I've said, standing in the magical environment of that dome, never dreaming I would ever meet the man who designed it… then meeting him and knowing that my life was changing yet again.

My Spiritual Job

Rather than listen to rock and roll music, I was now listening to John Denver's music. Whenever I listened to John sing *What One Man Can Do*, the song he dedicated to Fuller, I would ask myself over and over again: "What am I supposed to be doing with my life?"

Whenever I listened to rock and roll music, the only thing it inspired me to do was to go to the nightclubs of Waikiki.

When I listened to John Denver's songs, my thinking started in my heart. Rather than stay out late in nightclubs, I spent more time alone, surfing or hiking just being with the beauty of nature. On weekends, I spent time in personal development workshops learning how to become a better person, emotionally and spiritually. My more gentle side raised a few eyebrows among my Marine Corps friends and I found myself spending more time with business groups focused on solving social problems in communities around town than with associates in rock and roll or retailing.

Slowly it dawned on me that we go to school with the hope of finding a financial profession known as a job. After meeting Fuller, I realized I was looking for my spiritual profession, my spiritual work, my *spiritual job* and my life's purpose.

From 1981 to 1983, I studied with Dr. Fuller on three different occasions during the summers. Between summers, my new friends and I would get together to "group study" Fuller's books. His books are not very easy to comprehend, so we would agree to study a chapter each week then get together at one of our houses to discuss and "mind-map" Fuller's thoughts in that chapter.

Mind mapping is a method of using color and sketches, rather than words, to organize and prioritize Fuller's thoughts in the chapter. The sketches were done on large sheets of flip chart paper and started with a core or central concept. The key to mind mapping is color and sketches, using very, very, few words. Using very few words forces the participant to put words and thoughts into pictures, which intensifies the learning and discussion process.

As we all know, two or more minds are better than one... except in school, where two or more minds working together is known as *cheating*. The group study—using discussion, color, and pictures—was exciting, stimulating, challenging, and never boring. Rather than late nights in nightclubs, I was now spending late nights in book study groups. I knew this was my second chance to find my life's purpose. Rather than go to school to learn how to transport oil, or go to school to learn to rain terror from the skies, or go to school to learn how to manufacture and sell more rock and roll products, I was now "in school," a new second chance school, learning how to be a better human being, learning—possibly—to be a person who might make a difference in the world.

The problem was, I had no idea then what my *spiritual job* was... or was to be. From 1981 to 1983, I dedicated a lot of time studying Fuller's work. And 1983 was the last summer of events that I spent with him. He closed the conference with the words "Good-bye darling people. See you next summer." But he didn't see us the following summer. He died three weeks later on July 1, 1983.

Changes on the Horizon

By 1984, I knew I had to make changes… the problem was I was not sure what I was supposed to do… so I just decided to do something. As the saying goes:

> *"Sometimes you have to let go of what you love doing so you can do what you are supposed to do."*

I had also reread the book *Jonathan Livingston Seagull*, written by Richard Bach and first published in 1970.

The following is from Wikipedia, and gives you an idea of what the book is about:

> *"The book tells the story of Jonathan Livingston Seagull, a seagull who is bored with the daily squabbles over food. Seized by a passion for flight, he pushes himself, learning everything he can about flying, until finally his unwillingness to conform results in his expulsion from his flock. An outcast, he continues to learn, becoming increasingly pleased with his abilities as he leads a peaceful and happy life.*
>
> *One day, Jonathan is met by two gulls who take him to a 'higher plane of existence' in that there is no heaven but a better world found through perfection of knowledge, where he meets other gulls who love to fly. He discovers that his sheer tenacity and desire to learn makes him 'pretty well a one-in-a-million bird.' In this new place, Jonathan befriends the wisest gull, Chiang, who takes him beyond his previous learning, teaching him how to move instantaneously to anywhere else in the Universe. The secret, Chiang says, is to 'begin by knowing that you have already arrived.' Not satisfied with his new life, Jonathan returns to Earth to find others like him, to bring them his learning and to spread his love for flight. His mission is successful, gathering around him others who have been outlawed for not conforming. Ultimately, the very first of his students, Fletcher Lynd Seagull, becomes a teacher in his own right and Jonathan leaves to teach other flocks."*

Leaps of Faith

One important lesson I got from *Jonathan Livingston Seagull* is that sometimes a person needs to let go and let the currents of life carry them to where they are supposed to go.

From the summer of 1983 to end of 1984, I began preparing to let go and let the currents of life take me.

That process began with informing my two partners in my rock and roll business that I was "letting go" and moving on. When they asked where I was going, I mumbled something about letting the currents of life carry me. When that went over their heads, I simply said, "I'm taking a leap of faith into the unknown" and, in October of 1983, we began the buy-out process that would transition me out of the business.

In January of 1984, as I was tying up loose ends in Hawaii, New York, Taiwan, and Korea, I met the most beautiful woman I had ever seen. Her name was Kim and she wanted nothing to do with me. For the next six months, I kept asking her out and for six months her answer was always the same: "No."

Finally, she agreed to go out. We spent dinner and a long walk on Waikiki Beach together, talking until the sun came up. From late that night until early the next morning I talked about Bucky Fuller and the possibility of a life's purpose, a person's spiritual job. She was the first woman I had ever met who was interested in these subjects.

Over the next few months, we saw each other regularly. She was part of my "letting go" process. She was with me when I said a tearful good-bye to my partners and the workers in the Honolulu factory. Kim and I knew we, too, would soon be saying good-bye. She had her career in advertising in Honolulu and I was leaping into nothing. One day, as the day of reckoning approached, Kim said, "I want to go with you." In December of 1984, Kim and I held hands and took our leap of faith into the unknown. Without a doubt, 1985 was the worst year of our lives. Little did we know that, unfortunately, there would be years ahead that would make 1985 look easy by comparison.

We wish we could say it has all been easy, all peaches and cream. But it's been hell. Even today, in 2014, although financially and professionally "successful" we still have to deal with life in the real world, a world of greed, lies, dishonesty, legal hassles, and crime.

In spite of the hardships and heartbreak, the journey has been very much like the book *Jonathan Livingston Seagull* described. It has been a process to test our spirit and our dedication to our process... to see if we would quit when the going got too tough.

The great news is that we have met many great people, different types of people we might never have met if Kim had remained with the ad agency and I had remained in manufacturing.

Wikipedia best describes the people we meet and befriend along the way, in its summary of Part 2 of *Jonathan Livingston Seagull*:

> *"Jonathan transcends into a society where all the gulls enjoy flying. He is only capable of this after practicing hard alone for a long time. The learning process, linking the highly experienced teacher and the diligent student, is raised into almost sacred levels. They, regardless of the all-immense difference, are sharing something of great importance that can bind them together:*
>
> *'You've got to understand that a seagull is an unlimited idea of freedom, an image of the Great Gull.' He realizes that you have to be true to yourself: 'You have the freedom to be yourself, your true self, here and now, and nothing can stand in your way.'"*

There were many times in 1985 when Kim and I had no place to live and no money to eat. We survived by living in an old, brown Toyota and in a friend's basement. As I said, our faith was being tested.

In the fall of 1985, the stream of life carried us to Australia where we found people who loved what we were teaching. We were using games to teach socially responsible entrepreneurship and investing. By December of 1985, we actually made a small profit on a seminar we held in Sydney—and that is one of the reasons why Kim and I love Australia and will always be grateful to the people of Australia.

We had let go and the current of life carried us to Australia and Australians gave us chance to develop as teachers.

Change of Friends

One day in 1986, out of the blue, I received a call from John Denver's Windstar Foundation. John was hosting an event in Aspen, Colorado and wanted to know if I would be one of the guest speakers, along with several other entrepreneurs including Ben Cohen and Jerry Greenfield, founders of Ben & Jerry's ice cream. Of course I said "Yes."

Being in a large tent on John's property in Aspen was much like being in Bucky's dome in Montreal. The feeling of magic, wonder, and possibilities was the same. For some reason, I did not speak on my rock and roll business. It didn't seem to fit. For some reason—and totally unprepared—I spoke on education and learning. I spoke about the pain I went through in school, about knowing what I wanted to study but being forced to study subjects I had no interest in. I spoke about the emotional pain I went through in failing high school English twice, because I could not write well. I spoke for the kids like me, kids who wanted to learn but didn't like school. I spoke about how so many children have their spirits crushed in the traditional process of learning. At the end of my talk, I asked everyone in the group to close their eyes, join hands, and listen to Whitney Houston's latest release, *The Greatest Love of All*. The opening line of the song fit the mood and the message:

"I believe the children are our future…"

There weren't many dry eyes in the audience as I left the stage in silence. The audience, this group of "seagulls," were hugging each other, some crying, much as I had cried that day in 1981 when I was in the audience that first time with Bucky Fuller. The tears were of love, not sadness. They were tears of responsibility, not blame. They were tears of gratitude… gratitude for the gift of life. And they were tears of courage, knowing that changing the world requires courage, courage that comes from the heart. Many in this group of "seagulls" already knew that the word *courage* comes from the French word, "le coeur," the heart. Windstar was a gathering of gulls, most of whom already knew how to fly. They knew flying took courage.

Kim was waiting for me as I stepped down from the stage and we hugged silently. We knew we had found our spiritual profession, our spiritual job and our life's purpose. We knew then that we'd found what was to become, and still is, our life's work.

Ironically being a teacher was the not on my list of answers to the question "What do want to be when you grow up?" Being an attorney was "a higher calling" than being a teacher. It is not that I hated school. I hated being forced to learn what I did not want to learn. I hated not learning what I wanted to learn, which was to understand money and be financially free like my rich dad. I did not want to be a slave to a paycheck, job security, and a schoolteacher's pension, like my poor dad.

The Business Booms

Once Kim and I were clear on our spiritual jobs, our little educational company expanded to New Zealand, Canada, Singapore, Malaysia, and the U.S. business boomed.

Ten years later, in 1994, when we sold that business to our partner, Kim and I were financially free. Kim was 37 years old and I was 47. We achieved financial freedom without jobs, without government support, and without a retirement plan filled with stocks, bonds, and mutual funds.

When people began asking us how we achieved financial freedom without the traditional investment and retirement plans, Kim and I knew it was time for us to begin *our* new second chance.

Following one of Buckminster Fuller's *generalized principles*—a principle that is true in all cases, no exceptions—we began our next business. Today that business is known as The Rich Dad Company.

The generalized principle we followed was:

"The more people I serve, the more effective I become."

With the intent on serving more people, Kim and I began developing our *CASHFLOW*® game and I began writing *Rich Dad Poor Dad*.

On my 50th birthday, April 8, 1997, The Rich Dad Company was officially launched. Our mission:

"To elevate the financial well being of humanity."

A Second Chance for The Rich Dad Company

As I stated in Chapter One of this book, the world of money is changing and, unfortunately, millions of people are not. The reason Kim and I continued on with The Rich Dad Company, although we are both financially free, is because of the company mission, a mission of offering more people a second chance at money and life. Today, through the development of electronic games and apps, The Rich Dad Company finds itself poised for yet another second chance, a chance to serve more people using the tools and technology of the Information Age. The beauty of second chances is that you can have as many as you need or want… without any limits. Each of us has the power to choose to pursue a second chance, as opposed to whining about what might have been. And the more we learn, and the more aware each of us is about the ever-changing world we live in, the better our odds of succeeding as we commit to a second chance.

Dr. Fuller's last book was *Grunch of Giants*. GRUNCH is an acronym, which stands for **Gr**oss **Un**iversal **C**ash **H**eist.

Grunch was published after his death in 1983. *Grunch* was Fuller's only book to focus on many of the same things my rich dad was concerned about, *specifically how the monetary system is designed to steal our wealth.*

Reading *Grunch of Giants* in 1983 pushed me over the edge. I knew I could no longer be a manufacturer. Although I did not know what to do, I knew I had to do something. I knew too much and I could no longer stay silent. Fuller had taught us how to see the future and even then I could see this crisis coming, a financial crisis that began in our educational system.

In the following chapters, I will explain what I learned and why we are in a financial crisis we face today.

This *cash heist* is not new. It has been going on for a long time. For those who seek a second chance, understanding what Fuller calls the *Grunch of Giants*—and what he saw for the future—is essential to creating a brighter future for you and your family.

Chapter Three
WHAT CAN I DO?

---

*"I just invent, then wait until man comes around
to needing what I've invented."*

– R. Buckminster Fuller

It took me awhile to realize that Bucky Fuller's ability to predict the future had nothing to do with picking stocks, timing markets, betting on horses, or predicting who will win the World Series. His vision of the future had to do with god's view of the future.

Bucky was hesitant to use the word *god* because, for many people, that word carried a lot of "religious dogma," emotion, and controversy. Fuller did not think god was a white guy, a Jew, an Arab, or an Asian. Rather than use the word *god*, he preferred the Native American term, *the Great Spirit*. The Great Spirit is the invisible energy that binds all things in "universe," not just heaven and earth.

Whenever I use the term *god* in this book, please know I am not making religious references. I respect a person's right to choose—to believe in god, or not to believe in god or follow any religion. Simply said, I believe in religious freedom and the freedom to choose whether or not they believe in god.

The same is true for politics. I am not a Republican or Democrat. I have no dog in that fight. In fact, I like my dog more than I like most politicians.

Human Evolution

Fuller was not a futurist in the arena of money. He was a futurist on the Great Spirit's wishes for humanity's evolution. He believed humans were god's long-term experiment, placed here on "spaceship earth" to see if humans could evolve... if they could, or would, turn planet earth into a heaven on earth, or hell on earth.

Fuller believed Great Spirit wanted all humans to be rich. He often said, "There are six billion billionaires on earth." (That was in the 1980s. Today he would say "seven billion billionaires.") In the 1980s there were fewer than 50 documented billionaires. A far cry from the "six billion" that Bucky cited. By 2008 there were 1,150. Today that figure's projected at 1,645.

Fuller predicted that humanity had reached a critical evolutionary point. If humans did not evolve from greed and selfishness to generosity and abundance, humans—as an experiment on earth—would end. He often referred to the rich and powerful who hoarded "god's abundance" only for themselves as "blood clots." He believed that if humans did not "evolve" we would not only kill ourselves, but also kill the ecology of planet earth.

The reason Fuller sought to identify the Generalized Principles is because they are the invisible forces that run the universe. In other words, the Generalized Principles were the operating principles of the Great Spirit, and the Great Spirit wanted all humans and all life on planet earth to thrive. Fuller believed there were 200 to 300 Generalized Principles. At the time of his death he had discovered about 50. I am aware of and use about five of them.

In his writing and talks, he was critical of a few greedy, powerful people who used humans and the resources of planet earth only for their personal wealth. He believed that if humans did not shift from *greed* to *generosity*—humans working for a planet that worked for everyone and everything—humans would be "evicted" from "spaceship earth." The Great Spirit's experiment would be set back a few million years. He also said that god was patient and willing to wait for humans to evolve. Unfortunately, you and I do not have the luxury of waiting another million years for our fellow humans to "get the message."

Serving More People

As stated in the previous chapter, one of the Great Spirit's Generalized Principles that Fuller identified was:

"The more people I serve, the more effective I become."

As part of my own second chance, I do my best to follow this Generalized Principle when making business decisions. Rather than just work to make myself richer, I began to condition myself to think about how to enrich *others* while I was enriching myself.

That Generalized Principle was instrumental in our decision to sell the seminar business that Kim and I founded to our partner. Although that seminar business was successful, it was limited in terms of the number of people it could serve.

In 1994, it was difficult for us to sell that seminar business, a business we loved, were successful in building and making profitable. Yet, intuitively, we knew it was time to move on. It was time to seek ways to serve more people.

In 1994, we were financially free. That freedom came not from Bucky Fuller's lessons, but from following rich dad's lessons. Financial freedom gave us the time to develop our next business. In 1996, the first commercial version of our *CASHFLOW*® game was played in Las Vegas and, one week later, in Singapore. The next step was to develop a marketing plan to sell that game.

The *CASHFLOW* game had two inherent problems that made it difficult to sell. The first problem was that it was too complex. A game expert we hired advised us to "dumb it down" or it would not sell. We decided against that recommendation. The *CASHFLOW* game was designed to be an educational game, not a game for entertainment.

The second problem with the game was that it was very expensive to produce. The same game consultant told us the game should retail for $29.95. At $29.95 retail, our cost of manufacturing had to be no more than $7.00 per game. Our problem was that the first production run of the game cost over $50 per game to produce in China, landed, and warehoused in the United States. Against the advice of the game expert, we set the *CASHFLOW* game's retail price at $195, making it one of the most expensive board games on the market.

But adversity leads to innovation. To sell the game a $195 game, Kim and I had to be innovative. We went to our past seminar clients and offered a $500, one-day seminar featuring our game. During the seminar, the participants played our new game twice. The first time was to get familiar with the game. The second time to get into the game. The one-day seminar worked. Participants were excited, most claiming they learned more about money in one day than they had learned in a lifetime. When we announced the "used" games were for sale for $150, they were gone instantly. In fact there was a fight for used games, even though there were new games available for $195.

The business model worked and the "CASHFLOW Club" concept was born. In 2004, *The New York Times* ran an article, "The Rising Value of Play Money," on CASHFLOW Clubs and told us that they had identified over 3,500 clubs—all over the world. Many clubs are still in existence today, teaching and serving more people than Kim and I could ever do on our own.

Q: *If you want to serve more people, why didn't you offer the game for free?*

A: We considered using government grants to fund the manufacturing of the games, but that would have been following my poor dad's mindset, rather than my rich dad's entrepreneurial way of thinking.

Also, giving people things for free often keeps them poor. It encourages the "entitlement mentality" that destroys initiative and personal responsibility.

In spite of the high initial cost of the game, the online game is free to millions of people. One game can and has taught hundreds of people... for free, through CASHFLOW Clubs. Many CASHFLOW Club leaders around the world support the mission of Rich Dad, which is *to elevate the financial well being of humanity*, and teach the game to others. For them, not only is teaching spiritual, but the more they teach, the more they learn.

Most CASHFLOW Club leaders I have talked with report getting back far more than they give. They follow the religious principle of "give and you shall receive."

Unfortunately, there are clubs that only present the game to sell other products or business opportunities. If you encounter one of those clubs, just know that while I support free enterprise, I do not support people using my games as marketing tools.

Other Points of View

For about six months, I sat in the quaint, artist's town of Bisbee, Arizona… in an old jail that had been converted into an apartment. At one time, John Wayne owned that old jail, as a rental property. He loved Bisbee—and Southern Arizona, where he owned a large ranch.

During the day, I was working on my small ranch, converting an old stagecoach depot (a stopping point between Bisbee and the infamous town of Tombstone, where the gunfight at the OK Corral took place) into a one-bedroom home. At night I would sit in the jail, writing a book. It was a painful process. There were many starts and stops, fits and starts. Finally, late one night, exhausted from working on my property and tired of struggling with a book concept, my fingers began typing the opening lines of a new book. It began with the words "I had a rich dad and I had a poor dad."

And that's how the book, *Rich Dad Poor Dad,* was born. Most people don't know that *Rich Dad Poor Dad,* the book that started the Rich Dad series, was written as a "brochure" to market the *CASHFLOW* game.

On April 8, 1997, my 50th birthday, *Rich Dad Poor Dad* was launched and The Rich Dad Company was born.

Rich Dad Poor Dad floated around in the world of self-published books until early in the year 2000. It was selling virally, by word of mouth and one day it made *The New York Times* bestsellers list. It was the only self-published book on that prestigious list.

Soon after that, a producer from Oprah Winfrey's TV show called. But before she would book me for *Oprah*, she wanted to talk with rich dad's son. As soon as she verified the story of rich dad and poor dad, my guest appearance on *Oprah* was confirmed.

I was in Australia when the invitation came. It was a tough decision: should I stay in Australia, or fly to Chicago for the interview. Again the principle of "The more people I serve, the more effective I am" kicked in. Cutting my trip short, I flew directly from Australia to Chicago. I still remember walking onto Oprah's stage, sitting next to her for an hour, and talking about the need for financial education.

In that hour, my life changed completely. In one hour I went from an unknown to a world famous voice for financial education. It had taken only 55 years, years of many successes and failures and many second chances, to become an overnight success.

I tell you this story, not to brag or pat myself on my back, but as an example of the power of following Bucky Fuller's Generalized Principles and my rich dad's lessons on money.

The Rich Are Generous

A reporter once asked me if *Oprah* made me rich. I replied that I was already rich the day I stepped on her stage. I was rich financially because I had spent my life gaining knowledge, knowledge not taught in schools. All I was doing was sharing, being generous with what I knew.

My comment on being generous disturbed the reporter. His view was that a person had to be greedy to be rich. When I attempted to explain, the generalized principle of *unity is plural and, at minimum two*—that a person could be rich by being greedy *and* that a person could be rich by being generous—his eyes glazed over. His brain was rigidly locked around the idea that the only way to become rich was by being greedy. In his mind, it is not possible to become rich by being generous. In his mind, there is only one kind of rich person: a greedy rich person.

Q: *What happened after you became famous? Was it smooth sailing after that?*

A: No. Far from it. Fame and money made life harder, not easier. Many friends became jealous. Partners became greedy and began to steal. And many people came around to see how they could "help." It was tough trying to determine if people were coming to truly help with the mission or only to "help themselves" to what we had created.

The good news is that over the years many great people have come into our lives. Again: *Unity is plural* and we had to learn to take the good with the bad.

Bucky's Last Words

As I've said, Fuller died on July 1 in 1983. His wife Anne died 36 hours later. Both were 87 years old. Even in death, his life was supernatural.

He was speaking at an event, which would be his last, when he abruptly stopped and sat quietly for a moment. I was not at that event, but I did listen to an audiotape of his final words from that event. I will paraphrase his final words.

Bucky said he was cutting his talk short because his wife was gravely ill. He mentioned he'd had a premonition a few days earlier. His premonition was that he and his wife were to die together. Realizing death was near for both of them, he said "There is something mysterious going on." He encouraged everyone to continue on with the work, ending his talk with his usual parting words, "Thank you, darling people."

I later learned that he and his wife had made a pact that neither of them would ever see the other die. They kept their pact. Rushing to see her, Bucky sat at her bedside, where she was in a coma. As if on cue, he put his head down next to her, and silently passed on. She followed, 36 hours later, keeping their pact to never see the other die. He was a futurist who predicted how he and his wife would die. I guess he could hear the Great Spirit calling them home.

I was driving on a freeway in Honolulu when the news of their deaths came over the radio. The news so overwhelmed me that I pulled over on the side of the highway and cried. Looking back, it's clear to me that, as I was sitting on the side of the highway that emotional day, one phase of my life had ended and another had begun. I was given a new second chance. I was no longer to be an entrepreneur in manufacturing. I was about to become an entrepreneur in education.

Grunch of Giants

A few months later, Bucky's final book, *Grunch of Giants,* was released posthumously. As I've mentioned, GRUNCH stands for **Gr**oss **Un**iversal **Ca**sh **H**eist and refers to how the rich and powerful steal our wealth via our money, government, and banking system.

As I read this tiny, yet potent book, many pieces of the puzzle began to fall in place. My mind drifted back in time... when I was nine years old, in the fourth grade, and I raising my hand to ask my teacher, "When will we learn about money?" and "Why are some people rich and most people poor?"

In reading *Grunch,* the answers slowly seeped into my head. Fuller was very critical of the educational system, not only because of what it was teaching, but *how* it taught children to learn. He had this to say about every child and his or her special genius:

"Every child is born a genius, but is swiftly degeniused by unwitting humans and/or physically unfavorable environmental factors."

And...

"I observe that every child demonstrates a comprehensive curiosity. Children are interested in everything and are forever embarrassing their specialized parents by the wholeness of their interests. Children demonstrate right from the beginning that their genes are organized to help them to apprehend, comprehend, coordinate, and employ—in all directions."

Fuller recommended that students take control of their education process. In essence: do what Steve Jobs did at Reed College in

Portland, Oregon. Steve Jobs dropped out of school so he could drop back in, studying only subjects that interested him. Steve never went back to school.

Q: *Did Bucky Fuller say everyone has a genius?*

A: Yes.

Q: *But I don't feel very smart. I don't think I have a genius. Why is that?*

A: As Bucky says, schools and parents often *degenius* children. Fuller used the metaphor of school being a diamond mine. Teachers dig into the mine looking for "diamonds"—the kids they think are geniuses. The "tailings," or the dirt and rubble that tossed to the wayside, are the students the teachers believe have no genius potential. That is why so many students leave school feeling that they're not smart, not bright, not special… even angry at school and the school system.

Q: *So how does a person find their genius?*

A: There are many ways. One way is by changing their environment.

Q: *What does environment have to do with my genius?*

A: Let me give you some examples. Many students feel stupid in the environment of a classroom, yet their genius comes alive on a football field. Tiger Woods' genius comes alive on the golf course. The Beatles' genius came alive, with guitars and drums, in a recording studio. Steve Jobs dropped out of school, yet his genius came alive in his garage, where he and Steve Wozniak developed the first Apple computer.

Q: *So why don't I feel smart? Why can't I find my genius?*

A: Because most people go from home to school to work, environments that are not always the right environment for their genius to bloom. Many spend their lives feeling unfulfilled, untested, unappreciated, simply because they did not find the environment in which their genius could blossom.

Think of genius as three words, *genie-in-us*… the magician in us. The words genius, magician, and inspire are all related. Do you know someone who is a magician in the kitchen, someone who can take ordinary ingredients and create gourmet meals?

Q: *Yes.*

A: Do you know someone who has a "green thumb?" Someone who can take dirt, water, and seeds and create a magical garden?

Q: *Sure.*

A: Have you ever watched the Special Olympics, an event for physically-challenged children, and been inspired—spiritually touched—when they compete with all their hearts, undaunted and in spite of their disabilities and challenges?

Q: *I have.*

A: Those are examples of "genie-in-us," when the magician in us inspires others. We feel inspired when the spirit in someone else touches the spirit in us.

That is what genius is. When someone inspires us, we're reminded of the "genie-in-us."

Q: *So why don't most people find their genius?*

A: Because being a genius is not easy. For example, someone could be the next Tiger Woods, but if that person does not dedicate their life to developing their genius, their talents, their genie will never show its magic.

More Questions than Answers

For me, reading *Grunch* only raised more questions. And for the first time in my life, I wanted to be a student again. I wanted to go back to the fourth grade and find the answers to the flurry of questions I kept asking my teacher about money. I was hungry to learn, and I wanted answers to my questions: "Why is money not a subject taught in school?" and "What makes rich people rich?"

As I finished reading *Grunch* and went on to read Fuller's other books on education, I realized my questions in the fourth grade were caused by my natural curiosity. Money and why the rich are rich were my subjects of study. And, in my opinion, it's not by accident that the subject of money had been "sanitized" from academic study.

In 1983, the student in me came alive again and I did exactly as Fuller described. The student in me got back to my studies.

Over the years, my own studies verified Fuller's findings that the monetary system was designed to steal our wealth, making the rich richer, but not making you and I rich. This enslavement of others and theft of another's wealth has been going on ever since the first humans walked the earth. Fuller believed that intense greed and desire to enslave fellow humans was humanity's evolutionary test, a test to see if we could use our hearts and minds to create heaven on earth or if we would turn earth into a living hell and environmental wasteland.

In *Grunch of Giants*, Fuller described how the rich and powerful used money, banks, government, politicians, military leaders, and the educational system to implement their plans. Simply said, money is designed to keep people slaves to money and slaves to those who control the monetary system.

Ironically, and although Bucky Fuller and my rich dad would be polar opposites on the subject of money, they both would have agreed on the concept of money enslaving people. And their polarity supports and validates the generalized principle of *unity is plural*, both men disagreeing on substance, but agreeing in principle.

The Power of Knowledge

Soon after I appeared on *Oprah*, a mutual fund company offered me $4 million to endorse their mutual fund. While I like money as much as the next guy, accepting their money would have been selling out to GRUNCH. One of the great things about financial education is it gives people the power to choose… and to never need to sell their soul for money.

What Can You Do?

You and I both knew this was coming…

Q: *So what can I do?*

A: The answer is there are many things you can do. The world is filled with problems. A better question might be: What problem do you want to solve? What problem do you think god gave you unique gifts to solve? You can do it by yourself or you can join a group or an organization in solving the problem that causes you concern.

When you look at the world from the point of view of problems to solve, you will see that there is a lot to do and a lot *you* can do.

A more important question is: Are you willing to work on solving the problem? Or are you willing to work only if someone will pay you money?

In the next chapter, you will learn what I learned while looking for the answer of how our wealth is stolen via our money system and why there is no financial education in our schools.

By creating the *CASHFLOW* board game and writing *Rich Dad Poor Dad*, our wealth, income, and recognition went up exponentially. I mention this for those of you who are wondering when I will get around to what you can do for *your* second chance in life.

For those of you considering a second chance with your money and your life, you may want to ask yourself:

"How can I serve more people?"

rather than:

"How can I make more money?"

If you ask yourself how you can serve more people—rather than simply make more money—you are following one of the Generalized Principles of god.

Chapter Four

WHAT IS A HEIST?

---

*The dark ages still reign over all humanity, and the depth
and persistence of this domination are only now becoming clear.
This Dark Ages prison has no steel bars, chains, or locks. Instead, it is
locked by misorientation and built of misinformation.*
                                        – R. Buckminster Fuller

---

When I read this quote in this book *Cosmography*, another post-
humus book that followed *Grunch*, the idea that we were in the dark
ages rattled my brain. I wanted to learn more. My question was: How
does GRUNCH keep us in the dark ages?

For me, reading Grunch of Giants was like putting together the
first 100 pieces out of a 1,000-piece jigsaw puzzle. The 100 pieces
from Fuller's Grunch of Giants, interlocked with the other 100
puzzle pieces my rich dad had linked together for me years before.
The puzzle was beginning to take shape—and make sense. I began to
understand how our wealth was being stolen, via a heist of our money.

In 1983, I believed I had about 200 pieces of a 1,000-piece jigsaw
puzzle. I could see a picture forming and I wanted to learn more. For
the first time in my life, I was truly a student. I wanted to learn more.
And I knew I could not learn what I needed to learn by staying still,
so I decided to do what Fuller had done in 1927. I took a leap of faith
into the unknown.

Q: *Why the unknown?*

A: Because I really didn't know what the future would hold. My only thoughts were: If Bucky Fuller found his genius leaping into the unknown in 1927, maybe I should (and could) too. I wasn't too bright in school so I thought that maybe I'd be smarter in the unknown.

Q: *What was driving you? Why give up a good life for something that was unknown?*

A: Injustice. I grew up in the '60s, an extremely turbulent time. There were protests against the war in Vietnam and race riots at home.

In 1965, I left my sleepy hometown of Hilo, Hawaii and went to school in New York, at the Merchant Marine Academy. My roommate was a young black man, and who today—to be politically correct—I should refer to as African American. Tom Jackson was my first African-American friend, because in Hilo, there were no African Americans. With race riots in the news every night, Jackson would fill in the blanks, giving me the other side of the story.

We all know there is racial discrimination. There was discrimination in Hawaii, the Whites, called Haoles, versus Asians and Hawaiians—but it was not near the levels of discrimination my friend Tom experienced.

Q: *So it's racial discrimination that drives you?*

A: Yes and no. There will always be discrimination. It is injustice that drives me.

After graduating from Kings Point, the Merchant Marine Academy, in 1969 I went to flight school in Florida, not far from Alabama. A white classmate from flight school invited me to his home in Birmingham, the city at the epicenter of the 1960's race riots.

Q: *And what did you learn?*

A: That racial discrimination is financial discrimination. The blacks were fighting for the opportunity for a better life. In talking with other people in Alabama, both white and black, it became clear to me that they were struggling for the same thing: a better life.

You may recall that the protests and riots at the time was over integration of their schools. Both blacks and whites wanted better education for a better life.

Q: *So what is the injustice?*

A: The injustice is the lack of financial education in our schools. People go to school for a better life, yet few learn anything about money.

Q: *And today, the same problem exists? People still go to school but learn very little about money. Is that the injustice?*

A: Yes. Today, people of all races and all socio-economic classes—rich, middle class, and poor—are struggling for money. This causes people to panic over whether or not their child is getting the best education possible... so they can get a good, high-paying job. Ironically, their child will learn little, if anything, about money.

Q: *So... I'm not seeing what the injustice is...*

A: The injustice is financial ignorance. Today, almost everyone in every part of the world is having their wealth stolen via the financial system, via their money. And most do not even realize it. Their wealth is being stolen via their work, savings, and investments in the stock market.

If things do not change, I am afraid the rioting of the '60s will return, and this time it will not be race riots.

When I was 18, Tom Jackson, my roommate at Kings Point, took me home with him to Washington, DC. That trip disturbed me to the core.

And visiting my white friend's home in Birmingham, Alabama, right after race riots in that city, also disturbed me deeply.

Today, I see the same creep of panic and poverty bleeding into all corners of society. I know why drugs and crime are professions of choice in inner cities. Crime pays more than a job. And drugs relieve the pain people are in. At least drugs and crime can put food on the table and a roof over your head.

Today that pain has spread across all levels within our society. Money and ignorance do not discriminate. The lack of financial education is the injustice. And reading Grunch of Giants just made me want to learn more. As Fuller said:

"You can never learn less… you can only learn more"

So that is why Kim and I took our leap of faith in 1984. We really did not know what to do. All we knew was that we had to do something.

The Power of the Paycheck

Rich dad said, "The paycheck is one of the most powerful tools ever created by man. The person who signs the paycheck has the power to enslave another person's body, mind, and soul."

He also said, "When slavery was abolished, the rich created paychecks."

This is why chapter one in *Rich Dad Poor Dad* is titled The Rich Don't Work for Money.

Q: *So how do we end this injustice?*

A: It starts with words.

Words Are Tools

Fuller often said, "Words are tools." Since words affect our minds, he believed words are some of the most powerful tools invented by humans, which is why he chose his words carefully. Bucky believed many people struggled with life simply because they used words that dis-empowered them, made them weak, confused, fearful, sometimes even angry.

When rich dad wouldn't allow his son Mike and me to say "I can't afford it," he was echoing Bucky's belief that words can steal your power and make you weak. Instead, we were to ask ourselves "How can I afford it?" and challenge our brains to expand our means. The words we choose—and use—either open our minds or close them… make us feel powerful and creative or powerless victims of life. That's the power of words. My rich dad also agreed with Fuller when it came to financial words. For example, rich dad believed many people were poor simply because they used poor words. If you read *Rich Dad Poor Dad*, you may recall my poor dad often said, "My house is an *asset*." And my rich dad would say, "Your father may be a highly educated man, but his house is not an asset. It's a *liability*."

Millions of people are poor or struggle financially simply because they use "poor" or incorrect words. Millions of people struggle financially because they refer to their "liabilities" as "assets."

Rich dad's definitions were simple. They were:

Assets put money in your pocket.

Liabilities take money from your pocket.

He would then draw a simple diagram of a financial statement to illustrate his definitions. He used diagrams because "a picture is worth a thousand words."

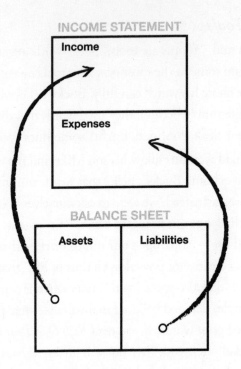

As you can see from the diagram, the key word that determines an asset or liability is *cash flow*. It's possible that these two words—*cash flow*—are the most important words in financial education.

Words Can Make You Rich

At the age of nine, I knew I was going to be a rich man, simply because rich dad taught me the meaning of financial words. I knew I was going to be rich because I knew the difference between assets and liabilities. At the age of nine, I knew my job was to acquire assets and minimize liabilities.

This was not rocket science. I was only nine years old and I could understand those concepts. The difference between most Americans (of *any* age) and me is that someone (in this case, my rich dad) took the time to teach me the words, the language of money, so I could feel knowledgeable and strong and in control of my money and—by extension—my life. Maybe this is where your second chance starts.

Rich dad began our financial education, learning the definition of words, by playing *Monopoly*. At the age of nine, I knew that one green house was an asset, when it produced, let's say, $10 of cash flow, money flowing into my pocket. Two green houses put $20 in my pocket. The math was not hard. Knowing the definition of financial words was powerful, and life changing. As I grew older and more experienced, my wealth increased as my financial vocabulary increased.

As I've stated earlier: *Knowledge is power.*

Knowledge begins with words. And the best news of all: words are free.

As Fuller said, words are tools, the most powerful tools created by humans. Words are fuel for our brains. Using poor words is like putting low-quality gasoline in a car—it affects long-term performance and can impact a person's entire life. Another way of putting this is: Poor people are not poor. They are using poor words to power their powerful brains.

Money alone can never end poverty. Many people give poor people money out of kindness. Often times giving money to poor people only keeps them poor longer. If we want to see an end to poverty, we should begin by upgrading the words poor people use.

Entitlement Mentality

An early lesson from my Sunday school class is:

> *"Give a man a fish, and you feed him for a day.*
> *Teach a man to fish and you feed him for life."*

Teaching people to become self-reliant begins with words of empowerment rather than words of entitlement.

Many in the middle class struggle because they, too, use poor words. Many in the middle class use the words "save money," which is ridiculous when banks and governments are printing money on 'presses' that are running at high speed.

Millions of middle class people and amateur investors "invest for the long term." That too makes no sense when professional investors, using HFT—High-Frequency Trading—are investing for milliseconds. For HFT traders, 'long term' is a half-second.

Financial Confusion

Millions of people struggle financially because they use words they do not understand.

Many times, so-called "financial experts" use financial terms or jargon to sound intelligent and to confuse their client. For example, I once attended a financial seminar and the "financial expert" was using words like *stochastic*, *moving averages* and *dark pools*. As the saying goes: *"If you can't dazzle them with your brilliance, baffle them with your BS."*

The reason so many people lose money when investing is because someone baffled them with financial BS.

One word that amused rich dad was the word "broker." He often chuckled when someone used that word, saying,

> *"The reason a person is called a 'stock broker' or a 'real estate broker' is because they are often broker than you are."*

Rich dad thought it was a high risk to take investment advice from someone who did not eat unless they sold you something. He also said,

> *"Most people get financial advice from sales people, not rich people. That is why most investors lose money."*

Rich dad had nothing against sales people. Instead he said:

> *"It is up to the investor to know the difference between good financial advice and a sales pitch."*

As Warren Buffett says:

"Wall Street is the only place that people ride to in a Rolls-Royce to get advice from those who take the subway."

The Power of Words

Rich dad would not allow his son and me to use words like "I can't... " and "I can't afford it." Rich dad would say that the people who use those words the most are poor people. He would often say, "People say 'I can't' work for people who say 'I can.'"

Rather than say, "I can't afford it" rich dad instructed us to ask, "How *can* I afford it?" And in place of the word *hope*, he preferred the words "I intend" or "I will."

Like Dr. Fuller, rich dad was very careful about the words he used. Although he was not very religious, he often used lessons from Sunday school to make his points. When reminding us of our word choices and the power they have, rich dad would quote from the book of John:

"And the word became flesh."

The Cash Heist

When Bucky used the word "heist" in the title of his book, I was a bit shocked. "Heist" is a very strong word and I was sure Fuller thought long and hard before incorporating that word into the title of his book.

I wondered if Bucky was angry when he chose that title or simply knew his time on spaceship earth was limited. It's clear that wanted to make a strong statement.

Finishing *Grunch of Giants* in 1983, I immediately looked up the word *heist*.

The simple definitions of the word heist are:

1. *Noun: a robbery*

2. *Verb: steal*

Again, I thought his use of the word *heist* was a bit strong, direct, and dangerous—because he was using the word *heist* in connection with institutions we trust, hold sacred… institutions that are at the core of our culture.

Until he wrote *Grunch of Giants*, Fuller was generally known as the "Friendly Genius." His use of the word *heist* was a departure from his reputation for benevolence. Accusing our schools, banks, legal system, government, politicians, and military of a "gross universal cash heist" was a departure for the "friendly genius."

It was at that point that I decided to do some of my own research. What I found deeply disturbed me.

The Heist of Education

The first two questions I asked myself were: Who controls education? *and* Who determines what is taught in our schools?

What I learned troubled me.

In 1903, John D. Rockefeller created The General Education Board. There was much controversy about why he created this organization. Some people say he created The General Education Board to improve education. Others say he created it to hijack the educational system of the United States. While *heist* and *hijack* are not the same words, they have similar meanings.

Around the same time, another of the Robber Barons, Andrew Carnegie, promoted his Foundation for the Advancement of Teaching. It seems both Rockefeller and Carnegie were working to influence the American education agenda, directing what students were taught in school.

The question is: What was their agenda?

I'm reminded, again, that the Generalized Principle, *unity is plural, and at minimum two,* applies. While some people will say Rockefeller and Carnegie were working for the good or our children, others say exactly the opposite.

In my search, I came across reports, written 60 to 100 years ago... inflammatory reports from credible people, reports that were hard to believe. What they accused Rockefeller and Carnegie of orchestrating, and the words they used, are best not repeated.

Today, looking back on those reports with decades of hindsight, there does seem to be some validity to the concerns. Those most critical of Rockefeller and Carnegie accused the two men of wanting to break the American spirit—and using the education system to do it.

Americans are individuals who left their countries of birth for freedom from oppression and for the opportunity of a better life. A shot at the American Dream. This made the DNA of Americans too strong, too independent, and too ambitious to be subservient to the rich and powerful. Those critical of Carnegie and Rockefeller believed that before the rich and powerful—people like Rockefeller and Carnegie—could gain further control over Americans and the wealth of America, the American spirit had to be weakened and Americans made dependent upon the government for financial support.

Q: *And is this why there is no financial education in our schools?*

A: It's certainly possible. Today, when you look at the chart I used in Chapter One, there does seem to be some validity to the concerns of credible people decades ago.

Dependent upon the Government

It's tough to argue with statistics. And it appears that Americans are becoming more dependent upon the government… and that the Entitlement Mentality is replacing the American Dream.

As we've seen before:

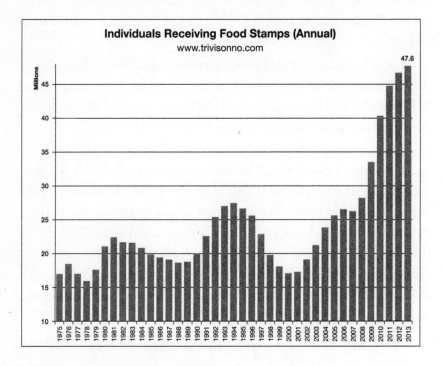

Decline of the Middle Class

Now look again at the chart on the next page on the decline of the middle class in America. And then take another look at the chart of the Social Security fund.

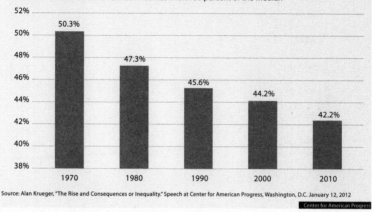

Fewer households are earning middle-class incomes

Not only have middle-class incomes stagnated, but the share of households that are earning middle-class income has also been in decline since the 1970s. The share of American households earning between 50 and 150 percent of the median income was 42.2 percent in 2010, down from 50.3 percent in 1970.

Percent of households with annual incomes within 50 percent of the median

Source: Alan Krueger, "The Rise and Consequences or Inequality." Speech at Center for American Progress, Washington, D.C. January 12, 2012

Center for American Progress

Dependent upon Social Security

Today in America, there are approximately 70 to 80 million baby boomers getting ready to retire.

Approximately 65 million Americans—38 million households—have little to nothing set aside for retirement. That means more than 60 million people may soon be dependent upon the U.S. government to take care of them.

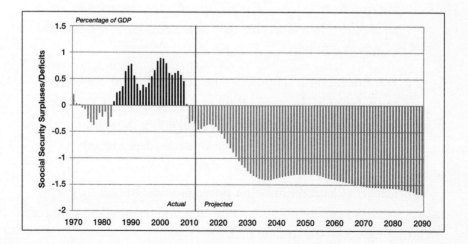

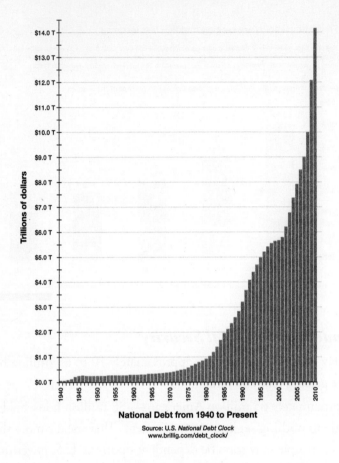

National Debt from 1940 to Present

Source: U.S. *National Debt Clock*
www.brillig.com/debt_clock/

Q: *Are you saying that, 60 to 100 years ago, the people who accused the rich, (the GRUNCH people) of using the education system to weaken the American spirit were ostracized, made to sound like quacks and heretics?*

A: Yes. Education is supposed to be pure, hallowed, for higher purposes only. To accuse Robber Barons such as Carnegie and Rockefeller of intentionally weakening the spirit of the American people via education was considered heresy.

Rockefeller's General Education Board proclaimed that they were taking young people out of the Agrarian Age and training them for the Industrial Age. And they did do that.

Yet, if you look at what's going on in America and the world today, it's not hard to see that Americans are becoming more dependent upon the government for life support. America today is less a democracy and more an oligarchy, a country with a few extremely rich, powerful people and a growing gap between the rich and everyone else. In many ways, America is becoming more like modern-day Russia, a land of oligarchs, than the democratic America our founders envisioned.

Regardless of whether you believe Rockefeller and Carnegie were working for good or evil, what I found through my research validated Fuller's concern about GRUNCH, the ultra rich and powerful, the oligarchs, taking control of important institutions such as education and why there is little if any financial education in schools.

In 1935 President Franklin D. Roosevelt introduced Social Security during the height of the Great Depression. Today, Social Security, Medicare, Food Stamps, and now Obamacare are part of the DNA of the American culture. It seems that more and more Americans today cannot survive without these government programs.

So why would the ultra rich and ultra powerful work to influence education and leave out financial education? I leave that to your imagination.

Teacher of the Year

In 1983, it was almost sacrilegious to criticize education. In many ways, education was on the same level as religion.

Yet, as I did my research, I came across teachers who were defecting, like priests walking away from their church.

One such teacher was John Taylor Gatto. And he was no ordinary teacher. He was named New York City Teacher of the Year in 1989, 1990, and 1991 and New York State Teacher of the Year in 1991. Also in 1991, he wrote a public letter in *The Wall Street Journal* announcing that he planned to quit teaching, saying that he no longer wished to *"hurt kids to make a living."*

He is the author of five books including *Dumbing Us Down* and *The Underground History of American Education.*

The Purpose of Education

There are three economic classes in America:

Rich

Middle Class

Poor

As stated previously, there was a time when it was illegal to teach a slave to write. Without education a slave would always be poor.

My research convinced me that the purpose of modern education was to take poor people and educate them in ways that would create a large middle class of educated workers, executives, professionals, and soldiers… more specifically: employees, consumers, and taxpayers.

The purpose of modern education was never to take the middle class and make them rich. That, in my opinion, is why there is no financial education in our schools.

This is why this chart tells an interesting story.

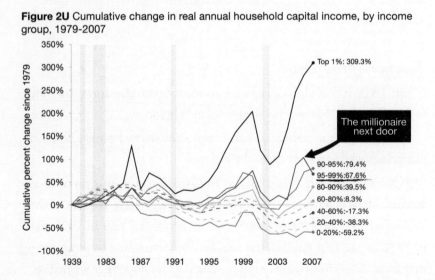

Figure 2U Cumulative change in real annual household capital income, by income group, 1979-2007

This chart explains why *The Millionaire Next Door*, described in that book as a person of the middle class who became a millionaire via inflation of their home and retirement account, may not be a millionaire in the near future.

And one of the ways GRUNCH steals our wealth begins in our schools, via the lack of financial education.

Why Savers Are Losers

Like education, saving money is held as sacred. Going to the bank to save money is a bit like going to the church and leaving behind an offering to the financial gods of GRUNCH.

Without financial education, how would the average person know that the banks steal their wealth via their savings? They wouldn't.

A saver's wealth is heisted via a banking mechanism known as the Fractional Reserve System. The concept of fractional reserve banking is thousands of years old. Why it isn't taught in school is no mystery to me. It's the way banks make money. And it's not pretty.

Thousands of years ago, when a merchant wanted to travel across the country, rather than carry gold or silver, the merchant would deposit their gold and silver with a 'banker' for safekeeping. The banker would then issue a 'claim' for that gold on a piece of paper. The merchant would travel from his home to a far away city, buy goods and pay for them with the piece of paper called a 'claim.' The seller of the goods would then go to his bank and could 'claim' the payment in gold or he could simply use the piece of paper, the 'claim,' and buy something else.

Bankers soon realized that people liked paper—the 'claim'—because it was more convenient to carry than gold or silver and easier to use in day-to-day transactions.

It was not long before bankers were "printing claims" and "lending claims" to borrowers who wanted money. Things worked well, as long as the owners of the gold and silver did not want their gold and silver back.

If and when the owners of the gold and silver realized their banker was lending out more "claims" to their gold and silver, a "run on the bank" occurred. A "run on the bank" occurs when the true owners of the gold and silver no longer trust their banker and turn in their "claims" for the return of their gold and silver. If the banker has more "claims" than gold or silver, the bank collapses and savers are losers.

This is why the Fractional Reserve System was created. Simply stated, a bank can only lend out a specified 'fraction' of the money that's in its vaults. There are specific limits to the amounts they can lend.

To keep things simple, let's use a fractional reserve of 10. This means, if you deposit $10 into your savings account, the bank can lend out $100 (or 10 times your $10) to people who want to borrow money.

A diagram of this fractional reserve system makes things a bit easier to understand.

The Bank	**You**

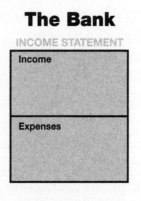

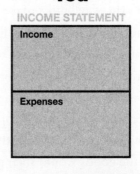

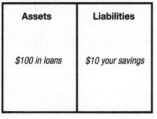

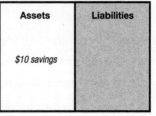

The diagram on the previous page illustrates two things:

1. Your $10 in savings is your asset

2. Your $10 in savings is the bank's liability.

Once again, you'll note: *Unity is plural, and at minimum two.* In this case, for there to be an asset there must be a liability.

Q: *Why is my $10 my asset but the bank's liability?*

A: By definition, assets put money in your pocket and liabilities take money from your pocket. In this example, when you save $10, the bank must pay you interest. So the cash, the interest, flows from the bank's pocket to your pocket. The diagram below explains the process.

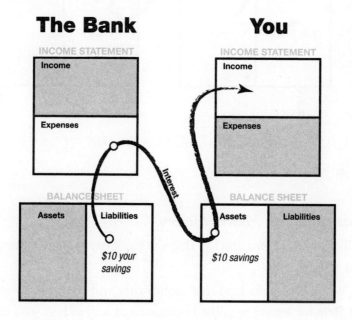

The Bank's Assets

If the fractional reserve is 10, the bank can lend your $10 ten times. And the $100 in loans made by the bank is an asset for the bank.

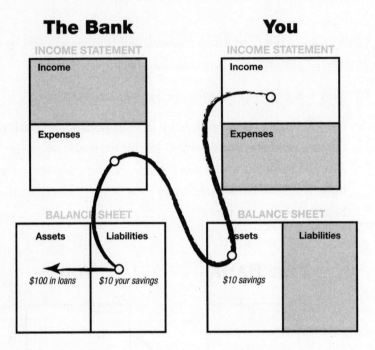

Q: *So the bank's assets are the loans it makes?*

A: Yes.

How the Bank Makes Money

Let's be generous and say that the bank pays you 5% interest on your savings.

When the banks lend that money they will charge between 10% and 50% for letting (qualified borrowers as well as high-risk ones) "use" your money.

That means the bank pays you:

Your $10 at 5% interest = 50¢ for one year

Let's say the bank charges 10% interest on the $100
(your $10 x 10) it loans:

$100 x 10% = $10

Q: *So the bank pays me 50¢ and they are paid $10 on my $10?*

A: Yes. This is an overly simplified example, but this is how the fractional reserve system works.

Q: *How does this steal my wealth?*

A: The fractional reserve system devalues the value of your savings. Your $10 now purchases less because your $10 is now $100 in the economy. It's known as inflation.

Q: *Is inflation bad?*

A: Inflation is good for debtors and bad for savers, which is why savers are losers. Inflation is why life is harder for millions of people today.

Q: *Why is life harder?*

A: Because life becomes more expensive.

Q: *So that's how my wealth is stolen via the banking system?*

A: This is one simple example. There are many more. If you take this fractional reserve system to the next level, you will understand why savers really are the biggest losers.

Q: *The next level? You mean what happens if the borrower of the $100 deposits that $100 back into the bank?*

A: Exactly. And then the bank lends out $1,000.

Q: *And what happens to my $10 in savings?*

A: It's worth less and less.

Q: *It's worth less and less?*

A: You got it. The entire modern monetary system is based upon inflation. The banks and governments want inflation.

Q: *Why?*

A: For many reasons. One reason is so that debtors can pay back their debt with cheaper dollars. Another reason is because consumers spend money faster if they expect prices to go higher.

Q: *Why is that?*

A: Think about it. If a person thinks cars will be 10% higher next year, he or she will buy a car this year. But if they expect the same car to be 10% less next year, they're likely to wait until next year.

Q: *Doesn't inflation cause people to be gamblers?*

A: Yes. Many people will buy a house this year hoping to flip it next year. The same is true with stocks and precious metals. Rather than have a stable, growing, and productive economy, we have an economy of speculators and gamblers.

People who "flip houses" or "trade stocks" add little value to the economy. While they make some money, "flippers" actually make life harder and more expensive for other people.

A person who buys a house for $100,000 and flips it for $120,000, doing little or nothing to improve the property, has added little to the economy, except to make life more expensive. The same is true for a person who buys a stock for $10 and sells it for $15 two days later. They have done little for the economy.

Q: *Are you saying that is bad?*

A: No. All I am saying is that's what happens when you have an economy that grows on inflation rather than production. Savers become losers and life becomes harder because life becomes more expensive. Inflation motivates many people to become consumers rather than investors. They eat, drink, and shop, because tomorrow prices may be higher.

When people wonder why the gap between the rich and everyone else is growing, some of the blame can be placed on our banks, the fractional reserve system, and of course, the lack of financial education in our schools… schools that actually encourage students to save money.

The Heist via Taxes

Many people believe paying taxes is being patriotic. Yet, if you study American history you'll learn that the American Revolution began in 1773 as a tax protest known as the Boston Tea Party. For years, America was pretty much a tax-free or low-tax nation.

Q: *Why do some people think paying taxes is patriotic?*

A: In 1943, during World War II, the U.S. government passed the Current Tax Payment Act. The government needed money to fight the war and needed tax revenue to pay for the war. Until 1943 the government had to wait for taxpayers to pay their taxes. To solve this problem, the Current Tax Payment Act was passed.

Q: *What did the Current Tax Payment Act do?*

A: It allowed the government to get paid before the worker got paid. Bucky Fuller said it allowed the rich to put their hands directly into the workers' pockets. Today, it's a giant, ongoing cash heist that gets bigger and bigger as the government gets needier and the rich get greedier.

Remember, the entitlement mentality did not start with the poor. The entitlement mentality started at the top, with GRUNCH and the plan to heist our wealth via the banks, government, and taxes.

The 1943 Current Tax Payment Act gave rise to the military-industrial complex that former General and outgoing President Dwight D. Eisenhower would later warn about in 1961. In 1943, with tax dollars now pouring into the government on a monthly basis, the military-industrial complex could declare war forever. The Cold War began and trillions in tax dollars went into producing weapons of mass destruction. Obviously, GRUNCH and friends of GRUNCH profit greatly from war and the fear of war. I've often thought that all GRUNCH has to do is use the media machine to whip up a potential threat from Iraq, North Korea, Russia, the Taliban, Al Qaeda or ISIS (Islamic State) and U.S. taxpayers feel that paying taxes is patriotic.

Q: *Are you saying the threats are not real?*

A: No. I know we have enemies. All I'm saying is that we will always be at war because war is profitable. For centuries, war is how nations have stolen the wealth of other nations. War is a giant cash heist on many levels… and on people, through blood, sweat, and taxes on both sides of the war, real or perceived.

Who Pays Taxes?

Pictured below is my rich dad's CASHFLOW Quadrant. It is also the title of book number two in the Rich Dad Series, *Rich Dad's CASHFLOW Quadrant.*

E stands for employee

S stands for self-employed, small business, or specialists... like doctors, lawyers, and consultants

B stands for big business, companies with 500 or more employees

I stands for professional investor (And while many people invest, they may not be professional investors. Professional investor is specific tax category.)

Taxes and the Quadrant

Taxes tell an interesting story.

TAX PERCENTAGES PAID PER QUADRANT

E and S: Those who go to school and get a job pay the highest taxes.

B and I: Those who operate according to the rules of GRUNCH pay the least taxes.

Again, this is why Lesson One in *Rich Dad Poor Dad* is The Rich Don't Work for Money. People who work for money, for paychecks, have their wealth heisted via taxes.

When President Obama promised to raise taxes on the rich, he raised taxes primarily on *high-income earners* in the E and S quadrants.

Heist via Bailouts

How many times have we heard this quote from former Federal Reserve Chairman Ben Bernanke repeated?

"One myth that's out there is that what we're doing is printing money. We're not printing money."

In 1994, G. Edward Griffin published his classic book *The Creature from Jekyll Island*. It is a long, yet easy-to-read history of the Federal Reserve Bank and includes the history of banks and the banking industry. If you love crime stories, you will love this book.

The title, *The Creature from Jekyll Island*, comes from the story of how the concept of U.S. Federal Reserve Bank was created in secrecy on Jekyll Island, Georgia. It had to be formed in secrecy due to opposition to the concept of a Central Bank in America. Many of the founders of America were vehemently opposed to a Central Bank, like the Bank of England, that would control the money supply in America. The founders feared a Central Bank would eventually have more power than the U.S. government.

As English banker named Amschel Rothschild stated:

"Let me issue and control a nation's money and I care not who writes the rules."

My take on the core theme of *The Creature From Jekyll Island* is:

"Bailouts are the name of the game."

In other words, *bailouts* are another method GRUNCH uses to heist our wealth. Make no mistake: bailouts are not accidents. GRUNCH designed bailouts into the system.

In 2008, when the bailout of the biggest U.S. banks began, many people thought "bailouts" were something new, an emergency procedure to save the economy. Nothing could be further from the truth. Bailouts allow banks to lend money to "friends and family members of GRUNCH." If "friends and family" lose the money, they don't pick up that tab—the taxpayers do.

Bailouts protect GRUNCH. The biggest banks aren't held accountable and do not have to pay for their mistakes. If you and I make financial mistakes, we suffer the consequences even to the point of declaring bankruptcy, going to jail, or losing everything.

The Bush Bailout

During the 1980s, there were the S & L (Savings and Loan) bailouts. One of the more interesting was the bailout of Silverado Savings and Loan. Neil Bush, another son of former President George H.W. and Barbara Bush, was a member of the board of directors of Denver-based Silverado Savings and Loan. Since his father was Vice-President of the United States at the time, Neil's role in Silverado's failure was a focal point of media attention.

The U.S. Office of Thrift Supervision investigated Silverado's failure and determined that Bush had engaged in numerous "breaches of his fiduciary duties involving multiple conflicts of interest."

"Breaches of his fiduciary duties involving multiple conflicts of interest" means the bank violated its responsibilities to its customers (savers) and made loans to Bush's friends for businesses in which he had an interest.

Although Bush was not indicted on criminal charges, a civil action was brought against him and the other Silverado directors by the Federal Deposit Insurance Corporation, the FDIC. The parties reached an out-of-court settlement, with Bush paying $50,000 as part of the settlement.

The point I want to make is this: The *Denver Post* reported that **Silverado's collapse cost taxpayers $1 billion.**

Once again, GRUNCH, the ultra rich and the powerful, wins… and taxpayers lose.

The Twinkies Bailout

In 2012, Hostess Brands, makers of Wonder Bread and Twinkies, an iconic crème filled sponge-cake snack, went out of business.

The retirement fund for the Hostess truck drivers was also in trouble. It could not make the retirement payments to the drivers.

In 2013, President Obama approved a "bailout" of the drivers' pension plan. While many hailed this "bailout" as benevolent, decent, and necessary to protect the drivers… keep in mind that there are always three sides to every coin. The question is, Who did Obama *really* bailout? The drivers or the Ottenberg family, owners of a 140-year-old bakery business? When the company went down, it meant the Ottenberg family would be the only contributors to the pension plan. If that happened, the Ottenberg family would go bust.

Q: *Are you saying President Obama "bailed out" the Ottenberg family, not the drivers?*

A: No. I'm saying Bucky would say, "Unity is plural, and at minimum two" and rich dad would say, "A coin has three sides, heads, tails, and the edge. Intelligent people stay on the edge and look at both sides."

Since GRUNCH controls the 4 Ms—*military, money, minds,* and *media*—most of the popular media report on only one side of the coin or the story, in this case the bailout of the drivers. Rarely will you see a news report that delivers two or more sides. Bear in mind that the entitlement mentality starts at the top, not the bottom. This is why GRUNCH wants the public to believe these bailouts are good for the everyday person—"Joe the plumber"—not the ultra rich.

Q: *You could replace the Bush family bailout with the Ottenberg family bailout couldn't you?*

A: I believe you can replace Bush and Ottenberg, as well as Rockefeller and Carnegie, the Clintons, Obama, and Romney with GRUNCH. And as I've said, repeatedly, this is why I believe there is no financial education in our schools.

People who are uneducated financially do not ask tough questions. All they hear is what they want to believe, and most want to believe the government is there to protect them. In reality, the government exists to protect the rich. That is why the Federal Reserve Bank bailed out the banks, not the homeowners.

That is why Fed Chairman Bernake began printing trillions of dollars as this chart from Chapter One shows.

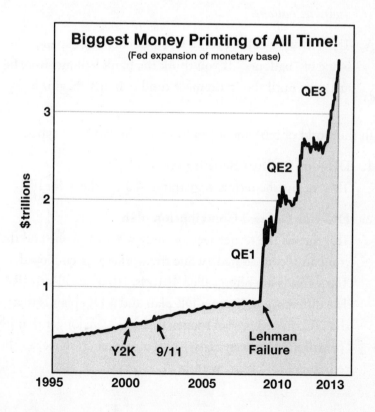

Q: *Was he lying when he said that?*

A: Not really. He just wasn't telling the full truth. Remember, all truth has at least two sides. It was true that the money in circulation was not changing. That's because the money he was printing was going to bailout the banks. The money he was printing was not going into circulation.

In 2014, the big banks are flush with cash, but they are not lending that money to small businesses or "Joe the Plumber." Again, Bernake bailed out the big banks, but not the homeowners, whose jobs, homes, wealth, and futures were stolen by the big banks. This is one more reason why I believe Fuller used the word *heist* in the title of his last book.

Q: *What is the difference between the bank bailouts and the Twinkies bailout?*

A: The Twinkies bailout sets a new precedent. It expands the scope of "bailouts." If you think the bank bailouts were big, just wait until the "retirement fund bailouts" begin.

In the world of retirement funds, there are two basic types.

1. **DB—or Defined Benefit plan**
   This means the retiree is guaranteed a paycheck for life.

2. **DC—or Defined Contribution plan**
   This means the retiree receives only what he or she and their company "contributed" while the worker was employed. These funds are often called 401(k)s, IRAs, and Roth IRAs. The difference between a DB plan and a DC plan is that the DC can run out of money if retirees live longer than the "contributed" money lasts—or if a market crash causes their retirement to "crash" with it.

The "Twinkies Bailout" was a bailout of a DB, a Defined Benefit plan. In theory, DB plans have professional management, while most DC plans are managed by the retiree.

Bailing out Twinkies can be viewed as yet another example of Wall Street protecting its own. These "professional money managers," many with advanced degrees from prestigious schools, should have been working for and protecting the workers but, in reality, they were working for Wall Street.

No one really knows just how many of these "professionally managed" DB funds are in trouble. By bailing out another DB retirement fund, President Obama reinforces the precedent for bailing out other DB funds in trouble. If the economy weakens or if the stock market crashes, the next bailout could be a multi-trillion dollar bailout.

Q: *Will the workers with a DC pension plan be bailed out?*

A: It's possible, but I doubt it. Most of the people with DC plans don't work for Wall Street or come from ultra rich families.

Q: *Aren't retirement plans protected by the government?*

A: Not really. The PBGC, the Pension Benefit Guarantee Corporation, is an insurance company. If pension funds go bust, the PBGC steps in. The problem is the PBGC cannot cover its obligations.

In 2014, PBGC's deficit was more than $35.6 billion and growing. The government may soon have to *bail out* the PBGC.

The same bailout provisions are found in The Affordable Care Act, known as Obamacare. The insurance companies involved in this program are protected by "government bailout" provisions.

Remember, a *bailout* means the rich and powerful make money. But if the rich and powerful *lose* money, the taxpayer guarantees their bailout.

Heist via Nixon

President Richard Nixon did a lot to contribute to today's financial crisis.

1971: Nixon took the U.S. dollar off the gold standard. This hurt the poor, the elderly, and anyone on fixed incomes. Taking the dollar off the gold standard also caused a massive boom in the global economy. Even the middle class *millionaire-next-door* got rich via pay raises, rising home values, and soaring retirement portfolios.

1972: Nixon traveled to China and opened the trade doors between the two nations. This was good for owners of factories, who moved their production to China. It was bad for American workers who now had to compete with a low-wage Chinese labor force.

1974: President Nixon resigned in disgrace on August 8 over his involvement in the Watergate Scandal.

A few days later, on September 2, 1974, ERISA—the Employee Retirement Income Security Act—was signed into law by President Gerald Ford, who had just replaced Nixon. ERISA morphed into the popular 401(k) plans that many U.S. employees now subscribe to.

Again, look closely at the titles of many government acts, such as the Affordable Care Act. Oftentimes, they are exactly the opposite of what the title implies. Specifically, we're learning that the Affordable Care Act actually made health insurance more expensive for many workers. And with ERISA, the security of an employee's retirement income became much less secure.

As stated in the earlier comparison between DB and DC pension plans, a DB plan (in theory) assured a paycheck for life. A DC pension plan funds retirement only as long as there is money in the employee's DC plan. Millions of workers are now counting on the stock market to keep their hopes and dreams of a secure retirement alive. That's gambling—not investing.

The chart from Chapter One poses some interesting questions. The question I ask is: What will happen in the near future? Will the stock market keep going up? Will it go sideways? Or will it go down?

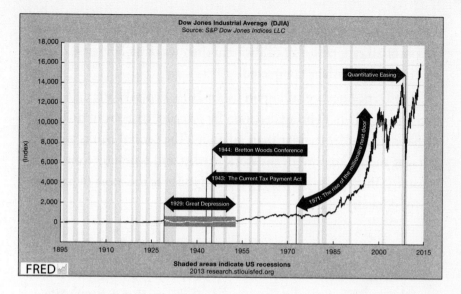

If the stock market crashes, what will happen to the millions of baby boomers with DC pension plans? Will the government bail them out like it bails out the rich and powerful, the members of GRUNCH?

Q: *If the market crashes, could there be another Great Depression?*

A: I will let you answer that question for yourself. From my point of view, millions are already in a great depression. They are the millions of people who are already relying on government support, or are among the working poor, or feel the stress of a shrinking middle class… all hoping a good education will save them and their kids.

The Dark Ages

As I've said I wondered when the Dark Ages began. How are we held in a prison that has no steel bars, chains, or locks? One way is a lack of financial education. My research found we the people have been warned for years. For example in 1802 Thomas Jefferson said "I believe that banking institutions are more dangerous to our liberties than standing armies.

"If the American people ever allow private banks to control the issue of their currency, first by inflation, then by deflation, the banks and corporations that will grow up around the banks will deprive the people of all property—until their children wake up homeless on the continent their fathers conquered."

The Dark Ages are still upon us. In 2014, central banks all over the world are fighting deflation by printing trillions of dollars. Deflation is harder to fight than inflation. The central banks are printing money to prevent the stock market and economy from crashing. This is why the crisis we are in today is the most dangerous in world history.

Boom then Bust

The middle class millionaires-next-door enjoyed the boom caused by inflation. What are they going to do if the market deflates? What happens if their home prices, stock prices and pay raises don't go up? What can they do?

How to Get out of the Dark Ages?

The question is: Who's next? What if this *cash heist* does start in our school system?

Q: *So what if education is the problem?*

A: Then that's good news—because then education can *solve* the problem for some people.

Q: *Some people? Not all people?*

A: No, not all people.

Q: *Why not?*

A: Because not all people are willing to learn. Most are hoping that everything will stay the same... and that tomorrow will be the same as yesterday. And that they'll get through another day, and week, and year.

Q: *Will tomorrow be the same as yesterday?*

A: I'll let you answer that question for yourself.

In Conclusion

Using Fuller's process of *prognostication*—looking at the past to see the future—it seems:

Class Warfare:

In 1971: The poor and working class had their wealth stolen when the U.S. dollar went off the gold standard.

In 2007: The middle class had its wealth stolen when millions lost their jobs, their homes, and their retirement savings.

Q: *Who is next? Are the rich next? Or, as Jefferson warned, "Will our children wake up homeless on the continent their fathers conquered?*

A: We'll look at answers to that question in the next chapter.

Chapter Five

THE NEXT CRASH

---

*"My ideas have undergone a process of emergence by emergency.
When they are needed badly enough, they are accepted."*
— R. Buckminster Fuller

In 2002, applying what Dr. Fuller taught me about predicting the future, *Rich Dad's Prophecy*, was published. The book was a combination of rich dad's warnings and Bucky's lessons from *Grunch of Giants*.

Basically, both men were saying the rich were playing games with money and a monstrous day of reckoning was approaching. They believed the game of stealing our wealth was spinning out of control and that even the rich could not prevent the inevitable.

In 2002, *Rich Dad's Prophecy* predicted a giant stock market crash that would occur sometime around the year 2016. The book also predicted that a secondary crash would occur prior to the giant crash of 2016.

When you look at the graph of the Dow, you can decide for yourself if the crash predicted in *Rich Dad's Prophecy* is possible.

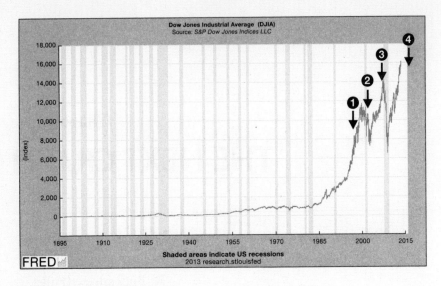

These are they key dates:

1. I began writing *Rich Dad's Prophecy* in 1998.

2. *Rich Dad's Prophecy* is published in 2002.

3. *Prophecy* predicts a secondary crash prior to the crash of 2016... and that crash occurred in 2007.

4. *Rich Dad's Prophecy* predicts the giant crash will occur around 2016.

Q: *Do you think a 2016 crash will occur?*

A: I would encourage you look at the chart and make your own decision. The reason Fuller is considered one of the world's greatest futurists is because he simply looked at the past to predict the future. You can do the same thing with this chart. While you are predicting the future, take a look at what the Economist magazine calls one of the biggest crashes in history, the crash of 1929.

If the giant crash of 1929 led to the Great Depression, which lasted 25 years, how long will the New Depression last, if *Rich Dad's Prophecy's* predictions comes true? What does your crystal ball say?

Q: *Let's say you're right. What does this all mean to me?*

A: If the prophecy is true, it means that the cash heist is becoming the giant cash heist. If Fuller and rich dad are correct, the next group to lose their wealth will be the rich who hold their wealth in the stock market. Once again… look at the past and you will see the future.

1971: The poor lost their wealth when President Nixon took the dollar off the gold standard. The poor lost because the money they worked for became worth less and less. When they earned more money, they paid higher taxes. As the money they work for loses value, prices keep going up. The harder the poor work, the further behind they fall. Today, in 2014, all across the world, the working poor are demanding a "living wage." Unfortunately, even if the minimum wage is increased, the poor will continue to be poor because they work for money that is no longer money.

2007: Those in the middle class lost their "biggest asset," their homes. For years, the middle class lived well, thanks to their credit cards. When the value of their homes increased they would take out a home equity loan and pay off their credit card debt. In 2014, housing prices remain low and mortgage, credit card debt, and student loan debt hang like an albatross around their necks. The heist took place via their home's drop in value.

2016: If the predictions in *Rich Dad's Prophecy* come true, many of the rich whose wealth is in the stock market will wiped out. Their wealth will be stolen in the next 'giant stock market crash.'

In 2007, as *Rich Dad's Prophecy* predicted, a massive stock market crash occurred. It was the secondary crash, the crash prior to the giant crash. A massive economic emergency wiped out millions of people.

Today the world remains in an economic emergency. The poor get poorer, the middle class is shrinking, and millions of highly educated young people cannot find jobs.

For others, the 2007 economic emergency was the best thing that eve happened to them. They emerged from the emergency richer, stronger, and more optimistic about the future.

The question is: Will the coming economic emergency be the best—or worst—thing for you?

According to Bucky Fuller, the word *emergency* is another very powerful word, but a word that's often misused and misunderstood. He said, "The base word within *emergency* is *emerge*," a generalized principle. Fuller said, "Out of emergency, new things, people, and societies emerged."

For those looking for a second chance in life, the good news is that many people *do* emerge from emergencies stronger, better, and richer.

As always, though, there's a second side to this 'coin.' The bad news is not all people emerge from financial emergencies. Many are wiped out.

How will you emerge from the coming economic emergency?

A Growing Emergency

Fuller believed humanity was facing more than just a run-of-the-mill emergency. He believed humans were at the edge of a massive emergency. He believed humanity was on the edge of an *evolutionary* emergency. Most important: He believed we still had the option to choose to "emerge" as a new form of humanity—or perish.

He was concerned that our leaders were not addressing these emergencies. Rather than address the emergencies facing them, our leaders continued to sweep the problems under the rug. They'd 'kick the can' down the road… pushing the problem onto the plates of the next generation. Ignoring today's emergencies is setting the stage for giant emergencies known as calamities, disasters, or collapses.

Fuller believed humans have been focused on money, power, and weapons development for too long. He believed it was time to change. Fuller believed it was time for all of us to make a conscious shift and put focus more on what he called "livingry," than "killingry." If we did not make that shift, Fuller believed, humans would become extinct, much like the dinosaurs.

Cooperate or Compete?

One step in this evolutionary process would require that humans learn to be *cooperative* rather than *competitive*.

Humans are naturally competitive. Since the days of cavemen, humans learned to survive by fighting, by being at war with other humans. Today, humans continue to invest trillions of dollars into war and weapons… while millions of people go to sleep hungry.

Fuller's solutions intrigued me. As I sat in the audience listening to him, I always wondered how many of our global emergencies could be solved if only we *cooperated* rather than *competed* with one another. It sounded simple, yet from personal experience, I knew that getting humans to *compete* was much easier than getting them to *cooperate*.

As a young boy, I remember my rich dad saying, "I don't need competition. Everyday, my employees come to work and we fight amongst ourselves. My hardest job is getting my own workers to cooperate. It seems each person wants his or her own 'turf,' their own 'rules,' their 'way of doing things' and especially 'their own opinion.' If we cooperated more and competed less internally, everyone would make more money."

Listening to Fuller, I realized *why* it would take global emergencies for humans to cooperate. Until there was a true emergency, it was human nature to compete or, even worse, do nothing.

Fuller's concern was that the coming emergencies would be bigger than our abilities, even if we did, finally, choose to cooperate.

Competing for Grades

As Fuller spoke, I realized schools taught students to *compete*, as opposed to *cooperate*. In school, I often wanted to cooperate… but that's often called *cheating*.

In many ways, the classroom is not much different than a Neanderthal man's cave. In the cave known as a classroom, young kids are taught to compete against their classmates, if they want good grades. Being an "A" student does not necessarily mean the student is smarter. An "A" means you won, you beat your classmates. It is no different than being the bully in the schoolyard, beating up on weaker classmates. Small wonder that many kids do not like school. If the "A" student cooperates and helps their classmates, they are thrown out of school for cheating.

Parents encourage this primitive academic behavior. They want their young, club-wielding Neanderthal to beat the brains out of his or her classmates. Although few will admit it, they want to make sure their child gets the good grades, good job, and high pay. Grades, in many ways, are about money.

After a child graduates at the top of the class, the next cave the "A" student enters is the corporate world. Once hired, the young executive's job is to "climb the corporate ladder," aka "beat on your peers." They don't dare cooperate because there is only one seat at the top, and they want to make sure that seat has their name on it. If businesses cooperate too closely, it can be called a monopoly or, if it is less formal but still anti-competitive, it can be collusion—both of which are often illegal.

In the world of politics, cooperation could be considered treason. Republicans do not dare cooperate with Democrats. In many cases, if a politician "reaches across the aisle," their own party cuts off their arm. This is why there is so much "grid lock"—versus real progress—in government. Nothing gets done and the emergencies grow into disasters.

As Fuller stated, humanity's next evolutionary challenge is to learn to cooperate and solve our global problems. The problem is, humans only know how to compete. We have yet to really *learn* to cooperate. Learning to cooperate would be evolutionary.

Q: *But can a person learn in a classroom where students cooperate rather than compete?*

A: Sure.

Q: *Can you give me an example?*

A: Sure. I'll give you two personal examples.

1. Cooperation is essential in team sports. As they say: There is no 'I' in team, but there is an 'I' in win. Too many students leave school understanding the 'I' in win, rather than the 'we win' in team.

    In team sports, the team supports each individual to be the best they can be, or the team doesn't win.

    In the classroom, the individual student does not want others to be the best they can be. The individual wants to the best.

2. In the Marine Corps Officer Candidate School (OCS), young officer candidates are evaluated *not* on how many times their team wins, but how well their team cooperates as a team.

    On some evaluations, winning or losing is not even mentioned.

    In other words, winning is not as important as cooperating in the Marine Corp. Marines know that if they cooperate, they win. This is why Marines believe they are the best branch of service. And although Marines believe they are the best of all the branches of the service, *no Marine believes he or she is better than another Marine.* Regardless of rank, Marines are taught to respect and value other Marines. This is why it's said, "Once a Marine always a Marine." The bond between Marines is spiritual, not financial.

So to answer your question—"Can you learn in a cooperative environment?"—the answer is "Yes." But that's not always true in an academic classroom. The world of academics is a world of "kill or be killed," a world of "survival of the fittest," a world of "winners and losers," a world of "I'm smart and you're not," a world of "I win," not "We win"... and a world where "cooperation is cheating."

Q: *Are you saying I should start cooperating?*

A: Not exactly. Again, the Generalized Principle is, "Unity is plural, at minimum two." The Marine Corps trains each Marine to be strong as an individual and as a team member. When it comes to money, many individuals are weak individually so no one wants them on their financial team.

In the world of money, the richest people in the world operate on teams. Yet most people operate as individuals. That's why most people are losers in the game of money.

To maximize your opportunity for a second chance, you have to get strong individually as well as learn to cooperate on a team.

The Big Problem

The problem is that our inability to cooperate is causing our emergencies to grow into giant, global emergencies. Fuller was concerned that these growing emergencies, if not addressed now, would overwhelm us and become bigger crises than humans could handle.

The following are some of the emergencies he felt were growing into giant disasters.

Environmental Emergencies

As far back as the 1950s and '60s, Fuller warned of the effects of global warming.

Today, rather than cooperate to solve our environmental problems, many leaders *deny* there are environmental problems. Whether you believe in global warming theories or not, the fact remains that our polar ice caps are melting, seas are rising, soil run-off is polluting our oceans, and fish that feed billions around the world are being depleted.

Whether a person believes in global warming or not, the facts are that our weather is becoming more violent. In recent years there have been horrific hurricanes like Katrina and Sandy, super-size tornadoes ripping across the Midwest, and ice storms shutting down southern

U.S. cities including New Orleans and Atlanta. Around the world, there is severe drought in some areas as well as massive flooding in other areas.

This state of emergency is growing.

Nuclear Emergencies

In the 1950s and '60s, Fuller spoke out against atomic energy. He said that the closest god wanted humans to be to atomic energy was 93 million miles, the distance from the earth to the sun.

Although nuclear power companies claim that nuclear power is "clean energy," what they do not say is that nuclear waste is lethal. Today, nuclear waste is stored in deep, underground caverns. The problem with nuclear waste is it takes hundreds of thousands of years to become inert or incapable of causing further damage. It also takes billions in taxpayer dollars to safely store that toxic waste.

In 2012, the tsunami that hit Japan spread atomic waste around the world via ocean currents. The effects of that single emergency will be with us for thousands of years.

Military Emergencies

In the 1970s and '80s, during the height of the Cold War, Fuller said, "Either war is obsolete, or we are." He meant, human intelligence had developed weapons of mass destruction so severe that if there were a nuclear war, only cockroaches would survive. There would be no winners and losers. In the next war, there will only be losers.

To Bucky, the idea that war was obsolete was a sign from the Great Spirit that humans needed to change direction, to evolve, to cooperate rather than fight.

Unfortunately, humans killing other humans continues. Today, terrorists have the power to take on the most powerful militaries in the world. Today, terrorists use cell phones to incite and recruit new soldiers to fight, use our airliners as weapons, and have access to information on how to build "suitcase-size" nuclear, biological, and chemical weapons. The United States spends trillions on its military, yet a simple, inexpensive "dirty bomb" detonated in New York, London, Tokyo, or Beijing could cripple the world economy.

In 1972, I saw one of my squadron mates shot down by a Chinese-made SA-7, a heat-seeking, shoulder-fired rocket known as the Strela. The Viet Cong soldier who fired the rocket did not need much training. All he did was point and pull the trigger, and the rocket did the rest—taking down a multi-million-dollar CH-53 Jolly Green Giant helicopter and killing 62 Marines. In 2014 a Malaysian passenger jet was shot down with the same weapon.

Today, the United States spends trillions on military training and new weapons. At the same time, an untrained terrorist with a $10,000, heat-seeking rocket fired at an airliner has the power to cripple, if not bring down, the world economy.

Unfortunately, fighting terrorism is not like fighting a conventional war, a war like World War II. We learned that lesson the hard way in Vietnam. Terrorists do not wear uniforms and they do not have to obey the rules of engagement of traditional war. Terrorists do not have factories, harbors, airfields, or towns that can be destroyed. They win because they have little to lose. Terrorists win because they can fight anywhere, everywhere, and forever. When we fight terrorism, we fight an ideology, not a country. Many believe that the more we focus on killing terrorists, the more terrorists we create.

Rather than evolving, getting the message that "war is obsolete," we continue to fight. This is why the emergency of terrorism grows.

Pandemic Emergency

Centuries ago there was the plague spread by fleas and rats and today we have Ebola spread by airliners.

Economic Emergency

Today, wars are fought with money, which is causing a massive economic emergency. Tragically, wars fought with money are often wars against innocent people, both young and old, rather than armed terrorists.

Today, billions of people live in day-to-day economic emergency.

It was this growing economic emergency that motivated Dr. Fuller to write *Grunch of Giants*, a book about how and why the rich and powerful intentionally steal the wealth of innocent people.

Maslow's Hierarchy of Needs

In 1943, Abraham Maslow, an American psychologist born in 1908, presented his paper on "A Theory of Human Motivation" in *Psychological Review*.

Although Maslow did not present his concepts as a triangle, today his *Hierarchy of Needs* is often represented as one.

Maslow's Hierarchy of Needs, pictured below, explains how economic emergencies affect our lives.

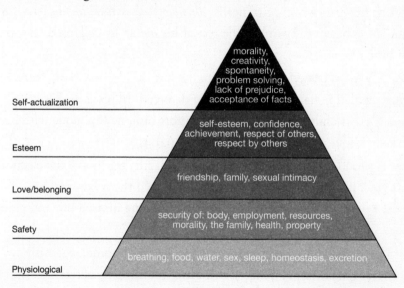

Maslow studied what he called *exemplary people* such as Albert Einstein, Jane Addams, Eleanor Roosevelt, and Frederick Douglass. According to Wikipedia, he explained his rationale for choosing his subjects by stating: "The study of crippled, stunted, immature, and unhealthy specimens can yield only a cripple psychology and a cripple philosophy." It is important to note that the two base levels of the triangle, *physiological* (or survival) and *safety*, affect the three top levels of *love/belonging, esteem,* and *self-actualization.*

Real Life Collapse

In 1973, I returned home to Hawaii from Vietnam to find my poor dad unemployed. He had resigned from his post as Superintendent of Education to run for Lt. Governor as a Republican against his boss, the Governor, a Democrat. After losing the election, the Governor black-listed my dad from future employment in state government.

To survive, he withdrew his life savings, cashed in his retirement savings, and bought a national ice cream franchise. Within a year, his business failed and my dad was an unemployed and out-of-money PhD.

It was painful to watch Maslow's Triangle collapse on my dad. When his first two levels of needs, *physiological,* (which means survival) and *safety* began to crumble, the rest of his hierarchy collapsed on top of him.

My mom passed away soon after he lost the election. Two years later my dad remarried, but was soon divorced. In his early 50s, as much as his children attempted to comfort him, he was alone with his grief, without much love or sense of belonging.

A proud and confident man most of his life, the loss of the election, his wife, his title, his power, and his job caused the collapse of his *self-esteem* preventing him from standing up, dusting himself off, and going back into the world.

Rather than become *self-actualized,* he sat at home, watching television, drinking, an angry and bitter man who was resentful of his friends who were more successful.

When you look at the top of Maslow's triangle, you see the word *morality.*

I am thankful that my dad never lost his morality. He had many questionable offers from people who wanted to use his past reputation and success, but he refused. He chose to struggle financially rather than sell his morality.

Many people do sell their morality. When the base levels of *survival* and *security* are weakened, many people turn to crime, selling drugs or sex, stealing, lying, and cheating. When people are desperate, frivolous lawsuits increase and ambulance-chasing attorneys get rich.

In 1973, I saw the future. Not the future of my dad's generation, but of my generation and that of our kids.

Rather than become productive and self-reliant, more and more people seem to believe they are entitled to government support. Their financial plan is to win the lottery, or hope for an accident so they can sue and live off the settlement.

When *survival* and *security* are weakened, a moral, ethical, and legal civilized society is the first casualty.

In my opinion, we are in an economic emergency. The questions are: Who will emerge from this economic emergency and who will not? Who will fortify their self-esteem, become self-actualized, and take a second chance at money and life?

Q: *What did Maslow mean by self-actualization?*

A: A self-actualized person is unstoppable. That is why he studied great people like Albert Einstein, Jane Addams, Eleanor Roosevelt, and Frederick Douglass. He did not study the mentally ill or neurotic people.

A self-actualized person will keep going no matter what obstacles are put in their way.

Q: *So a self-actualized person does not need to be motivated?*

A: Exactly. Today, when it comes to money, career, or finances, most people need to be motivated. They want incentives. They'll ask, "How much will you pay me if I work for you?" And "What is my bonus?" "When will I receive a pay raise?" and "What are my benefits?"

Many need "praise," which means "If you stroke my self-esteem, I will work harder." Many also say to themselves,

"If you do not make me feel good I'll quit or make your life miserable at work. I will gossip and spread rumors. And if you really upset me, I will take you to court and sue you for abuse or sexual harassment."

Others seek "punishment." Many only get back to work when counseled or reprimanded. Many need "performance reviews" to perform.

Q: *Doesn't this start at home?*

A: I believe it does. I hear many parents say, "I give my child $100 for every 'A' they receive on their report card." Others say: "I pay my child to read a book" or "I pay my child to do chores around the house." To me, this is training a child to work for money. This is why my rich dad refused to pay his son and me. He said, "Paying a child to work is training a child to be an employee."

Rich dad was training his son and me to be *entrepreneurs*, self-actuated boys who would grow up to build assets that produced income and created jobs. He was not willing to teach us to grow up to be adults who worked for money, job security, and benefits. He said, "If that is what you want to do when you grow up, then go to school, graduate, and work for people like me."

Fame, Success, and Money vs. Greatness

Simply said, fame, success, and money can be achieved by motivation, inspiration, intimidation, and compensation. For most people, being famous, successful, and rich are enough. But these achievements are not the same as greatness.

According to Maslow, greatness can only be achieved by *Self-actualization*. When you are self-actualized, you become unstoppable—even if you do not have money, a good job, a great education, professional credentials, good health, or a roof over your head.

When considering your second chance, you may want to ask yourself: "What would cause me to be self-actuated?" If you are self-actuated, you have a better chance of emerging stronger from the coming emergencies.

The Top of the Pyramid

Always remember, at the top of Maslow's pyramid is the word *morality*.

For many people, in their quest for fame, success, and money, the first casualty is their morality. This is why many ambitious and successful people fail to achieve greatness. For many people, the desire for fame, success, and money is so strong they are willing to do whatever it takes, including sacrificing their values and morals. We all know people like this. You may see them on TV, read about them in the paper, work with them... you may even go to the same church as they do.

In the real world, there are many great people who never achieve fame, success, or money. They are the billions of unsung heroes, people like my poor dad, who refused to sell their morality, no matter how tough their life became.

In your second chance, I hope you will choose to be one of these great people. Aspire to greatness, even if you do not achieve fame, success, and money. The world needs more great people, people who operate from "we win," rather than "I win." People who live by a strong moral code.

A Greatness Quiz

Ask yourself these questions...

Question: *Who do you know who has fame... but is not a great person?*

Answer:

_____

Question: *Who do you know that has success... but is not a great person?*

Answer:

_____

Question: *Who do you know who is rich… but is not a great person?*

Answer:

_____

Question: *Who do you know who is great… but may not be famous, successful, or rich?*

Answer:

_____

Question: *Have you told this great person that they're great and what they do that makes them great?*

Answer:

_____

Wouldn't it be great if you got in touch with them and let them know why you think they are a great person? And be sure to tell them what specifically they do that you believe makes them great. To just say "You're great" is nice, but lacks clarity and power.

If you personally acknowledge others for their greatness, the greatness in both of you increases. If one great person acknowledged 10 other great people, and those 10 great people each acknowledged 10 others, the power of Maslow's self-actualized greatness would spread around the world.

If greatness, rather than despair, spreads around the world, we the people will have the power to solve the coming emergencies, rather than wait for our leaders to solve them.

Of course the "I win" people won't like it, but it's time for them to step aside and let the *world* win.

The Next Economic Emergency

In the coming economic emergency, millions of people who are affluent today are likely to experience the collapse of their personal Maslow's hierarchy of needs.

In previous chapters, I wrote about the economic emergency the United States and most of the world are facing. In this next section I offer specifics on the looming economic emergency, who I believe will be the next casualties, and why.

The Poor

In 1971, the poor lost the War on Poverty when President Nixon took the U.S. dollar off the gold standard. When banks and governments print money, taxes, inflation, and poverty go up.

Unfortunately, many of these people will not emerge from their economic emergency.

The Middle Class

In 2007, the middle class lost the War on the Middle Class when millions lost their jobs, homes, and retirement savings.

On April 22, 2014, the front-page headline of the *New York Times* stated:

"The American Middle Class Is No Longer the World's Richest"

The article stated that the middle class in Canada is now earning more than the middle class in America, and that the poor in much of Europe earn more than the poor in America.

As of 2014, few middle-class Americans have emerged from the last economic emergency. Unemployment runs high among the educated young as well as the experienced and educated older workers. It is estimated that two-thirds of the unemployed who have found jobs earn less than they did prior to the 2007 sub-prime mortgage crash.

Who's Next?

In 2002, *Rich Dad's Prophecy* was published. It was a combination of rich dad's lessons on government, money and banking and Bucky Fuller's lessons on GRUNCH, Generalized Principles, and prognostication and how to predict the future.

Rich Dad's Prophecy predicted the biggest stock market crash in world history sometime at or around the year 2016. As you might guess, Wall Street's media machine attacked with a vengeance, doing their best to discredit the book and me. *Smart Money, Money* magazine, and *The Wall Street Journal* were not kind to my rich dad's prophecy, even though the predicted crash was more than a decade away.

Q: *Why do you think that the media went on the attack?*

A: *Rich Dad's Prophecy* is about the flaws in the 401(k) retirement plans that millions of workers contribute to every month. These flaws are among the reasons my rich dad predicted that the biggest stock market crash in history would hit around the year 2016. It's my opinion that the *Smart Money* reporter felt she needed to discredit my book (and me) because the media outlets needed to protect their advertisers who, by the way, are part of GRUNCH.

I understand protecting your advertisers, but why lie? Why sell your morality for money? *The Wall Street Journal* and *Money* magazine countered rich dad's prophecy without lying. I respect and expected that response. There are always two sides and an edge to every coin. *The Wall Street Journal* and *Money* magazine presented their sides. I surely did not expect them to agree with rich dad, my book, or me.

Q: *Who is going to be right?*

A: I am afraid rich dad and Bucky Fuller are already right. As I've stated often over the past 10 years: "The job of a prophet is to be wrong."

Q: *Why be wrong?*

A: Prophets sound warnings. They do not want to be right. They want people to take action, prepare, and make changes before the prophecy comes true.

Q: *Has that happened?*

A: I'm afraid not. GRUNCH and our government leaders have only made the coming emergency bigger and the looming prophecy more destructive.

Q: *How accurate is rich dad's prophecy?*

A: I will show you a chart you've seen before and let you decide for yourself.

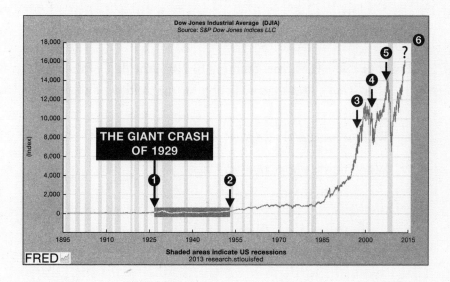

Point 1: Note the arrow pointing to the giant stock market crash of 1929. Many people today, even the *Economist* magazine, have gone on record saying the 1929 crash was one of the biggest crashes in history.

Point 2: The Great Depression actually lasted 25 years.

Point 3: Note the arrow pointing to 1997, when *Rich Dad Poor Dad* was published, stating 'your house is not an asset.'

Point 4: Note the arrow pointing to 2002, the date *Rich Dad's Prophecy* was published.

Point 5: Note the arrow pointing to 2007, the October peak of the Dow Jones Industrial Average. In *Rich Dad's Prophecy*, I clearly stated there would be one more giant crash before the monster crash in 2016.

The 2007 crash followed that prediction. The 2007 crash wiped out millions of homeowners, many finding out the hard way that their house is not asset—a warning statement first presented in *Rich Dad Poor Dad*. That book was published 10 years earlier in 1997.

The 2007 crash wiped out the middle class and many middle class millionaires-next-door.

Point 6: Note the arrow pointing to 2016, the date of the *Rich Dad's Prophecy* prediction for the mother of all crashes.

Q: *Will the prophecy come true?*

A: Who knows? I hope not.

Chapter Six

HOW MUCH IS A QUADRILLION?

---

*"You cannot get out of the way of things
you cannot see moving toward you."*
– R. Buckminster Fuller

Many of us know there are giant problems ahead. The problem is, we cannot *see* them. If we could see them, we would probably get out of their way.

The Invisible Age

In 1974, the financial future for millions of workers changed.

In 1974, the Congress of the United States passed ERISA, the Employee Retirement Income Security Act, today known as to the mandate that led to the creation of the 401(k). Today, most Western nations have some form of Defined Contribution plans for workers. For example, Australia calls its plan the Superannuation, in Canada it's known as the Registered Retirement Savings Plan (RRSP), and in Japan it's known as the Defined Contribution Pension Plan.

That year, 1974, signaled the end of the Industrial Age retirement plan for employees. Industrial-Age workers had DB (Defined Benefit) pension plans. A DB pension plan paid the employee for life.

A DC or Defined Contribution pension plan is exactly that, the worker *contributes* to the plan. And only funds in a DC pension plan are those contributed to the fund. If the plan runs out of money after the employee retires, the worker is out of luck. And, possibly, in financial trouble.

A DB pension plan is an Industrial Age pension plan; a DC pension plan is an Information Age pension plan.

And in the Information Age, it's easy to watch the markets. In additional to TV and radio reports, we can check stocks and markets 24/7 on the Internet or with an app on our phone. If the stock market is up people feel good, and if it's down they worry.

Giants You Cannot See

Without financial education, few workers are aware that there are financial markets that are much, much, bigger than the stock market. These giant markets are invisible to the financially uneducated. If any of these giant markets catches a cold, coughs, and sneezes, the hopes and dreams of a comfortable retirement for billions of people may be wiped out by giants they cannot even see.

Later in this chapter I will go into further detail about one of these invisible giants, a giant known as the derivatives market, an invisible giant that nearly brought down the world economy in 2007.

Before focusing on that giant, it is important to understand why Fuller said:

> *"You cannot get out of the way of things*
> *you cannot see moving toward you."*

One of the more important lessons I learned from Fuller was to train myself to see what most people cannot see.

How to See the Invisible

I remember a story Fuller told about seeing his first automobile as a young boy. He recalled how terrified people were—and how terrified the horses were. Many people believed the automobile was just a novelty for the rich, a fad that would soon pass. As we all know, the automobile soon replaced the horse as the primary transportation for the masses… and the world changed. The automobile made lives easier and made many people extremely wealthy. The horse is now the novelty of the rich.

He told us that story to make a point: That humans could *see* the automobile. The automobile was the new technology that transitioned the world from Agrarian-Age transportation, *the horse*, to Industrial-Age transportation, *the horseless carriage*.

His point was that in years past, *we could see the changes that would change our lives*. In the Information Age, we *cannot* see the changes that are changing our lives. In many ways, the Information Age is the Invisible Age.

Increasing Unemployment

One reason why unemployment is increasing and high-paying jobs are harder to find is because in the Information Age, humans are being replaced, much like the horse was replaced by the automobile. In photography, for example, humans were once needed to process film into prints. I still remember taking my roll of exposed film to the local drug store, dropping it in a little paper bag, and coming back a week later to pick up my pictures.

Digital photography not only eliminated tens of thousands of jobs, it wiped out the Eastman Kodak Company. Not that long ago, Eastman Kodak was a Fortune 500 Company, an Industrial-Age giant that went bankrupt because it was not able to transition from an Industrial-Age company to an Information-Age company.

Eastman Kodak was made obsolete by a new technology known as digital photography. Ironically, it was Eastman Kodak that developed digital photography in 1975. The company poured billions into the development of digital photography, but, unfortunately, an old, employee-heavy business model was not compatible with new technology. The company declared bankruptcy in 2012.

The point Fuller was making decades ago is that the loss of jobs will continue as the Information Age marches on. The problem is that people will not see the technology that is replacing them, nor will they see that technology coming. Millions will be happily employed today and suddenly out of work tomorrow, run over by the invisible.

As you plan and prepare for your second chance in life, you must be able to *see* what's ahead... even if it can't be seen with your eyes.

The Blind Leading the Blind

A bigger problem is that our leaders cannot see the changes that lie ahead. They are as blind as the rest of us. This *invisibility of change* is one reason why there is gridlock in Washington with extreme adversarial positions being taken in our nation's capital and in capital cities around the world. Our leaders cannot see the changes... all they can see is each other. So they attack each other, rather than the problem.

Today our leaders promise many things. They promise to:

"create more jobs"

"retrain workers"

"spend money on infrastructure projects that will create jobs"

"raise test scores so our kids can compete in the global economy"

"keep kids in school longer"

"teach more math and science in schools"

"raise the minimum wage"

"stop bailing out the banks"

"tax the rich"

"reduce corporate taxes"

... and other political plans, promises, and ideas hoping to prove to you and me that they know what they're doing, that they are "the man (or the woman) with the plan"—and that they will lead us out of this mess. Yet, in reality, many are only the blind leading the blind.

The ability to 'see' the changes we *cannot see* is the challenge in the Information Age.

Learn to See the Invisible

Your second chance in life may hinge on your ability to learn to see the invisible.

Q: *Why do I need to learn to see the invisible?*

A: Because the future belongs to those who can see the invisible. Those whose minds can see what their eyes can't.

Brain vs. Mind

Fuller often spoke about the difference between a human's brain and a human's mind. To him, they are not the same thing.

Simply said, the brain is used to see *tangible objects*. The mind is used to see the *invisible*. Fuller said the brain sees *objects* and the mind sees the invisible *relationship between objects*. The example Fuller used in his talks was the relationship between the planets. The brain sees the planets while the mind senses the presence of gravity, the invisible force that keeps planets orbiting each other.

In the game of golf, golfers will use their brains to see the ball, the hole and the undulations of the green before striking a putt. The best golfers will use their mind and are able to see an invisible line, as the ball travels over the green to the hole. The golfers who can see that invisible line are the golfers who win tournaments and earn the most money.

In overly simplistic terms, human intelligence is located in the mind, not the brain. That may be why F. Scott Fitzgerald said:

> *"The test of a first-rate intelligence is the ability to hold two opposed ideas in the mind at the same time, and still retain the ability to function."*

Unfortunately, most people are trained to use their brains, but not their minds.

Only One Right Answer

Schools teach students that there is only one right answer. When people believe there is only one right answer, we have arguments, disagreements, divorces, fights, murders, court battles, and wars. Schools teach "answers" that the brain can memorize, versus relationships that the mind can explore.

As rich dad said:

"When you argue with an idiot, there are now two idiots."

Two idiots appear when each idiot thinks there is only one right answer.

When parents and schools teach children that there is only one right answer, the top of Maslow's Hierarchy of Needs is squashed and individual self-actualization is retarded. Self-actualization requires:

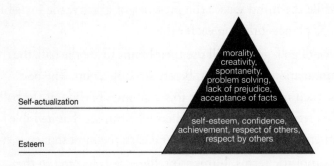

A Second Chance

A shot at a second chance in life requires a person to have the courage to see what most people cannot see. A second chance requires a person who dares to be creative and spontaneous, a person who can come up with multiple answers to solve problems, a person who can accept facts and isn't prejudiced.

A second chance requires self-esteem, confidence, achievement, respect for others as well as earning the respect of others. In a single word, self-esteem requires courage. The word courage is derived from the French word *le coeur,* which means *heart.* Courage does not come from the brain. The world is filled with highly educated "brains" that lack the courage to venture into the unknown or take risks—because courage comes from the heart, not the brain.

A second chance requires knowing the difference between what the brain sees and what the mind sees. A second chance is not about being right or having the right answers. A second chance is about taking action, making mistakes, correcting your course, and bouncing back from failure until you succeed.

Unfortunately, this type of behavior is not validated as intelligent behavior in our schools. In fact, it's the exact opposite that is viewed as "intelligent."

The Mystery of the Invisible

Fuller believed that 99% of the universe is invisible. If that is true, then humans have based much of their existence on less than 1% of what exists... what we can see.

Humans have always been aware of the invisible. For thousands of years, humans across the globe have sensed the existence, mystery, and power of the invisible.

That is why humans have idolized gods, sanctified sacred places, worshiped animal forms, symbols, and humans such as Jesus, Abraham, Mohammed, Buddha, and others. It was through these physical incarnations that humans tapped into the mystery and power of the invisible.

When diseases caused epidemics and widespread death, humans went on "witch hunts" looking for the evil person that brought this evil upon them. The invention of the microscope gave researchers such as Louis Pasteur the ability to see the "invisible"—the germs and bacteria that were killing people, as opposed witches and other evil forces.

Modern-Day Witch Hunts

Today, there are modern day financial witch hunts called *class warfare*. Many people want to believe that it's the rich who are making them poor. While it is true there are some "rich witches," people who have committed crimes against other people, most rich people have done good things that have made them rich.

During the French Revolution, the era that made the guillotine famous, the poor chopped off the heads of royalty, including Marie Antoinette. The poor also rolled the heads of "entrepreneurs," the innovators, risk-takers, job-creators—the future of the French economy. That is what happens when the gap between rich and everyone else gets too wide.

Today, the French economy has yet to recover from the days of the guillotine. Once a world power, France is now a socialist state that still vilifies the desire to be rich.

Q: *Is America getting closer to civil unrest? And class warfare?*

A   Yes. If the poor and middle class keep blaming the rich for their problems, the gap between rich and everyone else will only grow wider in the Information Age.

Q: *Why is that?*

A: In my opinion, there are two reasons.

Reason number one is that the rich can hide their wealth in the realm of the invisible. The rich have the resources to move their wealth. When the rich move their wealth, there is less invested in the economy, making life harder for the poor and middle class. Many companies such as Apple earn billions outside of America, but do not bring that money back to America. They keep that money offshore (legally) because U.S. corporate tax laws would take a large percentage of those earnings. If corporate tax rates were reduced, it's likely that more money would return to America and prosperity would increase.

Reason number two is that if you are angry at the rich, it makes it harder to see what the rich do that makes them rich.

Q: *If I am angry I will be less able to see and do what the rich do?*

A: Yes. That's my opinion. You will see only one side of the coin: *your side.* For an opportunity for a second chance, it's important to understand what the rich do that makes them rich. If you are angry or jealous, you are blind to what the rich do. Knowledge allows people to see. Anger and ignorance causes blindness.

The Evolution of Wealth

To better understand what causes the gap between the rich and everyone else, it helps to look at the evolution of wealth over the four ages of humanity—the Hunter-Gatherer Age, the Agrarian Age, the Industrial Age, and the Information Age.

The Hunter-Gather Age

During the Hunter-Gatherer Age, humans were equal. It was a one-class society. There was no rich, middle class, or poor. The tribal chief lived in a cave, hut, or tent like everyone else. The chief's cave, hut, or tent did not have hot and cold running water. The chief did not have a private jet. It was true communism, where everyone was equal in one commune, one tribe, one community. No one owned anything. The chief lived, ate, and traveled like the rest of the tribe. The chief did not have access to better hospitals and the chief's kids did not go to better schools. Things were fair and people were equal. When food or game became scarce, or the weather changed, they simply moved. Land had no value.

The Agrarian Age

The Agrarian Age began when humans domesticated animals and planted crops. Land became valuable and a two-class society was born, the rich and the poor, those who owned land and those who did not. The phrase *real estate* comes from the Spanish language meaning *royal estate.* The word *peasant* is derived from French words *pays* and *sant,* which means "person of the land." Now that land was valuable, the concept of "tax" and who paid "taxes" was born, peasants paying the king a tax for the privilege to live and work the king's land. In return for the peasant's tax money, the king promised to protect the peasants from other kings.

To keep the peasants under his control, the king would grant large tracts of land to his friends, who were called *barons* and *lords*. This is where the term *landlord* comes from. The landlord collected taxes from the peasants and sent the king his portion of those taxes. With these taxes, the king and his lords could now afford to live in castles, while the peasants lived in huts. The royals rode horses and the peasants walked.

In time of war, the lord would round up his peasants, buy them weapons, train them, and send them into battle, fighting to protect the property of the rich.

The Agrarian Age was the beginning of a two-class society, rich and poor; royals and peasants. In the Agrarian Age, the royals got richer; peasants worked harder, paid their taxes, and fought the king's wars for conquests and expansion. Not much has changed.

The Industrial Age

The Industrial Age ushered in a three-class society: the rich, the middle class, and the poor.

In the Industrial Age, a new kind of land became valuable. In the Agrarian Age, fertile land was valuable. In the Industrial Age, fertile agricultural land was not required for factories, which is why Henry Ford chose the rocky, less expensive, non-agricultural land that is now Detroit to build his automobile factories. Around factories, middle class suburbia spread as the middle class become homeowners and lords of their own castles, their homes.

As industrialization over took agriculture, the kings and lords began selling pieces of the royal estate, becoming bankers and offering "mortgages" to the middle class, so they could buy their own piece of the royal estate. Today, a mortgage payment is the largest expense of most middle-class people.

The poor continue to make rent payments to their landlords.

The Industrial Age gave rise to a new royalty, known as bankers and industrialists. A few ambitious American bankers and industrialists became known as Robber Barons.

Wikipedia offers the following description of Robber Barons:

"In social criticism and economic literature, robber baron became a derogatory term applied to wealthy and powerful 19th-century American businessmen that appeared in North American periodical literature as early as the August 1870 issue of The Atlantic Monthly magazine. By the late 1800s, the term was typically applied to businessmen who used what were considered to be exploitative practices to amass their wealth. These practices included exerting control over national resources, accruing high levels of government influence, paying extremely low wages, squashing competition by acquiring competitors in order to create monopolies and eventually raise prices, and schemes to sell stock at inflated prices to unsuspecting investors in a manner which would eventually destroy the company for which the stock was issued and impoverish investors."

People want to believe *greed* increased exponentially in the Industrial Age. And it did. Greed and ambition increased because the ability for a poor person to become extremely rich increased dramatically during the Industrial Age. Many Robber Barons started out poor and became richer than many kings and queens of the Agrarian Age.

Some of the more famous (or infamous) Robber Barons are:

- Andrew Carnegie (steel)—Pittsburgh and New York

- James Duke (tobacco, energy)—Durham, North Carolina

- Andrew W. Mellon (finance, oil)—Pittsburgh

- J. P. Morgan (finance, industrial consolidation)—New York

- John D. Rockefeller (oil)—Cleveland, New York

- Leland Stanford (railroads)—San Francisco, California

- Cornelius Vanderbilt (water transport, railroads)—New York

Bucky Fuller pointed out that several of these Robber Barons founded some of the most prestigious colleges and universities in America. Robber Barons such as Stanford, Duke, Vanderbilt, Carnegie, and Mellon had their schools named after them. Fuller referred to Harvard University as JP Morgan's School of Accounting. John D. Rockefeller founded the University of Chicago in 1891 and the General Education Board in 1903.

Rockefeller claimed to have started the General Education Board for the purpose of transitioning bright farm boys and girls from the Agrarian Age, into the Industrial Age. Some of these bright young men and women probably became the new "lords" for the Robber Barons, known today as CEOs, CFOs, accountants, and attorneys.

Many suspected that Rockefeller's real purpose for founding the General Education Board was to control the nation's educational curriculum. As stated earlier, the creation of the General Education Board appears to be a "heist" of our educational system. People suspect Rockefeller wanted to educate the best and brightest young people to be employees and executives, but *not* entrepreneurs like him. The good news is, many colleges and universities are now offering programs for students who want to be entrepreneurs, rather than executives and employees. Slower to change and evolve was the large-scale integration of financial education into all school curriculums.

Class Warfare

Today, there is class warfare in America and across the world. Many people believe that today's rich are reincarnations of the Robber Barons of old, no more than crooks and thieves.

Yet, if you are looking for a second chance in life, it is important to stand on the edge of the coin, and see both sides of the coin, both heads and tails. If you see only one side of the coin you may never fully understand what made the Robber Barons extremely rich, richer than kings and queens of old. If you see only one side of the coin, you may wind up on the poor side of this growing war among classes.

Wikipedia supports The other-side-of-the-coin point of view quoting television journalist John Stossel's comments:

"They weren't robbers, because they didn't steal from anyone, and they weren't barons—they were born poor…

"Vanderbilt got rich by pleasing people. He invented ways to make travel and shipping cheaper. He used bigger ships, faster ships, served food onboard. He cut the New York–Hartford fare from $8 to $1. That gave consumers more than any "consumer group" ever has…

"Rockefeller got rich selling oil. First competitors and then the government called him a monopolist, but he wasn't. At the time he had well over a hundred competitors. No one was forced to buy his oil. Rockefeller enticed people to buy it by selling it for less. That's what his competitors hated. His finding cheaper ways to get oil from the ground to the gas pump made life better for millions. Working-class people, who used to go to bed when it got dark, could suddenly afford fuel for lanterns, so they could stay up and read at night. Rockefeller's greed might have even saved the whales, because when he lowered the price of kerosene and gasoline, he eliminated the need for whale oil. The mass slaughter of whales suddenly stopped."

In spite of the good things these capitalists did, many people refer to them derogatorily as Robber Barons rather than people who made life better for people. In other words, the Robber Barons were not greedy. They were generous. If you want to become richer, you may want to find ways to become more generous. Ways to serve more people.

The Information Age

In 1957, the Soviet Union launched Sputnik, the first satellite to orbit the earth. Many people mark this event as the start of the Information Age, the Invisible Age. We all knew the satellite was there, we just could not see it. Today, there are thousands of satellites—satellites we cannot see—running many facets of our lives.

The Information Age caused wealth to evolve yet again. Today there is a new type of real estate: *invisible* real estate. Some people call it "cyber real estate." Cyber real estate is why there are 19-year-old billionaires who never finished school and 59-year-old college-educated executives out of work and looking for a job.

Cyber real estate is found in our mobile devices such as a smart phones, iPads, and computers. When you and I go to Google or Amazon we are no different than a person who lands on Park Place or Boardwalk in the game of *Monopoly*®.

A few of the new Robber Barons, the Invisible-Age entrepreneurs who never finished school, are:

1. Steve Jobs   Apple Computers

2. Steve Wozniak   Apple Computers

3. Bill Gates   Microsoft

4. Larry Ellison   Oracle

5. Tom Anderson   My Space

6. David Karp   Tumblr

7. Dustin Moskovitz   Facebook

8. Mark Zuckerberg   Facebook

9. Michael Dell   Dell Computers

Who Do You Blame?

In many ways, you could blame these individuals for the growing gap between rich, poor, and middle class. You could blame them for high unemployment. You could even blame them for the growing numbers of people on government support programs.

And we can blame ourselves.

As I've stated earlier, when humans cannot see changes, because the changes are invisible, people blame other people. People burn witches, cut heads off with guillotines, and attack each other (think Republicans and Democrats) rather than solve problems they cannot see.

Why the Rich Are Getting Richer

In 1967, when my classmate Andy and I hitchhiked to Montreal, Canada, we weren't only going to see Bucky Fuller's dome, the U.S. Pavilion at Expo 67, the World's Fair on the Future. We wanted to better understand why Fuller often said, "God wanted all humans to be rich." Fuller also said and wrote about in his 1981 book *Critical Path*, "Technologically we now have 6 billion billionaires on Spaceship Earth..." To our 20-year-old brains, that statement was outside our reality. It definitely was not an idea taught in school. In school, we were taught only a few people could be "rich."

Although we stood inside the U.S. Pavilion in Montreal for hours, we did not get the answers we came for. All our *brains* could see was this massive structure, a sphere that seemed to hang in space, a massive dome with very little visible support. It was unlike any other building we had ever seen. The dome enclosed large volumes of space, yet it seemed as light as a feather.

Although our *brains* did not get the answers we were looking for, our *minds* could sense the possibility of the world Fuller could see. Andy and I left Montreal with a profound sense of possibility, of the belief in the prospect of a world that could work for everyone, a world that didn't have to be a win-lose or you-or-me world. A world where we didn't have to kill or steal from others in order to live. A world that could be win-win... you *and* me.

As many of you know, I believe that anyone can take control of their financial future—if they are willing to learn, take action, make mistakes, learn from those mistakes and remain unstoppable. I've proven that a not-so-school-smart kid from Hilo, Hawaii could beat the odds... and I know you can, too. There can be a second chance for you, if you believe in yourself and are willing to put action behind the knowledge you gain.

The Generalized Principle of the Rich

The Generalized Principle of the rich is the principle of *ephemeralization.* In the simplest of terms it means, "to do more with less."

The kings of the Agrarian Age became rich by doing more with less. Rather than move from place to place in search of food, they stopped moving in search of food and began producing food. By caring and cultivating the land, they could produce far more food from the land, feeding more and more people.

The American Robber Barons of the Industrial Age followed the same principle of ephemeralization. They did more with less.

Think back to John Stossel's words (on page 131) on why the Robber Barons were generous people. He is describing the generalized principle of *ephemeralization.*

Q: *So some people say the Robber Barons were greedy and others say they were generous?*

A: Yes. Again, all coins have three sides. Intelligence is being able to stand on the edge of the coin—the edge of the idea or the issue—and see both sides.

Q: *The new Robber Barons are entrepreneurs like Steve Jobs, Mark Zuckerberg, and David Karp? Did they follow the Generalized Principle of ephemeralization?*

A: Yes. Always remember, the horse was replaced by the horseless carriage. In the Information Age, humans are being replaced by technology they cannot see.

Today, cyber-real-estate retailers such as Amazon and Alibaba are wiping out traditional 'real estate'—the retail stores, like Sears and JCPenney. In cities all over the world, millions are losing their jobs.

Q: *And that's why the gap between rich, poor, and middle class is growing?*

A: It's one of the reasons.

Q: *Are you saying some people are operating by Industrial Age ideas and others are operating by Information Age ideas?*

A: Yes. Many highly educated, unemployed executives are still looking for that high-paying job with benefits in the Industrial Age. Unfortunately, most schools and schoolteachers operate by Industrial Age ideas on business and employment. Most schoolteachers want more pay to teach smaller classes. This idea goes against the generalized principle of ephemeralization. They should, instead, be looking for ways they can do more (serve more kids, with better types of teaching, and better results...) with less.

Q: *Aren't some teachers are using the Internet to teach more students at lower prices?*

A: Yes. A few teachers are earning millions doing this—as they should. These teachers are following the principle of ephemeralization. They are doing more with less.

Q: *What will happen to the teachers, or anyone, who does not follow the principle of ephemeralization?*

A: I'll let you can answer your own question. Personally, I believe the days are numbered for people who want to be paid more and do less. Many of the unemployed or underemployed continue to have that Industrial-Age idea running their *brain*, which causes their *mind* to be blind to opportunities around them.

Q: *And our leaders have the same problem? They cannot see the changes?*

A: Yes, which is why the next crisis will be a quadrillion-dollar crisis.

The Invisible Giants

Some of the biggest markets in the world are:

1. The Derivatives Market

2. The Currency Market

3. The Bond Market

4. The Stock Market

5. The Commodities Market

6. The Real Estate Market

The three biggest markets are the top three: Derivatives, Currency, and Bond markets, in that order.

There is disagreement about where the other markets—Stocks, Commodities, and Real Estate—rank in terms of size. For me it's enough to know that they are all giant markets, and markets that overlap, which is why they're often difficult to measure. For example, many people invest in real estate via REITS, Real Estate Investment Trusts, which are technically stocks. The same is true for commodities, stocks, and bonds. It can be confusing.

The Derivatives Market

The important point is: the biggest market in the world is the derivatives market. It dwarfs all other markets. It is the monster few people know about, understand—or can see.

Q: *How big is it?*

A: Prior to the 2007 crash, the derivatives market was estimated to be $700 trillion.

Q: *Why is that important?*

A: Because the crash of 2007 was not really a real estate crash or stock market crash. It was a derivatives market crash.

Q: *So, what is a derivative?*

A: Before answering that question, I will quote comments from a few very knowledgeable experts on derivatives.

Warren Buffett, the world's richest investor says:

"Derivatives are financial weapons of mass destruction."

George Soros, one of the most successful investors in the world, avoids using the financial contracts known as derivatives:

"Because we don't really understand how they work."

Felix Rohatyn is the investment banker who saved New York from financial catastrophe in the 1970s. He describes derivatives as:

"Financial Hydrogen Bombs."

The Other Side of the Coin

Not surprisingly, some people like derivatives. Former Fed Chairman Alan Greenspan, aka The Maestro, who served four U.S. presidents (Reagan, Bush 41, Clinton, and Bush 43) had only good things to say about financial derivatives:

"Concentrations of risk are more readily identified, and when such concentrations exceed the risk appetites of intermediaries, derivatives and other credit and interest rate risk instruments can be employed to transfer the underlying risks to other entities.
As a result, not only have individual financial institutions become less vulnerable to shocks from underlying risk factors,
but also the financial system as a whole has become more resilient."

– Alan Greenspan in 2004

During confirmation hearings in 2005, as Ben Bernanke was poised to replace Alan Greenspan as the new Federal Reserve Chairman, the following Q and A took place:

Senator Paul Sarbanes: Warren Buffett has warned us that derivatives are time bombs, both for the parties that deal in them and the economic system. *The Financial Times* has said so far, there has been no explosion, but the risks of this fast growing market remain real. How do you respond to these concerns?

Ben Bernanke: I am more sanguine about derivatives than the position you have just suggested. I think, generally speaking, they are very valuable. They provide methods by which risks can be shared, sliced, and diced, and given to those most willing to bear them. They add, I believe, to the flexibility of the financial system in many different ways. With respect to their safety, derivatives, for the most part, are traded among very sophisticated financial institutions and individuals who have considerable incentive to understand them and to use them properly. The Federal Reserve's responsibility is to make sure that the institutions it regulates have good systems and good procedures for ensuring that their derivatives portfolios are well managed and do not create excessive risk in their institutions.

Fast Forward to 2007...

When the stock and real estate markets suddenly began collapsing in 2007, causing millions of families to lose their jobs, their homes and their retirement investments, the problem was not really caused by subprime borrowers, bad real estate, or even fraudulent subprime debt. The real problem was derivatives known as CDS, Credit Default Swaps, and CDOs, Collateralized Debt Obligations.

Warren Buffett spoke out saying:

"(Derivatives are) carrying dangers that, while now latent, are potentially lethal."

When the subprime-debt bomb exploded, derivatives were upgraded from "latent" to "lethal."

Derivatives were the invisible Black Death of the financial markets causing banking giants such as Lehman Brothers and Bear Sterns to collapse, and millions to lose their jobs, homes, and futures.

Q: *What are derivatives?*

A: In extremely simple terms, derivatives are insurance policies, like the insurance policy you have on your home or your car.

When subprime borrowers stopped paying on homes they could not afford, these weapons of mass destruction began exploding. The explosions were like Hurricane Katrina hitting New Orleans or Hurricane Sandy hitting New York and New Jersey. The difference is: Insurance companies are regulated and have the resources to pay on claims.

The derivatives market, the biggest financial market in the world, is largely unregulated and enforcement is virtually nil. It's the taxpayers who pay if derivatives go bad, not the banks or the people who sold and profited from the derivatives.

The Real Robber Barons

The Chairmen of Federal Reserve Bank, the U.S. Secretary of the Treasury, and CEOs of our biggest banks could be viewed as the real Robber Barons. They used the Generalized Principle of ephemeralization to make themselves richer, at the expense of the world economy. They were greedy, not generous. And, in my opinion, they violated a Generalized Principle to rip people off, rather than use the principle to make life better.

Today, the gap between the rich and everyone else continues to grow wider. Millions have lost everything, including their dreams. Tragically, only one banker has been prosecuted so far, while Greenspan and Bernanke enjoy their retirement and income from speaking fees.

Q: *Who is responsible for this derivatives crisis?*

A: In the year 2000, President Bill Clinton signed a bill creating the Commodity Futures Modernization Act, the CFMA, which paved the way for a much larger derivatives market. Between 2000 and 2007, the derivative market grew from $100 trillion to $700 trillion. Then the explosions began.

Q: *How big is the derivatives market today?*

A: According to Bert Dohmen, publisher of the respected *Wellington Letter*, in 2014 the derivatives market had grown to $1.2 quadrillion.

Q: *How much is a quadrillion dollars?*

A: It's a s*** load of money.

In the next chapter, I will go into other markets and government manipulation of markets, exploring what very few people know about or see.

Q: *Why would I want to know about that?*

A: So you can have the time to get out of the way of things most people will never see coming.

Chapter Seven

HOW TO SEE THE INVISIBLE

"Words are tool… the most powerful tools made by man.
— R. Buckminster Fuller

In his books and in his talks, Bucky Fuller often spoke about the power of words. During an extremely low point of his life, he realized that many of his problems began with words. "I became very suspicious of words," he said. At that point he decided to be silent until he was sure of the meaning of every word he spoke. His silence lasted for more than two years.

As Fuller spoke, I could hear my rich dad saying over and over again, "Your house is not an asset."

Rather than attempt to explain the difference between assets and liabilities, rich dad would draw this simple diagram:

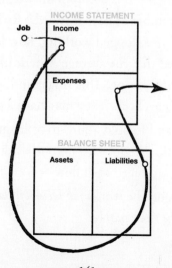

As Fuller spoke to our class, I realized how much of a head start I had, just by simply knowing the difference between the words *asset* and *liability*. Rich dad's simple drawings—the diagrams he sketched time and time again—allowed me to *see* what most people cannot see. Millions of people are in financial trouble because they call their homes and cars *assets* rather than *liabilities*. Worst of all, most people have no idea what an asset really is.

Fuller became very suspicious of words, and so should you.

It's possible that the two most important words in the world of money are *cash* and *flow*. Cash flow determines whether something is an asset or a liability. If you understand the meaning of the words, *cash flow, asset,* and *liability*, your chances for a richer life are greatly improved. The reason most people struggle financially is because they have lots of cash flowing out—and very little flowing in.

I encourage you to take the time to write down every asset and liability you have. The test of an asset or liability is this: If you stopped working, what brings money in and what pulls money out? Most poor and middle-class people only have liabilities—but no assets.

Most retirement plans are not assets. They are unfunded liabilities that will, hopefully, flow money out when your working days are over.

The moment a person begins to look for assets they can acquire or build, their world begins to change. They begin to see the invisible.

Another important word is *wealth*. Fuller defined wealth as "your ability to survive X number of days forward." Rich dad defined wealth by asking, "If you stopped working, how long could you survive?" It's estimated that the average American can survive less than a month without working. This is why millions cling desperately to a job and a steady paycheck. They may have a job, but no wealth.

The reason Kim and I could afford to retire at 37 and 47, respectively, was because we focused on our wealth. We focused on acquiring assets that produced cash flow.

We did not focus on the words *job security, paycheck,* or *investing for the long term in the stock market.*

Rather than focus on the word *saving*, we focused on the word *debt*, and used debt to acquire assets.

Examples of Opposites

When kids are programmed to "go to school, get a job, work hard, save money, buy a house (because your house is an asset), get out of debt, and invest for the long term in the stock market," they are blinded by words. They cannot see the world of the rich on the opposite side of the coin.

Here are some examples of *opposites*...

Employee	Employer
Saver	Debtor
Taxed income	Tax-free income
Liability	Asset
Self-employed	Entrepreneur
Paycheck	Cash flow
Gambler	Investor

Schools train students to use the words on the left. The rich focus on the words in the right-hand column. If a person would take the time—just as Fuller sat in silence for over two years studying the precise meaning of words before speaking them—they would *see* the invisible world of money, a world few people ever see.

Q: *I can see the difference between asset, liability, and cash flow. But what's the difference between a person who is self-employed in the S quadrant and an entrepreneur in the B quadrant?*

A: The self-employed work for money. Entrepreneurs in the B quadrant work for assets.

For example, a real estate agent is self-employed because they work for money, or income in the form of commissions. A real estate *entrepreneur* works to acquire real estate assets that produce cash flow.

The real estate agent will pay the highest percentage in taxes. The real estate investor may pay zero percent in taxes on his or her cash flow.

The real estate agent works for taxed income and the real estate investor works for tax-free income.

Real estate agents will save their money. Real estate entrepreneurs will borrow money to buy their real estate.

If the real estate agent sells 10 houses a year and the real estate entrepreneur acquires 10 rental houses a year, in 10 years, the self-employed real estate agent may have made more money than the real estate entrepreneur, but the real estate entrepreneur will be far *wealthier*, enjoying tax-free cash flow.

Q: *Is this true all over the world?*

A: More or less. Tax laws are basically the same all over the world. Always remember the golden rule: The person with the gold makes the rules.

Q: *Why don't most people know this?*

A: Because most schools only teach students the words listed on the left side of the comparisons on the previous page. That is why most people want a paycheck, while the rich want cash flow. Based upon the principle that *unity is plural*, there are always at least two sides to every coin… the universal duality of yin and yang.

You'll notice this plurality in the CASHFLOW Quadrant. Those on the E and S side work for money; those on the B and I side work for assets.

E stands for employee

S stands for self-employed

B stands for business owner

I stands for investor.

The economic crisis has hurt Es and Ss, but in many cases it has benefited Bs and Is. Those in the E and S quadrants lost because the value of their money and savings went down due to the printing of money, inflation, and higher taxes. Many lost liabilities they believed were assets, liabilities like their homes and the stock value of their retirement accounts.

As I've stressed: When you study the CASHFLOW Quadrant, relative to taxes, you can *see* the bigger picture.

TAX PERCENTAGES PAID PER QUADRANT

Q: *What is the primary reason for the difference in taxes?*

A: One reason is that Es and Ss work for money, they save money, and they invest their money for the long term in the stock market.

The Bs and Is work to create assets. Rather than save money, they borrow money. And rather than invest, they produce the assets that the Es and Ss invest in.

Q: *Why is this so confusing?*

A: Because you are seeing the *opposite* side of the *invisible world of money.* It is like being right-handed and being asked to use only your left hand. It takes a while to adjust.

Q: *How do I begin to retrain myself to see the opposite side of money?*

A: I always suggest playing *CASHFLOW.* The more you play the game and teach others to play, the more you will *see* the difference between a paycheck from a job in the Income column and cash flow from your Asset column. Remember, Es and Ss focus on the Income column and Bs and Is focus on the Asset column.

CASHFLOW is the only game that teaches players the power of debt. The player who can use debt will beat those who are afraid of debt. The better you get at playing the game, the more clearly you will understand why debt and taxes make the rich richer, while those same things (debt and taxes) make the poor and middle class poorer. Once you *see* the opposite side of the coin, your confusion will clear and a whole new world will open to you. A world that's invisible to most people.

Q: *So the difference begins with paying more attention to the words I use?*

A: Yes… and being aware of what GRUNCH is doing—being aware of the things that most people don't see.

As we use the past to see the future, there are new voices that are sharing their thoughts on what the future will look like. I like to call them "the new Chicken Littles"… and I'm interested in what they have to say about the future.

The future is about what we see… and what we don't see. It's about how the evolution from the Industrial Age to the Information Age represents more than changes in the way we do business. We live in a 24/7 world and much of what drives today's fast-paced change is invisible. We train our minds to see what our eyes can't when we pay attention to words… and who's using them.

Before introducing a few of the new Chicken Littles, I want to review the story of *Chicken Little*. It's a very old but timeless folk tale, told in many languages, and is more relevant today, perhaps, than ever before. Here's one of the most widely recognized versions.

The Story of Chicken Little
Chicken Little was in the woods.
A seed fell on his tail.
Chicken Little said,
"The sky is falling. I will run and tell the king."

Chicken Little met Henny Penny.
He said, "The sky is falling, Henny Penny."
Henny Penny said,
"How do you know, Chicken Little?"
Chicken Little said,

"Some of it fell on my tail."
"We will run." Said Henny Penny.
"We will run and tell the king."

They met Turkey Lurkey.
Henny Penny said,
"The sky is falling, Turkey Lurkey."
"How do you know, Henny Penny?
"Chicken Little told me."

"How do you know, Chicken Little?"
"I saw it with my eyes.
I heard it with my ears.
Some of it fell on my tail."
"We will run." Turkey Lurkey said,
"We will run and tell the king."

They met Ducky Lucky.
Turkey Lurkey said,
"The sky is falling, Ducky Lucky."
"How do you know, Turkey Lurkey?"
"Henny Penny told me."

"How do you know, Henny Penny?"
"Chicken Little told me."

"How do you know, Chicken Little?"
"I saw it with my eyes.
I heard it with my ears.
Some of it fell on my tail."
Ducky Lucky said, "We will run.
We will run and tell the king."

They met Goosey Loosey.
Ducky Lucky said,
"The sky is falling, Goosey Loosey."
"How do you know, Ducky Lucky?"
"Turkey Lurkey told me."

"How do you know, Turkey Lurkey?"
"Henny Penny told me."

"How do you know, Henny Penny?"
"Chicken Little told me."

"How do you know, Chicken Little?"
"I saw it with my eyes.
I heard it with my ears.
Some of it fell on my tail."

Goosey Loosey said,
"We will run and tell the king."
They met Foxy Loxy.
Goosey Loosey said,
"The sky is falling, Foxy Loxy."
"How do you know, Goosey Loosey?"
"Ducky Lucky told me."

"How do you know, Ducky Lucky?"
"Turkey Lurkey told me."

"How do you know, Turkey Lurkey?"
"Henny Penny told me."

"How do you know, Henny Penny?"
"Chicken Little told me."

"How do you know, Chicken Little?"
"I saw it with my eyes.
I heard it with my ears.
Some of it fell on my tail."
Foxy Loxy said,
"We will run.
We will run into my den,
And I will tell the king."

They ran into Foxy Loxy's den,
But they never come out again.

A Story of Courage

There are different endings to this story, as well as many
different interpretations of its meaning. In this ending, Foxy Loxy
eats the feathered creatures. In other endings, Chicken Little and his
friends escape.

The story of *Chicken Little* is a story of courage. It takes courage
to speak out.

As the old saying goes:

"The only thing necessary for the triumph of evil
is for good men to do nothing."

We all know people who do nothing, people who choose not to speak out about things that concern or upset them. And I suspect that there's a reason for that. It's not easy being Chicken Little. I learned that first hand when *Rich Dad Poor Dad* was published in 1997. When I wrote that "Your house is not an asset," I was ridiculed and challenged. And when, in 2002 in *Rich Dad's Prophecy*, I stated there was going to be the biggest stock market crash in history sometime around the year 2016—and that there would also be an earlier crash in between 2002 and 2016—I became labeled a Chicken Little, a guy running around shouting "The sky is falling!"

Bucky Fuller, rich dad, and I were not credible Chicken Littles, at least when it came to money and the economy. We were not trained economists, bankers, or stockbrokers; we didn't work on Wall Street. So it's understandable that we were not taken seriously.

New Chicken Littles

Soon after Y2K, the year-2000 millennial computer-crash scare, a new breed of Chicken Littles began warning, "The sky is falling." And they got people's attention. Why? They truly were a new breed of Chicken Littles. There were educated at great schools and had high-level career experience in the world of business, banking, finance, and the military... the world Fuller said was run by GRUNCH.

The good news is more and more people are paying attention to their warnings. The bad news is they are saying the same things—albeit from different perspectives—that Fuller, rich dad, and I have been saying for years.

Q: *Is that fair?*

A: I didn't say it was fair. I'm saying a little financial education may assist you in seeing both sides of every Foxy-Loxy story.

Q: *Can this go on forever?*

A: It's possible, but I doubt it. There are forces in play that are more powerful than words, manipulations, and lies.

Q: *What kinds of forces?*

A: I will introduce you to three new Chicken Littles who have the courage to speak out. They may give you insights into the forces that are building, forces more powerful than phony unemployment and inflation reports, false promises to voters, and intentional market manipulations by the Plunge Protection Team. I'll go into more detail on these forces and the manipulations of the PPT later in this chapter.

The New Chicken Littles

There are three new Chicken Littles who have joined the growing chorus of Chicken Littles throughout history. They are men who have the courage to speak out. These new Chicken Littles have been educated in great schools and have worked in the higher levels of banking, within the military, and in corporate America. All three have written books that express their views on today's crises.

The three are:

Richard Duncan *The Dollar Crisis* and *The New Depression*

James Rickards *Currency Wars* and *The Death of Money*

Chris Martenson *The Crash Course*

Richard Duncan

Richard studied economics at Vanderbilt University, graduating in 1983. He studied International Finance at Babson College, graduating in 1986.

He worked for the World Bank in Washington D.C. and has been a consultant to the IMF, the International Monetary Fund. Richard is the author of *The Dollar Crisis* (2002) and *The New Depression* (2012).

The *Economist* reviewed both books saying:

"His analysis, again highlighted in his latest book,
The New Depression, still seems acute."

After reading his book, *The Dollar Crisis*, in 2003, I have become fast friends with Richard. It is nice having a friend in high places who can explain the world economy from the points of view of the World Bank and the IMF. We have shared the stage at events in many parts of the world, explaining how 'money' is making the world poorer.

In his books and his presentations, Richard explains how "hot money" flows from country to country, causing booms and busts. For example, when this "hot money" flowed into Japan, the economy of Japan boomed. Management experts from corporations and top universities flocked to Japan to study the "Miracle of Japan." Many thought it was Japanese management that caused the boom, when it was really "hot money."

In 1991, the "hot money" left Japan and the Japanese asset bubble burst. Japan has not yet recovered. In fact, Japan's economy is still in flux and it appears that neither political nor banking actions can save their economy.

The "hot money" flowed into Southeast Asia, creating the Asian Tigers or Asian Dragons, countries like Thailand, Indonesia, Taiwan, South Korea, and Hong Kong. And the same thing happened. The economies of these countries boomed, then busted in the 1997 Asian Financial Crisis.

The "hot money" then flowed into America. Fannie Mae, Freddie Mac, and the nation's biggest banks took that "hot money," made subprime loans, created derivatives out of these subprime loans, and in 2007 the U.S. economy collapsed—exactly as Richard predicted, in 2003, that it would.

The "hot money" flowed into Europe and today once rich and powerful nations like Ireland, Greece, Italy, and Spain are financial basket cases that may not recover.

In early 2000, Richard also warned the world of the growing threat of derivatives. Unfortunately, his warnings have gone unheeded.

In looking at the world from Richard Duncan's viewpoint, it is easy to see that "hot money"—money created after 1971, when Nixon broke the Bretton Woods Agreement and took the U.S. dollar off the gold standard—has caused pain and poverty in South America, Mexico, Asia, the United States, and Europe.

Q: *Why does "hot money" cause poverty?*

A: The same way 'subprime mortgages' caused the American economy to nearly collapse. When money flows in, the banks must lend. Always remember your savings are your asset, but the bank's liability. Due to the Fractional Reserve System, explained earlier in this book, the banks lend multiples of their reserves. For example, let's say that the fractional reserve rate is 10—which mean banks can lend 10 times their reserves. The fractional reserve rate can vary depending upon how much money the Federal Reserve wants to put in or pull out of the economy.

When banks lend, prices go up. When prices go up, banks lend more and more and more… until the economy cannot handle any more 'credit' or 'debt.' In other words, foolish people keep borrowing until they can no longer pay the money back, then the "hot money" leaves.

I encourage you to read Richard Duncan's books and listen to his interviews with me on Rich Dad Radio if you want to see the world economy from his point of view.

James Rickards

James graduated from Johns Hopkins University in 1973 with a B.A. and in 1974, from the Paul H. Nitze School of Advanced International Studies with an M.A. in International Economics.

He received his Juris Doctor from the University of Pennsylvania Law School and an LLM in taxation from New York University School of Law.

In 1981, James was involved in the Iran hostage crisis. As general counsel for the hedge fund Long-Term Capital Management (LTCM), he was the principal negotiator in the 1998 bailout of LTCM by the Federal Reserve Bank of New York. And he worked on Wall Street for 35 years.

In 2001, James began using his financial expertise to aid the U.S. national security community and the U.S. Department of Defense advising them on the coming currency wars.

Forbes magazine reviewed of his book saying:

> *"History well may view James Rickards as the Paul Revere of the Currency War."*

The reviewer from the *Financial Times* summed it up this way:

> *"Let's hope he's wrong."*

In his book, James explains how countries are fighting wars with money, hence the title: Currency Wars.

In the old days, countries killed their enemies with weapons. Today, countries kill their enemies with money. Unfortunately, leaders are also killing their own people with their own money.

The number one fear among political leaders is unemployment, because unemployment leads to social unrest and violence. This is why the United States has stepped up its "Food Stamp" programs. Hungry people riot; people with enough to eat do not.

Chris Martenson

Chris Martenson received his PhD degree in neurotoxicology at Duke University in 1994. He obtained an MBA degree in finance from Cornell University in 1998.

He worked as a corporate finance analyst for Pfizer, a Fortune 300 company.

Chris co-founded Peak Prosperity, a financial education company, with Adam Taggart, a former vice-president with Yahoo.

Peak Prosperity is a company that publishes information and educational material on the economy. Chris is the author of *The Crash Course* (2011).

The Rich Dad Company held a two-day workshop, a book study, earlier this year and invited Chris and Adam to lead the study of their book. People came from all over the world.

Ken McElroy, Rich Dad Advisor on real estate, said this to me after the seminar:

> *"Disturbing, enlightening, and empowering.*
> *I am making changes today, not tomorrow."*

Chris uses his background as a scientist to explain the challenges the world economy faces. I believe that's why his views are very close to those of Dr. Fuller. The best news about *The Crash Course* is that Chris makes science and the economy easy to understand.

The book is filled with ideas that are worth studying and considering. Here are three key ideas:

Looking at the future is not about being right. It is about taking action. Too many people will wait for proof rather than prepare. Chris does not say he's right, he simply explains why he is taking action and preparing for what he sees in the future.

He explains the '4 Es' that are affecting all of us today. They are the Economy, the Environment, Energy, and the word Exponential. The word exponential (Martenson's "honorary" fourth E) is important because he explains (very simply and in great detail) why the coming changes are accelerating exponentially—not linearly—in speed. People will not know what hit them or have time to prepare, if his findings are correct.

His recommendations are simple, realistic, and practical. They're steps that almost anyone can implement.

He tells you what Foxy Loxys are not telling you… from a scientific point of view.

One of his more controversial predictions is his prediction on the prices of energy, especially oil and coal. Many corporate and political Foxy Loxys want Americans to believe America is now energy independent, and Chris agrees to a certain point.

Chris states what Foxy Loxy is not saying is that the era of cheap energy is over. In other words, the United States and the world have a lot of energy, but from now on the cost of energy will continue to climb. If Chris is correct, the rising cost of energy will wipe out financial markets, such as the stock market.

Paul Revere

In American history, the story of Paul Revere's ride—and his warning, "The British are coming!"—is a Chicken Little story. In this story, the British *were* coming and Paul Revere went down in history as a hero. This quote seems very appropriate here, related to what it takes to do what Paul Revere did:

> *"Courage is being scared to death, but saddling up anyway."*
>
> – John Wayne

Who is Foxy Loxy?

An important question for today is, "Who is Foxy Loxy?"

Foxy Loxys are everywhere, doing their best to lure you into their dens. Most of us have run into one or more real Foxy Loxys in our own lives. Many of us have been scammed by a Foxy Loxy, or fallen in love with and married one. Many of us work with Foxy Loxys. And, just maybe, some of us *are* Foxy Loxys.

Today, Foxy Loxy can enter your home via the radio, television, newspapers, and the Internet. Foxy Loxys can now enter your home from anywhere in the world.

The Tools of Foxy Loxy

This thought begs new questions.

Q: *How does Foxy Loxy get into our lives?*

A: There are many ways. The primary way is through words. Simply put, Foxy Loxy says what you want to hear and want to believe. Words are the tools of Foxy Loxy. For example, we have all seen television commercials promising, "All you have to do is take this little pill and you will lose 10 pounds in one week." I am a sucker for that one. Although I know the ad is probably a scam, I want to believe it's true. I want to believe I can continue to eat, drink, and avoid exercise—and still look as good as the models on TV.

Rich Dad on Words

Rich dad was also cautious about the words he used. He, too, knew that words had tremendous power. As I've stated earlier in this book and in most of my books, rich dad's respect for the power of words was the reason he wouldn't tolerate his son or me saying, "I can't afford it." He would say, "Poor people say 'I can't afford it' more than rich people. That's why they're poor."

Rich dad also said, "The difference between the rich, poor, and middle class are the words they use. The poor and middle class use working-class words, words like *job, career, benefits*, and *paycheck*. They do not use the words or the language of money. So they work for money, rather than have money work for them."

Your second chance can start with your decision to learn and choose different words. Words that can deliver the outcomes you're looking for.

Both Bucky Fuller and rich dad agreed that one of the most powerful words is the word *responsibility*. For both of them, *responsibility* was a spiritual word. Rich dad would say, "Rather than politicians speaking about the rights of every citizen, politicians should speak of the responsibilities of every citizen."

President Kennedy did that when he said,

"Ask not what your country can do for you,
ask what you can do for your country."

Unfortunately, today's political leaders speak more of "entitlements" rather than "responsibilities." Our economy will not change until our words change... and the word responsibility replaces entitlements.

Q: *So my second chance begins by observing and being aware of the words I use?*

A: Yes. If you will invest the time to notice the words in your thoughts and the words you use when you speak—and consciously work to change, improve, and upgrade your vocabulary—your life may change and you may notice many changes around you. It's not an overnight process, it's a day-to-day process. But if you change your words, you change your life. The most important thing is that you *control* the changes by controlling the words you put in your head and speak from your mouth. Remember the words of the Bible, "And the word became flesh."

You will eventually *become* your words and your thoughts.

Q: *Can it be that easy?*

A: I'm not saying it will be easy. But it is that simple. If it was easy, everyone would do it... but most won't. Millions find it easier to say, "I'll never be rich." Or "I'm not that interested in money." Many choose to make the rich wrong, saying, "The rich are greedy." Or "The rich should pay more taxes." Or "I am entitled to more money." And their lives reflect those thoughts and words.

Q: *How can I improve my financial vocabulary?*

A: A good start might be subscribing to *The Wall Street Journal*. Read an article or two every day. Keep a financial dictionary by your side. Make it a goal to look up two new words each day. Use those two new words in your conversations that day. In one month, you will have approximately 60 new words in your head. Keep that up for a year and your life may be very different. But remember... there are never any guarantees.

Q: *Why no guarantees?*

A: Because you have to use the new words. You have to put them into action, before they "become flesh," become a part of you. Too many people memorize words, use those words to sound intelligent, but do not really understand them or put those words into action.

After reading *Rich Dad Poor Dad*, millions of people know that "assets put money in their pocket." Although they know the definition, millions still have not taken action to acquire or build assets. Many do not take action for fear of making mistakes, losing money, or looking foolish. So they know the definition of the word *asset,* but for many, the word has not yet become flesh.

Changing your future is like learning to play golf. If you want to be a better golfer, you have to take lessons, practice those lessons, and then apply them when you play the game. Many people take lessons, but never practice and never play, so their golf game remains the same.

Q: *Why are people so afraid of making mistakes?*

A: Many reasons. One reason is that, in school, the people who make the fewest mistakes are labeled 'smart.' And people who make lots of mistakes are labeled 'stupid.'

In real life, people who make the most mistakes and learn from those mistakes are more successful than those who do not make mistakes.

You cannot learn the words of money if you are afraid of using them—afraid of putting the words into action, making mistakes, and learning from them. As John Wayne said: "Courage is being scared to death, but saddling up anyway."

Q: *What happens to people who do not know the words of money?*

A: Foxy Loxy lures them into his den and has fried chicken for Sunday dinner, deep-fried turkey for Thanksgiving, roast goose for Christmas, and sesame duck for Chinese New Year.

Q: *How does he do that?*

A: With words. He just tells them what they want to hear. Without financial education, people will follow the Foxy Loxy who whispers sweet nothings in their ears… because without financial education, there's probably very little between their ears. That is what Bernie Madoff did. He told people what they wanted to hear and $50 billion followed him into his cave as part of the biggest Ponzi scheme in history.

The bigger Ponzi schemes are the stock market, real estate market, lotteries, and Social Security… but they are *legal* Ponzi schemes.

Q: *What are Ponzi schemes?*

A: That might be a good word to look up and use in conversation today. Ponzi schemes are important to understand because Foxy Loxys love Ponzi schemes. People love Ponzi schemes because they want to believe the money they put in today will grow into more money tomorrow. In reality, Ponzi schemes are unsustainable.

Real Foxy Loxys

When Fuller wrote of GRUNCH he wrote of the "invisible giants" that control the world's economy. These invisible giants control our laws, politics, and politicians.

The following are some examples of how the invisible giants of GRUNCH have affected the economy of the United States and the world.

In many ways, all politicians are Foxy Loxys. They believe they need to tell you what you want to hear. If they told us the truth and showed us both sides of the coin, they would never be elected. For them to be able to lure you into their dens, politicians need voters without financial education. Without financial education, most voters see only one side of the coin or the issue, the side the politician knows the voters want to see. They dare not tell voters the truth, or look at issues from both sides.

The following are some examples of how the invisible giants of GRUNCH have affected the economy of the United States and the world. Consider the duplicity from the last 10 U.S. presidents.

President John F. Kennedy (1961-1963)

It was President John Kennedy who changed the numbers on unemployment. Today, when the Fed reports on unemployment, the fact is that the numbers do not reflect the truth. Today's unemployment numbers do not include the number of discouraged workers, the workers who have stopped looking for work. The unemployment numbers only reflect those who are "currently" or "actively" looking for work. That is why a report citing 7% unemployment should probably read more like 20% or higher.

Q: *Why did he do that?*

A: Again, there are many reasons. One reason may be that he wanted to look like he was doing a good job. He probably wanted to run for a second term and high unemployment could hurt his chances of reelection.

Another reason is that the boom in the U.S. economy after World War II was ending. Japan and Germany were back on their feet and competing against us, causing the U.S. economy to shrink.

A lesser-known reason is that the Federal Reserve Bank needed to look good. High unemployment would also mean that the Fed was not doing its job. In 1977, Congress amended The Federal Reserve Act, specifying this "dual mandate" of the Fed.

Q: *Why is that?*

A: The dual mandate stated the Fed now had two things it must do: lower unemployment and lower inflation.

Q: *So rather than admit unemployment is high, President Kennedy (and then the Fed) change the numbers? Changed the definition of how unemployment and how it is measured?*

A: Yes. That's one way to look at it...

Q: *Why would they do that?*

A: To tell people what they want to hear. That is what Foxy Loxy does. The problem is, *real* unemployment is much higher than *reported* unemployment.

Q: *What's wrong with that?*

A: It doesn't solve the problem or even really identify or address the scope of the problem. It just makes unemployment a bigger problem.

President Lyndon B. Johnson (1963-1969)

Some people believe that President Lyndon Johnson allowed funds from Social Security to be rolled into the General Budget of the United States. The problem was that Social Security money was spent, not invested. In other words, money ear-marked for retirement was used to pay bills. That's why the Social Security fund is empty, filled with IOUs from the U.S. Treasury. This is why millions of baby boomers and their kids may face uncertainty when they're ready to retire.

Bucky Fuller noted that if Social Security contributions had been put into the stock market back in the 1930s today's retirees would be multi-millionaires. Now it's too late. Social Security, a giant Ponzi scheme, is out of money (more accurately: in "deficit spending") just as 75 million baby boomers stop working.

Q: *How will the U.S. government pay the millions of people who have been paying into Social Security and Medicare?*

A: I don't know. All Ponzi schemes collapse when new money coming in is not enough to pay for the old money that wants to get out.

President Richard M. Nixon (1969-1974)

After taking the U.S. dollar off the gold standard, President Richard Nixon needed to manipulate the truth on inflation. To distort the true numbers on inflation, he redefined the Consumer Price Index, or CPI, the government's (manipulated) measure of inflation. Rather than tell the truth about inflation, he had energy and food removed from the CPI.

When President Barack Obama took office in 2008, the price of gasoline was approximately $1.78 a gallon. By his second term, in 2012, gasoline was approximately $3.50 a gallon.

And although gasoline had nearly doubled in price, the government is allowed to report that the CPI indicates no inflation.

Since many fertilizers come from oil, and since oil is required to plant, harvest, and transport food, the price of food has gone up as the price of oil went up. Although every shopper knows that food costs more today, the CPI still reports that there is no inflation.

Q: *Is this the second mandate of the Fed? Low inflation?*

A: Yes. Again, it is what people without financial education want to hear, even if it's not true. One advantage of not having financial education in schools is that the masses of people are easily deceived. When people are uneducated financially, it is easier to steal their wealth.

Q: *Leaders can steal people's wealth via financial deception?*

A: Yes. Inflation is one way wealth is stolen. Inflation devalues your work, the money you work for, and the money you save.

President Gerald Ford (1974-1977)

President Ford was the new President who replaced President Nixon when ERISA, the Employee Retirement Income Security Act, was passed in 1974. ERISA paved the way for the 401(k).

Q: *Why is ERISA so important?*

A: ERISA is another way the rich put their hands in the pockets of employees. In other words, ERISA allowed Wall Street to be paid before the employee gets paid.

Q: *How is that? Why does Wall Street get paid first?*

A: The 1974 ERISA legislation is very similar to the 1943 Current Tax Payment Act. The 1943 Act gave the IRS, the government tax department, the power to deduct taxes from an employee's paycheck before the employee received his or her pay check. ERISA allowed the bankers of Wall Street to do the same thing. For people with 401(k)s, it meant the bankers on Wall Street were paid before the employee was paid.

Q: *What did Fuller say about the stock market?*

A: He said investing in the early days of the stock market was only for the rich. The saying behind closed doors of the exchanges was "Keep the pikers out." The term *piker* comes from medieval times. A piker was a peasant foot soldier who carried a long staff with a metal tip, or pike. Simply put, "Keep the pikers out" meant "Keep the poor people out."

Once GRUNCH realized the pikers had money, they opened the doors of the stock market (via ERISA) and other pension plans to the pikers. When "piker's money" entered the stock market, the rich became extremely rich.

President Jimmy Carter (1977-1981)

President Carter may be the most straight-shooting, straight-talking President in recent history. It appears that he meant what he said, and said what he meant. That may be why he is sometimes considered the 'forgotten President.'

He probably was a little ahead of his time. It took until 2014 before an openly gay football player was selected in the National Football League draft.

Today we have drone strikes. How long will it be before terrorists use drones rather than airliners? President Carter's thoughts on war:

> "War may sometimes be a necessary evil.
> But no matter how necessary, it is always an evil,
> never a good. We will not learn how to live together
> in peace by killing each other's children."

Today, the U.S. Senate and Congress are at war, rather than at work.

"Unless both sides win, no agreement can be permanent."

President Carter left office actively supporting projects for social justice and human rights. Habitat for Humanity calls the former President and Mrs. Rosalynn Carter "our most famous volunteers."

President Ronald Reagan (1981-1989)

President Reagan was in office during the 1987 stock market crash, known as Black Monday. The chart of that crash is pictured below.

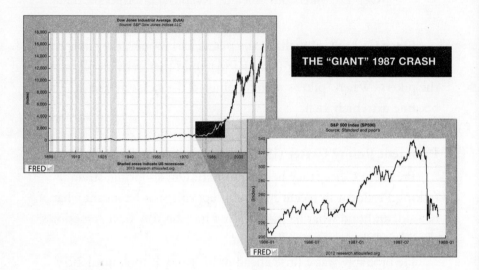

To prevent future stock-market crashes, in 1988, President Reagan created The President's Working Group on Financial Markets. Today, it is known as The Plunge Protection Team, or the PPT.

Q: *What does the Plunge Protection Team do?*

A: No one really knows… or few people are willing to talk about it.

Q: *What happens?*

A: Today, whenever a crash occurs, a mysterious no-name-buyer enters the game, via futures markets, purchasing massive quantities of "derivatives" through giant banks such as JP Morgan, Goldman Sachs, and off-shore accounts. These mysterious, invisible buyers have the power not only to stop a crash, but prevent other markets, such as the gold and silver markets, from rising. The next time you see a market crash that "miraculously" recovers, it could be Foxy Loxy in action. The government's Plunge Protection Team at work, keeping the markets propped up… until the day when the manipulations will no longer work.

Q: *Is this why rich dad's prophecy of a giant crash in 2016 may not occur?*

A: Correct. Manipulated markets can be propped up, preventing the crash.

Q: *For how long?*

A: Who knows?

Q: *What's wrong with manipulating the financial markets?*

A: It protects gamblers. And goes against the free market forces. Today, millions of people invest foolishly because they know the government will not let the markets crash.

Q: *So what's wrong with that?*

A: It prevents investment money from going into businesses and factories that create jobs. The money stays in the markets— the *casinos*—not the economy.

Foxy Loxy will tell you he's protecting you, but he's really protecting the big banks and their casinos.

Q: *How does he do that?*

A: Again, there are many ways. One way is through the FDIC, the Federal Deposit Insurance Corporation.

Q: *What does that organization do?*

A: It insures savers' deposits. When the 2007 crash began, the banks were afraid that people would start withdrawing their savings. So the government instructed the FDIC to increase the deposit insurance ceiling to $250,000.

Q: *What's wrong with that?*

A: It makes savers careless. Rather than assess the soundness of the bank, the saver blindly puts their money in any bank that offers FDIC insurance.

Q: *And what's wrong with that?*

A: The FDIC is broke. It does not have enough money to cover the next crash.

Q: *What's wrong with that?*

A: If there is another crash, the FDIC will go bust. And the taxpayers will once again bail out the banks—to the tune of up to $250,000 per savings account.

Q: *So what's wrong with that?*

A: The losses will be in the trillions. Your children and their children will be bailing out the banks via their taxes for years and years.

Q: *So Foxy Loxy says, "Your savings are insured," but he fails to say that the FDIC is broke and the taxpayer will foot the bill if those insurance payments need to be made?*

A: Yes. Foxy Loxy will always say what you want to hear and want to believe. Even *The Economist* magazine states the $250,000 FDIC insurance program needs to be reduced soon. That article stated that every bank should have a rating so the savers will know how sound a bank is and how safe their money is. At $250,000 per account, *The Economist* believes the risks are too high for taxpayers and future generations— and that the FDIC protects the banks, not the savers.

President George H.W. Bush (1989-1983)

"Bush 41" promised: "Read my lips, no new taxes." But he raised taxes and was not reelected for a second term.

President Bill Clinton (1993-2001)

Few Presidents have done more for the modern banking industry than President Bill Clinton. If there were not so many people who share responsibility for the financial crisis of 2007, it would be easy to blame him for most of the crisis. Simply put, he made his banking friends very, very rich—at the expense of the poor and the middle class. The irony is that millions believe he is a friend of the poor.

One of two important things President Clinton did while in office was repeal the Glass–Steagall Act. That 1932 Act prevented commercial banks from being investment banks. The act is also known as The Banking Act of 1933.

In 1998, after Citibank was allowed to affiliate with Salomon Smith Barney, President Clinton publicly declared, "The Glass–Steagall law is no longer appropriate."

Q: *Why is that important?*

A: It allowed commercial bankers to be investment bankers. They could now make more money by investing savers' money.

Q: *Why did they do that?*

A: To make more money. The bankers could make more money in the stock market than by lending money to borrowers. And once that happened the stock market took off. The casino was open for business, with investor losses protected by the government and taxpayers. If the market went down, President Reagan's Plunge Protection Team would pump it back up.

Q: *Then what happened?*

A: A new class of Americans emerged: the investor class. They were not rich, they were not poor, and they were no longer middle class. Most were well-educated and had high-paying jobs or professions, such as doctors and lawyers, and most had the extra money to invest in a 'no-lose market.' They did well during the 2007 crash because they were not among the millions who lost their jobs, homes, and retirements.

Q: *This is the group that will lose if your rich dad's prophecy comes true in 2016, or whenever it happens?*

A: Unfortunately, yes.

Q: *What was the second thing President Clinton did?*

A: I wrote about it in the previous chapter. In the year 2000, President Clinton signed a bill creating the Commodity Futures Modernization Act, or CFMA, which paved the way for a much larger derivatives market. Between 2000 and 2007, the derivative market grew from $100 trillion to $700 trillion.

Remember that Warren Buffett called derivatives, "… financial weapons of mass destruction…"

And in 2007, the explosions began.

A Picture of the Past

On the chart on the following page you can see the size of the 1987 stock market crash during the Reagan years. You can also see the duration of President Clinton's eight years in office.

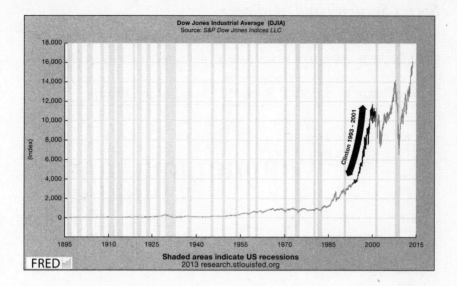

President George W. Bush (2001-2009)

Few Presidents have added more to the national deficit than President Bush II. Prior to the 2004 election, his popularity and job-approval ratings were slipping. Many thought his reelection was doubtful.

It is rumored he cut a deal with the pharmaceutical drug industry and put the weight of his office behind The Medicare Prescription Drug, Improvement, and Modernization Act (also called the Medicare Modernization Act or MMA). It is a U.S. federal law enacted in 2003. It produced the largest overhaul of Medicare in that public health program's 38-year history. The Act made seniors happy and the drug industry *very* happy. In my opinion, the act virtually guaranteed the bankruptcy of the United States.

The U.S. Comptroller General David Walker has called the Act:

"The most fiscally irresponsible piece of legislation since the 1960s."

President George Bush II was reelected to a second term in 2004.

Social Security and Medicare

You have seen the chart on Social Security a number of times. The chart below is a snapshot of the future of Social Security and Medicare.

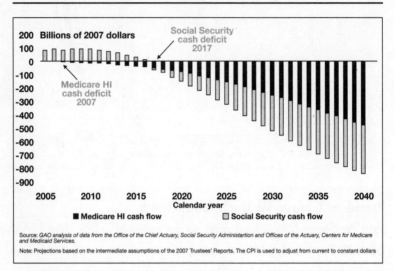

Medicare and Social Security Face Large Deficits

Source: GAO analysis of data from the Office of the Chief Actuary, Social Security Administration and Offices of the Actuary, Centers for Medicare and Medicaid Services.

Note: Projections based on the intermediate assumptions of the 2007 Trustees' Reports. The CPI is used to adjust from current to constant dollars

Q: *What story does this chart tell us?*

A: It depends. For the millions of people who are counting on the government to take care for them, the story may not have a happy ending.

President Barack Obama (2009–2017)

President Obama rode into office in 2008 on the power of hope. By the 2012 election, much of that hope had turned to disappointment.

President Obama is a polished Foxy Loxy. He is a great orator. When he speaks, people either love him or hate him. Very few are on the edge of the coin.

President Obama pushed through The Affordable Care Act, aka Obamacare.

Always remember, the titles or names of most government legislation are a Foxy-Loxy trick. The name is often the opposite of what the legislation really does. For example:

The Social Security Act made life more secure for the World-War-II generation, but not for millions of the Vietnam-War generation. Social Security and Medicare will be a social liability for the children, grandchildren, and great-grandchildren of the Vietnam War generation.

ERISA, the Employee Retirement Income Security Act which led to the 401(k), made bankers richer, but may not make employee retirements more secure.

The Affordable Care Act known as Obamacare has already made healthcare more expensive for millions of people. Only time will tell when it comes to evaluating the impact of Obamacare.

As the story of *Chicken Little* goes:

Foxy Loxy said,
"We will run.
We will run into my den,
And I will tell the king."
They ran into Foxy Loxy's den,
But they never come out again.

President Obama lured people in with the words "affordable health care." What he did *not* say is that the "Affordable Healthcare Act" is really a tax act.

Q: *How is it a tax act?*

A: President Obama raised taxes on the investors in E and S quadrants.

Q: *The quadrants that work for money?*

A: Yes, especially the Es and Ss who invest their money in the stock, bond, and mutual fund markets. He raised taxes on interest, dividends, and capital gains—primarily from paper assets.

Q: *Who was spared from Obamacare's taxes?*

A: One group that was spared from Obamacare tax increases are the investors who use debt to acquire real estate that produces *cash flow*.

Real estate investors who flip properties for *capital gains* are now likely to see tax hikes as a result of the President's Obamacare legislation.

Q: *So that's another difference between capital gains and cash flow?*

A: Yes. Capital gains occur when you sell an asset, such as a stock, bond, real estate, or business, and take the profits. Your profits from the sale, your capital gains, are taxed. Real estate investors who invest for cash flow, are not taxed on their cash flow. In fact, if they have good tax advice, their cash flow may be tax-free income.

Q: *Is this fair?*

A: Sure it is. The same tax laws are available for everyone. What is unfair is the lack of financial education in our schools, and the education that would make people aware of this.

Q: *Is it the same all over the world?*

A: Yes, for the most part. As I've said: terminology and government policies differ, but in general, the tax laws are the same.

Recently, I was in Scotland. Friends of mine, Graeme and his wife Leanne, purchased a 150-year-old, historic church for £200,000 British pounds. The Scottish government gave him £350,000 in the form of a government grant to fix it up. It's money they do not have to pay back.

Q: *He paid £200,000 and was given £350,000 by the Scottish government? You mean the project was free?*

A: Yes and no. He has to do what the government wants him to do, which is restore the church and provide low-income housing. The key words are: *he is doing what the government wants him to do.*

He plans to restore the church and convert it into low-income housing for 16 families, using £400,000 in investor money, called *equity*. He will then borrow £700,000 from a bank, known as *debt,* to complete the project.

After two years, when the project is up and running and cash flow is coming in from the renters, the business plan is to go back to the bank, show the bank the increase in cash flow, and ask for another loan to refinance the project based on the increase in cash flow.

With the new loan, all investors are expected to get their money back and continue to receive tax-free income—cash flow—for the life of the project. In other words, their return on investment will be *infinite* because after two years they'll have no money in the investment. On top of that, the money they get back via the refinance is tax-free because the money they put into the deal is returned to them from debt on the property, debt the tenants will pay off via their rent.

As my friend, partner, and Rich Dad Advisor Ken McElroy stood there with us in Scotland evaluating the old church property, at least 20 people walked past the For Sale sign, never seeing the opportunity that was right in front of their eyes. Ken was very proud of Graeme and Leanne because, through his books and seminars, he had taught them how to structure this type of investment.

This method of investing is used all over the world. The problem is, the people who walked by the old church everyday, on their way to work and the pursuit of their paychecks, could not see the *invisible flow of cash* that Graeme and Leanne had trained themselves to see.

Q: *Ugh… why does my head hurt?*

A: Because your mind and brain are beginning to see the invisible. You're beginning to see how the *invisible* giants of GRUNCH control the world via the money supply—free to print as much money as they want, devaluing our work, our savings, increasing taxes and inflation and making life harder for those who work for money. You're beginning to understand why the truly rich do not invest for the long term in the stock market. Remember: things are opposite. The rich sell stocks, shares in their businesses, and the poor and middle class buy stocks. And you're beginning to see how our schools blind us financially by teaching students to work for a paycheck.

Q: *And all this begins with words?*

A: Yes. Words allow your mind and brain to see the other side of the coin, to see the invisible. It's a world most people walk by every day, on their work… never seeing how the rich are getting richer. They believe tax laws are unfair—even when tax laws *are* fair, with tax advantages available to anyone with the financial intelligence to *use* the tax laws to their advantage. The differences between rich, poor, and middle class begin with words. Words make the rich richer and words make the poor and middle class poorer.

If you're serious about a second chance in life, start by changing the words you use.

Forbid yourself from ever saying, "I can't afford it." Those are the words of a poor person. Don't say, "Live below your means." Those words damage the rich spirit in you.

Starting today—right now—use the words of the rich, rather than the words of the poor and middle class. Start using the words *assets, liabilities,* and *cash flow* rather than the words *job security, paycheck* and *savings.*

HOW ARE YOU GOING TO ACHIEVE FINANCIAL FREEDOM?

ASK A RICH DAD COACH

"Having a Rich Dad Coach is like having your very own rich dad—someone to give you feedback, hold you accountable, and to encourage your success. The focus is on you and how you will personally get out of the rat race—just like rich dad did for me.

Your coach will help you get there. By going through this process, you will come away with a real, workable plan—customized to your strengths and passions."

— **Robert Kiyosaki**

Get your Free Introduction to Rich Dad Coaching and a Special Bonus Offer by calling 1-800-240-0434 ext. 2739 or visit
www.RichDadCoaching.com/BeRich

If you are ready to **TAKE CONTROL OF YOUR FINANCIAL FUTURE**, leverage the power of a Rich Dad Coach to help you…

- *Formulate a personal investment plan*, laying out the steps that will help you become financially secure, comfortable and rich.

- *Identify your strengths and leverage them* to become a successful investor.

- *Achieve your goals by providing one-on-one attention* and give you invaluable feedback, motivation, and accountability.

- *Focus your efforts* on the best wealth generating opportunities in your area.

- Map out where you want to go financially and *what you'll need to do to get there!*

www.RichDadCoaching.com/BeRich

SUCCESS STORY

"We are proud to say we reached our goal of acquiring passive income over expenses in our own personal lives. This was no easy task since we had LOTS of expenses and NO true assets."

Lisa R., Tennessee

CASHFLOW® The Web Game

Interactive Financial Statement
Learn what's really important in entrepreneurship and investing: Your Financial Statement.

Play **CASHFLOW® The Web Game** with up to six players online. Meet and interact with players who have the same goals and aspirations as you do. Test your skills and strategy against the rest of the world.

Anytime. Anywhere.
Play CASHFLOW® anywhere you have an Internet connection—any time of day.

The Best Part?
Learn to be wealthy by playing CASHFLOW online for **FREE**! Visit **www.RichDad.com** and start playing today!

Teach Your Future Entrepreneurs

CASHFLOW For Kids teaches you the difference between an asset and a liability and the principal of cash flow versus capital gains.

Kids get to practice real-world investing scenarios with play money.

Play CASHFLOW For Kids at home with your kids and friends. Visit the online store at **www.RichDad.com**

Asset or Liability?
Kids can tell if their investments were good or not.

Bucky Fuller believed that words are "the most powerful tools created by man." You can change your life by changing your words. And the best news of all is that words are free.

Q: *What can I do right now?*

A: That is what the rest of this book is about. So far, this book has been about the past. The next part of this book is about the present and the future.

Parts Two and Three of this book are about your second chance. They're about financial education. But unlike old-style education, financial education is not about being smarter than everyone else, or being the person with all the right answers. It's about working cooperatively, rather than competitively. Financial education requires your personal vision for the future and your commitment to what you need to learn to have the future you desire and deserve.

Financial education is not about being right and not making mistakes. Financial education is about having courage and taking action—even if you're afraid—and knowing you *will* make mistakes and possibly stumble or fail on your path to success and the life you want for yourself and your family. Your second chance is about picking yourself up when you fall and learning from your stumbles and missteps, your mistakes.

Parts Two and Three of this book are about empowering yourself—regardless of what you did or did not do in the past—and using the present to prepare for a brighter future. Your second chance starts today.

As Bucky Fuller said,

"We are called to be architects of the future, not its victims."

Part Two
The Present

Are you sane or insane?

"The definition of insanity is doing the same thing over and over again and expecting different results." —*Albert Einstein*

Part Two: The Present

INTRODUCTION

Government Insanity

Does it make sense that our governments continue to print money when printing money is what caused this crisis?

Personal Insanity

Does it make sense for you to keep working for money, saving money, and investing for the long term in the stock market when governments of the world *are printing money just to keep the stock market propped up?*

Time to Get Sane...

Part Two of this book is about your present financial condition. Your second chance begins when you evaluate where you are *today*... and then decide where you want to be in the future.

Chapter Eight
BEFORE AND AFTER

---

*"One picture of a caterpillar does not tell you it is
going to transform into a butterfly..."*
— R. Buckminster Fuller

People love before and after photos. Television weight-loss
commercials often show a 290-pound person in one picture alongside
a newly-svelt, 115-pound goddess in a bikini. The announcer says, "If
this 52-year-old grandmother can do this, so can you." The phones start
ringing and websites buzz—and millions of dollars change hands.

Before and *after* photos inspire us. The photos remind us of who
we are on the inside. And they remind us of the god-given gifts we
were born with... the potential to be anything we want to be. We
remember there is a butterfly in each of us, waiting to be set free.

"Makeovers" have also become a very popular formula for TV-
show success. There are programs that take a frumpy, unattractive
person, change their clothes, hair, and makeup and—like magic—a
"Cinderella" or "Prince Charming" steps on to the stage. There are
TV programs that take run down old houses, paint them, remodel
the kitchens and baths, transforming the spooky old house into a
dream home.

My Own Show

For years, television producers have called, asking if I would do a
TV makeover show. They've wanted me to take a "poor person" and

make them over... transforming them into a rich person. Over the years, I have had serious discussions with at least a dozen TV producers. The discussions always ended with the same questions: "Can it be done?" And "How can we do it?" Discussions always stopped at the same question: "How does a caterpillar become a butterfly?"

Interior vs. Exterior

There are differences between exterior makeovers and internal makeovers. It's pretty easy to paint an old house or put nice clothes on a person. Those are exterior makeovers. But how does a person transform from poor to rich? There's more to it than a coat of paint. It requires an internal makeover.

Going from poor to rich is an invisible transformation—and much more than simply a paint job. Internal makeovers don't make good reality TV because the changes are invisible. These transformations are internal context shifts, changes in the way people think about themselves and their money, and the choices they make. I know it can be done, but so far the TV producers and I have not yet found the magic formula.

Economic Crisis

Much of today's economic crisis is caused by people who want to look rich on the outside but who are not rich on the inside. The subprime mortgage crisis is a prime example of this human desire. Millions of poor and middle-class people were given NINJA loans, (*no income, no job, and no assets loans*) so they could buy a house, or refinance their existing house with loans they most likely could never repay. The banks then repackaged these "subprime loans" into *derivatives* and sold these "weapons of mass financial destruction" to a money-hungry world. In other words, the desire to look rich on the outside can cause real estate and stock market booms and busts and cause consumer credit card debt (and even student loan debt) to soar.

There is nothing wrong with wanting to look rich. I've never wanted to live below my means. In my opinion, living below your means kills your spirit. Instead, I look for ways to expand my means and find news ways of making money that can give me the means to enjoy the finer things in life.

I love my nice homes and cars. I think that's true for many people. The problem is that without financial education, most people will never be rich on the inside… and that is the real crisis.

A Second Chance

This book is not about an exterior "make over." A true second chance is not about updating a kitchen, a fresh coat of paint, new clothes, losing 10 pounds, or going back to school to get a higher-paying job.

A true second chance is a metamorphosis, the same type of transformation a caterpillar goes through before emerging as a butterfly. The potential to transform from caterpillar to butterfly is in all human beings, which is why before and after photos work so well in advertising and television shows. Those *before* and *after* photos remind us of our power, the power deep inside us.

Turning Caterpillars into Butterflies

Q: *Have you ever been broke?*

A: Yes, a number of times.

Q: *So you know what it feels like?*

A: I do.

Q: *Do you feel sorry for poor people, people without money?*

A: No, I don't feel sorry for poor people. I *empathize,* but I don't *sympathize.*

Q: *Why not? Why don't you feel sorry for them?*

A: Because I know that inside each human being is the god-given power to change and improve their lives, if they want to.

If I feel sorry for them, I am saying they don't have that power. If I feel sorry for them, I am saying God short-changed them. And I know He didn't. I know we all have the power of free choice.

Q: *Isn't that a bit idealistic?*

A: Yes, it is idealistic. And it's also realistic. I know because I have felt sorry for myself. I have thrown my own pity parties. The problem with pity parties is the people who enjoy them.

Q: *And who is that?*

A: Other victims, losers, and people who enjoy feeling sorry for themselves.

Pity parties also attract "rescuers" and the "do-gooders." Many "do-gooders" actually *do* help people. But unfortunately, not all "do-gooders" empower people to find their God-given powers. Many "rescuers" keep people helpless. There is a difference between helping, comforting, feeding, and empowering people.

As I've said many times: Simply giving money (or entitlements) to poor people only serves to keep them poor longer.

Don't get me wrong. We all need a bit of sympathy and compassion now and again. We all need words of encouragement when we fall down and we often need help getting back on our feet. It's OK to feel sorry for ourselves for awhile. It's part of the healing process.

Q: *So you* have *felt sorry for yourself?*

A: Sure. Many times. But feeling sorry for myself has never helped me in the long run. Feeling sorry for myself has only made my problems bigger and last longer.

Q: *So what happened when you fell down in business and lost everything?*

A: Once my pity party was over, I stood back up and got back to work.

Q: *Without money? When you were broke?*

A: Sure. Not having money made me stronger, smarter, and more resourceful. Without money I had to think and be creative. Obviously, my recovery would have been easier if I'd had money, but not having money actually empowered me to use and develop talents I probably never would have developed.

I believe we all have strengths and weaknesses. If I feel sorry for myself. I strengthen my weaknesses. If I wallow in self-pity for too long, my strengths grow weaker... and, at the same time, my weakness grow stronger.

Q: *So government entitlement programs and charities cause people's weaknesses to become stronger and their strengths to become weaker?*

A: That's my belief. Many people will disagree with my beliefs. There *is* a time to give a person a hand up. And there are times when a person needs a swift kick in the butt. I've had my butt kicked many times and although I did not like it at the time, all of them have made me stronger.

Q: *So being poor could make you rich, if being poor inspires you to find your strengths?*

A: Yes.

Q: *And being rich could be a weakness?*

A: It could. We have all seen families that spoil their children. Giving a child everything may make the parent and child feel good, but parents runs the risk of weakening the child and, possibly, arresting the development of their core internal strengths, strengths that will give them the power to stand up when they fall down.

On my Rich Dad Radio Show, I interviewed Donald Trump's two sons, Don Jr. and Eric. For nearly an hour they talked about how they were raised as rich kids of fame and privilege. They had advantages few of us will ever have, yet their lives were not easy. Their dad had both boys working on the docks and on construction crews as laborers. Not quite the life of privilege you'd expect for sons of a wealthy man. On occasion, I have spent time with both young men. Speaking from personal experience, I can say that they are rich young men, but not spoiled brats. They are more down to earth than most of my friends' kids, who have been given everything.

Topic:
Raising Entrepreneurs
Guests:
**Don Trump, Jr.
and Eric Trump**

The Rich Dad Radio Show
download the free app
www.richdad.com/radio

Triggers for Tragedy

I live in an affluent neighborhood in Phoenix, Arizona. It is a small neighborhood, a circle of big homes around a golf course. There are fewer than 40 homes on the circle. Yet, soon after the markets crashed in 2007, there were three suicides and a fire in that small community.

Q: *Who committed suicide?*

A: One was a young guy who took over his father's multi-million dollar business and lost it. The other person married for money and lost his wife's fortune. Apparently, suicide was a less painful prospect than facing his wife in divorce court. The fire was a real estate "flipper" who bought a house for $3.5 million and tried to flip it for $5 million. When he couldn't do that and could no longer make the payments, he apparently set a fire and saw the insurance pay-off as his only alternative. He went to jail and, I've heard, he committed suicide.

Q: *These were people who looked rich on the outside but who were not rich on the inside?*

A: That's my opinion. And it's interesting that, at the same time, many of my wealthy neighbors became even wealthier. They found opportunities during the crash. The crash—while devastating for many—was a good thing for them.

There was also one neighbor who got into a lot of financial trouble when the market crashed, but he did not commit suicide. Instead, he weathered the storm, worked his way out, and today is stronger, smarter, and richer.

Q: *So he found new strengths and strengthened them?*

A: That's my belief. Falling down can be a good thing—if standing up again makes you stronger. It's my experience that if you just give people money after they fall down, they'll stand up again but will be weaker, not stronger. This is what happened when taxpayers bailed out the biggest banks. Today, our big banks are reportedly 37% larger. They grew bigger, but not stronger. As Einstein said, *"We can't solve problems by using the same kind of thinking we used when we created them."*

Q: *Does this mean that the next crash will be a monster?*

A: I am afraid it might.

Q: *So how do I find my strengths—and strengthen them?*

A: That is one the many secrets to life. I wish I had the easy answer. I wish I had a magic wand, but I don't.

Q: *Do you think God created crashes so we'd have the opportunity to stand up stronger?*

A: I think so. At least that's one way to look at it. As I've stated in an earlier chapter, one of Bucky Fuller's Generalized Principles is the *emergence through emergency*. I believe we are on the edge of the biggest financial emergency in world history. The question is: How will we emerge?

Flat Broke

In December of 1984, Kim and I left Hawaii with nothing. Our combined financial statement looked like this:

INCOME STATEMENT

Income
0
Expenses
?

BALANCE SHEET

Assets	Liabilities
0	$820,000

We were adrift in San Diego. We had no jobs and no income. Our expenses were low because we lived in a borrowed car or in friends' spare bedrooms. We ate whenever money came in, which was not often. Everyday was a financial emergency.

I had no assets. Before leaving Hawaii I had sold everything (which was primarily real estate in Hawaii) to keep my nylon surfer-wallet business going.

The $820,000 we had in liabilities was investor loans, also used to keep the wallet business afloat. When I left the business, I assumed responsibility for paying the loans back. I called my investors to let them know what I was doing, informing them I would pay them back when I got back on my feet. Some told me to forget the loan. Others, I knew, I needed to pay back.

Being in the Present

I tell this story of being broke in San Diego because Part Two of this book is about the Present. Before Kim and I could move into the future, we had to have a clear picture of where we were today, in the present.

Many people are *not* in the present with their finances because, without financial education, they do not know what financial statements are. Many highly educated people are financially illiterate because they cannot read or use financial statements.

If you have read *Rich Dad Poor Dad* and played the *CASHFLOW* game, you have a better understanding of how financial statements work than many highly educated people. As you look to the future, you can put that knowledge to work.

Second Chance

By 1994, our financial statement looked like this:

INCOME STATEMENT

Income
$10,000 rental home

Expenses
$3,000 personal expense

BALANCE SHEET

Assets	Liabilities
52 apartment rental units	**$85,000 residence**

We were not rich. We were "net-worth millionaires" with $120,000 in annual passive income from cash flow from our assets. We didn't need a job. In the 10 years between 1984 to 1994 we had achieved financial freedom.

We still lived in a small house and lived the lifestyle of most middle-class people. The difference was we never had to work again. We were no longer slaves to money. Money now worked for us. We were transforming from caterpillars to butterflies, but we knew we were not *yet* butterflies. We were aware that a metamorphosis was taking place inside of us and we knew that it was not yet complete. We still could not fly and we knew we had more work to do. Most important of all, we knew our wealth was growing on the inside, not the outside.

People Look Richer

During these years, many people looked richer than we did. Their financial statements probably looked like this:

Income
High salary **from a job or profession**
Expenses
High expenses **of a luxury lifestyle**

Assets	Liabilities
Stocks, bonds, **savings**	**Big house** **Nice cars** **Credit car debt** **Student loans**

The problem is that many people who look rich on the outside are in financial trouble on the inside. To look at them, you might never know that they struggled to make ends meet, perhaps even living paycheck to paycheck. Many of them even survived the 2007 crash. They may not be so lucky in the future. And if rich dad's prophecy is accurate, this group may be the next victims of the turbulent times ahead.

Q: *Tell me again why this group is at risk...*

A: Sure. In his book, *The Crash Course*, Chris Martenson states
that there are three levels of wealth:

3. Tertiary Wealth

2. Secondary Wealth

1. Primary Wealth

The people who have high-paying jobs, nice homes, and money in
the bank and the stock market own tertiary wealth. Chris states that,
in the next crash, it will be those with tertiary wealth—the paper
wealth of the affluent investor class—who will be hurt the most.

Q: *If tertiary wealth is paper wealth, what is the difference between
primary wealth and secondary wealth?*

A: Primary wealth is *resource wealth*. Examples of resource
wealth are oil, gold, silver, fish, trees, fertile land.

Secondary wealth is *production wealth*. Examples of
production wealth are entrepreneurs who are farmers who
produce food, fishermen who catch fish, oil drillers who
produce oil, gold miners who produce gold, and factory
owners who produce products.

You may be too young to remember the TV sitcom *The
Beverly Hillbillies*, but I'll tell you the storyline and use
it as an example of the three types of wealth.

One day, when a poor mountaineer named Jed Clampett was
out "shootin' for some food" on his property, the shot he fired
changed the course of his life. That shot hit paydirt, literally,
and Jed watched the crude oil ("black gold... Texas tea")
bubbling up from the ground. The OK Oil Company paid Jed
a small fortune for the rights to drill on his land. And, as the
story goes: "the next thing you know old Jed's a millionaire."

He owned the *resource*—the primary wealth of the land and oil itself. OK Oil Company, once it acquired the rights to drill on Jed's property, owned the secondary wealth, the *production*.

So where did the oil company get the money to pay Jed for his crude? They got it from the stock market and private investors... from tertiary wealth.

Q: *So those with tertiary wealth are savers and stock investors who work for or own shares in these resources and businesses?*

A: Yes. As Chris states in his book, paper investors own "claims" to wealth, but not the wealth itself. For example, the U.S. dollar is not wealth. It's a "claim" to wealth. A shareholder in a company like General Mills owns a "claim" to the company, but he or she does not own the farms on which the food is grown.

Q: *And what is wrong with that?*

A: If the stock market crashes, shareholders are the first losers.

Q: *Shareholders are the first losers? Why is that?*

A: Well... I'll try to explain, as simply as possible. Let's say a company goes out of business. If there is any money left, the first people to get paid are employees. After that it's the suppliers. The third group to be paid is creditors, people who loaned the company money or extended credit. And last to be paid—assuming there's any money left—are shareholders.

Q: *Are things riskier for shareholders today?*

A: Yes.

Q: *Why?*

A: Investing in stocks has been pretty much a safe bet since 1954.
Since 1954, the stock market has been on a steady upward
climb. There have been a few dips, bumps, and crashes, but the
market has always recovered and shareholders who invested for
the long term generally did well. Many did extremely well.

Q: *Tell me again what happened in 1954?*

A: The stock market crashed in 1929 after reaching an all-time
high of 381, triggering the Great Depression. It took 25 years,
until 1954, for the stock market to reach 381 again. The
market has been going up now for 60 years and millions have
made fortunes. Once again, you can see that climb in the
chart below.

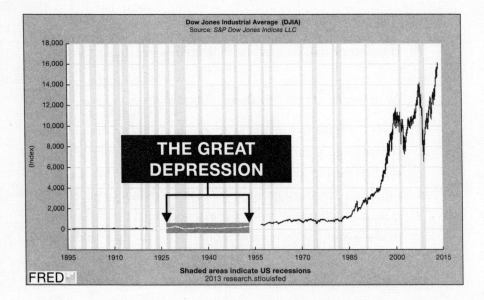

Since 1954 you can see why millions have made fortunes and why
millions hold their wealth in the stock market. This is why so many
people continue to believe the old advice of "Invest for the long term."

Q: *So the problem is they're investing for the long term in tertiary wealth, in paper wealth? Right?*

A: Yes, and if any one of the new Chicken Littles is correct— people like Chris Martenson, James Rickards, or Richard Duncan—the stock market is going to come down and those who are rich in tertiary wealth will pay the price.

Q: *And those who invest in primary and secondary wealth have a better chance of survival?*

A: Yes. But again, there are no guarantees.

Q: *If tertiary wealth is wiped out, what will the world look like?*

A: I imagine that major financial cities such as New York will be hit the hardest.

Q: *Why is that?*

A: Because cities such as New York are built on tertiary wealth. Much of the wealth of New York residents is held in tertiary wealth. There are few farms, factories, or oil wells in Manhattan. If their tertiary wealth goes down, so does the value of their condos, co-ops, and brownstones. If residents owe more on their New York residences than they're worth, we could face another mortgage crisis, but this time it will not be the subprime mortgages of poor people, it will be jumbo-mortgages of rich people.

Q: *What do you think the odds of this happening are?*

A: As long as governments continue to print money to pay their bills, pay people not to work, and keep the financial markets artificially propped up, the problem grows.

James Rickards, in his book *Currency Wars,* writes about this *increasing complexity.*

Q: *What does he mean by that... increasing complexity?*

A: Rather than working to solve our problems, governments are coming up with more and more complex solutions as ways to keep the economy propped up.

James uses the example of snow piling up on a mountain. Rather than setting off small explosions to create small cascades of snow, governments are building taller, bigger, and stronger barriers, hoping to prevent the accumulating snow from becoming an avalanche. Their complex solutions then require more and more complex, new solutions—making the problem worse, not better.

As you might guess, one day we will run out of complex solutions, and the barriers will give way. And rather than a series of small, intentionally created avalanches, the entire mountain will come down.

Q: *So what's the solution?*

A: One answer is to personally step back from *complexity,* tertiary wealth, and get back to *simplicity,* or secondary and primary wealth.

Q: *Have you pulled back from tertiary wealth?*

A: I never got into it. I have almost nothing in savings, stocks, bonds, mutual funds, and other paper assets. Most of my wealth is in primary and secondary wealth.

Q: *Why is that?*

A: Because my rich dad taught his son and me to invest in primary and secondary wealth, in resources and production. Primary and secondary wealth is the wealth of the truly rich. It always has been, and always will be.

Q: *Can you give me a few examples?*

A: Sure. Rather than save money, which is tertiary wealth, I save gold and silver bars and coins, primary wealth known as resource wealth.

Rather than invest as a shareholder in oil company stocks, tertiary wealth, I invest as a partner in oil production, which is secondary wealth. I do not own the oil company; I own a percentage of the oil. If the price of oil goes up I get paid, and if the price of oil goes down I still get paid.

I own real estate, primarily apartment complexes, which is secondary wealth. I do not own shares in REITS, Real Estate Investment Trusts, which are tertiary wealth.

As an entrepreneur, I do not buy shares of companies. I sell shares of my companies to investors, as tertiary wealth.

Q: *Sounds complicated and expensive. Can anyone participate in primary and secondary wealth? Even if they have very little money or financial education?*

A: Sure. Anyone can. For example, anyone in the world can invest in real silver, which is primary wealth.

As I write this book, silver is selling for approximately $20 an ounce—down from a high of almost $40 per oz. If someone cannot afford $20, they can still find pre-1964 U.S. dimes made of silver. In other words, for 10 cents anyone in the world can become an investor in primary wealth, silver.

Q: *Why is that a good investment?*

A: Prices of gold and silver will always go up and down due to market demand and government manipulation. But as long as governments are printing money, saving silver and gold—primary wealth—makes much more sense to me than the tertiary-wealth strategy of saving dollars. As long as governments are printing money, saving money is the riskiest thing you can do.

Silver has one advantage over gold and paper money: The supply of silver is declining. Supplies of gold remain relatively constant, and the mountains of paper money are increasing. Paper money can now be created in microseconds. It takes years and millions of dollars to find, develop, and bring new gold and silver mines into production.

Stockpiles of silver are declining because silver is an *industrial metal* as well as a *precious metal.* Silver is used in medicine, water purification, electronics, and has hundreds of other applications.

Don't forget that silver and gold have been real money for thousands of years. It's hard to say with certainty how long the U.S. dollar will be around.

Q: *Is that why Bitcoin has become so popular?*

A: Probably. Anytime people lose faith in government, new forms of currency will appear.

Q: *Are you investing in Bitcoins?*

A: No.

Q: *Why not?*

A: Because I do not understand Bitcoins, and for me, gold and silver are easy to understand and hard to reproduce. It is difficult to counterfeit real gold or silver.

In my opinion, and I could be wrong, Bitcoins are tertiary wealth. I do not understand how they could be primary or secondary wealth, except for the people who *produce* Bitcoins and other forms of cyber-currency.

The Good News

There is good news for people who shift their focus from tertiary wealth to secondary and primary wealth. They are actually moving backwards, back towards the real wealth that makes the ultra-rich rich.

In a previous chapter, I wrote about the four ages of humanity, which are:

1. Hunter-Gatherer Age

2. Agrarian Age

3. Industrial Age

4. Information Age

In some ways, primary wealth is the wealth of the Agrarian Age. Secondary wealth is the wealth of the Industrial Age. And tertiary wealth is the wealth of the Information Age, the Invisible Age.

Regardless of whether the wealth is visible or invisible, the truly rich invest in the same forms of wealth: primary and secondary. Even in the Information Age, the truly rich—people like Bill Gates and Mark Zuckerberg and Oprah Winfrey—own resources and production. In the Information Age, the invisible resources are *intellectual property*, invisible assets yet very real property, much like real estate. Intellectual property can be patents, trademarks, or contracts, all invisible yet real property nonetheless—and extremely valuable property.

The Rich Don't Work for Money

Chapter One of *Rich Dad Poor Dad* states, The Rich Don't Work for Money. Saying it another way, the rich work for primary and secondary wealth, not the 'money' that is tertiary wealth. They work hard to own resources and production. They are entrepreneurs. And these entrepreneurs take an idea, find the resources, build a business that turns resources into products, and these products become money. Their wealth is not in their money. Their wealth is in their ownership of primary and secondary wealth, resources and production that are both visible and invisible.

Our educational system teaches students to go to school, get a high-paying job, work hard for money, save money, and invest for the long term in the stock market. These are all forms of tertiary wealth.

In many ways, the gap between the rich and everyone else is the gap between those who own primary and secondary wealth and those who own tertiary wealth.

Q: *So if I start focusing on primary and secondary wealth, I move closer to the wealth of the truly rich, the rich Fuller referred to in* Grunch?

A: Yes. You can focus on the wealth of GRUNCH without being dishonest and deceptive. There is nothing wrong with wealth. But keep in mind that there are right and wrong, legal and illegal, moral and immoral ways of acquiring wealth.

Q: *And if I focus on going to school, landing a higher-paying job, working harder, saving money, and investing in the stock market, I move further away from the wealth of the truly rich?*

A: Correct.

Q: *And is that why there is no financial education in schools?*

A: Correct, again, in my opinion.

Q: *How do I begin focusing on primary and secondary wealth?*

A: That's what I want to hear! Your second chance can now begin.

Q: *So how do I start?*

A: You start in the present. You start with where you are today.

Q: *How do I do that?*

A: The same way Kim and I did in 1984. We filled out our
financial statement to get a picture where we were financially.

Rich dad often said: *"My banker has never asked for my report card.
My banker does not care if I had good grades or bad grades. My banker
wants to see my financial statement because he wants to know how smart
I am with my money."*

You can start by taking time to fill in the blanks of the financial
statement below. It is your report card on where you are, financially, today.

Second Chance Exercise:

Take a blank sheet of paper and draw the following diagram:

INCOME STATEMENT

Income
Expenses

BALANCE SHEET

Assets	Liabilities

Important Note:

Remember that rich dad's definition of an asset is:

"Assets put money in my pocket."

His definition of a liability is:

"Liabilities take money from my pocket."

For this exercise, list only assets that actually *cash flow* money into your pocket, the income column. And for liabilities, list all your liabilities and how much money each one costs you each month. Record those costs in the expense column as pictured in the example below.

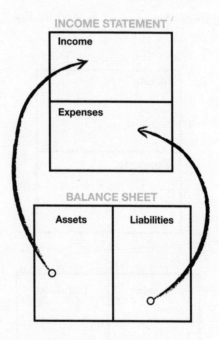

The Power Is in the Present

The present is where your second chance begins. And it can start today.

For many people, this is a very difficult process. It is also the most important first step in the process of transforming from a caterpillar into a butterfly.

For many people, putting their present financial condition down on paper is painful. You may be experiencing that same pain. I encourage you to take a deep breath, and stick with it. A little pain can be a good thing, if it wakes you up to your real world.

You may want to ask for help from a trusted friend, someone you can talk with while you fill out your financial statement. Money is an emotional subject. Your friend is probably less emotionally attached to your finances than you are and he or she can offer a more objective point of view.

Always remember, the power to change begins in the present.

If you skip this process, you lose your power. Once you commit to taking on this process, you may find your power coming back. Your power returns when you find the courage to face your true financial condition. That's the point at which you hold your future in your hands... and your second chance at life can begin.

Q: *Is this why you said you empathize but do not sympathize with those who are struggling?*

A: Yes. I have been through this process many times. You saw one of my financial statements, the one with $820,000 in liabilities. Feeling sorry for myself would not make that number go away. As I've said earlier, I have had a number of second chances, times when I had to start over again. A second chance is never easy, but at least I grew smarter by solving my problems—rather than pretending I had no problems or looking to others to solve them for me.

And everyone—as long as they are willing to make changes and commit to a course of action—deserves a second chance, if they want one.

Q: *So by focusing on my personal financial statement, I begin to see my strengths and my weaknesses?*

A: Yes.

Q: *And rather than feeling sorry for myself, which makes me weaker, I can now begin to find my strengths, get out of my current situation, and move into the future?*

A: Yes. When you focus on strengthening your strengths, your internal make-over begins, as does your metamorphosis from caterpillar to butterfly.

Remember that your financial statement today, is your *before picture.* Now we're ready to move into the future and look at your *after picture... your Future.*

The Future

Now that you've taken a good, honest, hard look at your present, it's time to look towards your future.

On another sheet of paper, draw this diagram of a financial statement again. You will create the Financial Statement for your Future.

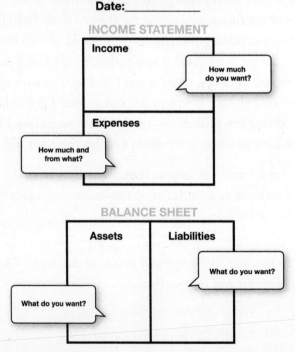

Choose Your Asset

There are four basic asset classes in any financial statement. They are:

Business

Real Estate

Paper

Commodities

Take a moment and ask yourself which asset class (or classes) you are most interested in. There is no right or wrong answer.

Let me share with you my personal choices.

My first choice has always been commodities. I love gold and silver. I began collecting silver coins when I was nine years old. I went to school in New York to be a ship's officer. My specialty was oil, and I became an officer on oil tankers.

The point I want to make is that *love* is important in investing. I love gold, silver, and oil. Love makes it easier for me to *study* gold, silver, and oil. As you know, market prices are always going up and down. I do not mind price fluctuations because I love my assets. I want to own more. So when prices go down, I buy more.

My second choice is real estate. I love real estate because it is easy to use debt to acquire properties. It's a bonus that the tax laws are favorable for real estate investing.

I love real estate, especially old buildings. And it's that love that makes it easy for me to be a student of real estate and real estate finance. I am always a student, as I encourage you to be, because I can never say I know it all. Again, market prices go up and down. When they go down, I buy more. I rarely sell because I love my real estate assets and the cash flow they deliver.

My third choice related to asset classes was to be an entrepreneur, someone who started businesses. I have started many businesses, but most of them never survived those first critical years. The ones that did survive were my nylon and Velcro surfer wallet business, my rock-and-roll business, my education company, a gold mine, a silver mine, an oil company, and today, The Rich Dad Company.

Of all the asset classes, business is the toughest. That may be why the richest people in the world are entrepreneurs. It can be a long road—and a tough one—but when they win, they often win big.

My fourth choice is paper assets. I have attended many classes on stocks and options. I am not good at it. I don't love reading annual reports or watching stock prices going up and down.

As an entrepreneur, I have formed three companies and taken them public, via an IPO, an Initial Public Offering, just for the experience. I wanted to look behind the curtains at how companies are created and then sold to the public. It is a dirty game and I did not enjoy it… but you might. So I have millions of shares of stocks, but stocks of *my company*, not shares in someone else's business.

Take the Time

Your second chance begins inside of you. I encourage you to take the time to look at all four asset classes and to drill down a little and study them. Then decide which one you love the most.

If you find that you don't love any of them, then take a break and wait till you find an asset class you can love.

And be very careful. The most important aspect of choosing an asset class is love, the love of study, the love of being a student. I have gone to too many 'seminars' that sell investments that promise magical returns to gullible and naïve people, people who dream of getting rich quick. While a few may be good investments, most are scams, deceptions, and maybe even lies from promoters who only want your money.

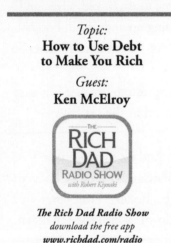

Topic:
**How to Use Debt
to Make You Rich**

Guest:
Ken McElroy

The Rich Dad Radio Show
download the free app
www.richdad.com/radio

Always remember this: The best investments are never advertised… and I do mean *never*. The best investments, regardless of asset class, are *always* sold to insiders, those *in the know*. For example, when my partner Ken McElroy has a new investment, he simply calls a few people and the investment opportunity is gone. Fully-funded and closed. He does not need slick brochures or the dog-and-pony-show hype of investment seminars to promote and sell his projects to outsiders.

One of your goals should be to become such a good investor, a rich and knowledgeable investor, that you'll have an inside track and get in on the inside.

As you may know, *insider trading* is illegal in the public market, known as the stock market. But *insider investing* is legal for private markets. For example, when the Chinese company Alibaba went public, it was sold to outsiders. The real profit had already been made by insiders, long before Alibaba was offered to the public.

As a friend of mine often says, *"All* investing is insider investing. The only question is, how close to the inside are you?"

Choose Your Game

Bucky Fuller often said, "They're playing games with money." He did not like the game of money or the games that governments and GRUNCH play.

My rich dad said, "Find the game of money you love and play to win." His game was to be an entrepreneur in restaurants, hotels, convenience stores, and—especially—real estate. As I wrote about in *Rich Dad Poor Dad*, Ray Kroc, founder of McDonald's said, "I am not in the hamburger business. McDonald's is in the real estate business." In other words, his hamburger business buys his real estate, and his real estate is some of the most expensive real estate in the world. That was also my rich dad's game and it's my game today.

Rich dad also said, "Most people do not like the game of money. That is why they choose job security and a steady paycheck over playing the game.

"Rather than play the game of money, they turn their money over to a financial advisor, hoping they've chosen the right advisor."

He added, "The reason most people are not rich is because they go through life *playing not to lose* rather than *playing to win* in the game of money."

My poor dad did not like the game of money. He played not to lose. His game was to go to school, become a government employee, and have the government take care of him. Unfortunately, he lost because he never played to win.

What game do you want to play? If you decide to play rich dad's game, start by choosing the asset you love, the asset you want to study and the game you want to play. You'll want to commit yourself to becoming the very best you can be, playing the game of money that you love.

The Future

If cash is trash...

...then what is Financial Education?

Part Three: The Future

INTRODUCTION

The best introduction to Part Three, in my opinion, is a summary of Parts One and Two…

DOES IT MAKE SENSE to **go to school** and learn little about money?

Why would you go to school, to get a job, to work for money—yet never *learn* about money? Education exerts a powerful influence in all our lives every day. That is why some types of education were denied to slaves prior to the Civil War and to women in many parts of the world even today.

Chapter One of *Rich Dad Poor Dad* states, The Rich Don't Work for Money. The rich do not work for paychecks. As rich dad said, the person who signs the paycheck has tremendous power over the person who receives it. On top of that, the more money you earn, working for money, the more you'll pay in taxes. That may be why Steve Jobs' paycheck was only $1 a year.

In addition to the fact that they learn little about money in school, many students leave school deeply in debt. Student loan debt is the most onerous of all types of debt.

The chart below shows the rise in student loan debt.

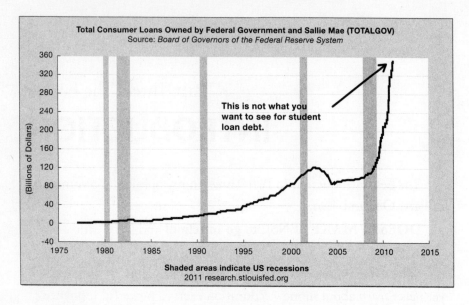

Making matters worse, paychecks for college graduates are getting smaller.

The chart below shows the drop in income for college graduates.

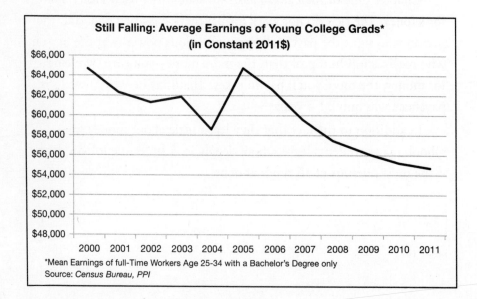

DOES IT MAKE SENSE to **work hard for money**, when the reward for working harder is only to pay more in taxes on the money you earn?

The chart below shows that the higher-income middle class pays the highest percentage in taxes. The top 20% pay 50% of their income in taxes, while the top 1% pay only 13%.

This is one reason why the middle class is shrinking.

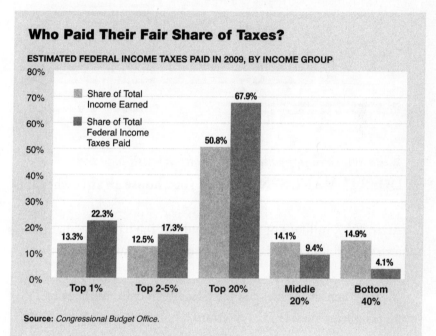

Who Paid Their Fair Share of Taxes?

ESTIMATED FEDERAL INCOME TAXES PAID IN 2009, BY INCOME GROUP

Share of Total Income Earned

Share of Total Federal Income Taxes Paid

Top 1%: 13.3%, 22.3%
Top 2-5%: 12.5%, 17.3%
Top 20%: 50.8%, 67.9%
Middle 20%: 14.1%, 9.4%
Bottom 40%: 14.9%, 4.1%

Source: *Congressional Budget Office.*

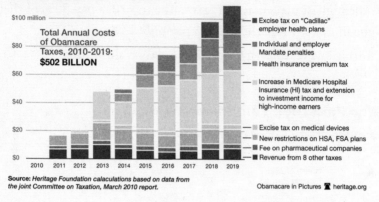

Taxed Enough Already? Just wait until Obamacare kicks in

To pay for generous subsidies to purchase health insurance, a huge expansion of Medicaid, and other new spending, Obamacare raises taxes and adds 17 new taxes or penalties that will affect all Americans.

Total Annual Costs of Obamacare Taxes, 2010-2019: **$502 BILLION**

- Excise tax on "Cadillac" employer health plans
- Individual and employer Mandate penalties
- Health insurance premium tax
- Increase in Medicare Hospital Insurance (HI) tax and extension to investment income for high-income earners
- Excise tax on medical devices
- New restrictions on HSA, FSA plans
- Fee on pharmaceutical companies
- Revenue from 8 other taxes

Source: Heritage Foundation calaculations based on data from the joint Committee on Taxation, March 2010 report.

Obamacare in Pictures ☎ heritage.org

When you work for money, your wealth is stolen via taxes.

DOES IT MAKE SENSE to **call your house** an asset when it is really a liability?

After 2007, millions of people found out the hard way that their homes were liabilities. Today, millions of people owe more on their homes than they're worth.

Making matters worse, due to college loan debt, millions of young people are unable to even afford a home.

The chart below shows the drop in home values.

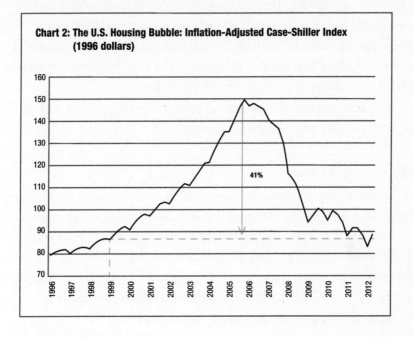

Chart 2: The U.S. Housing Bubble: Inflation-Adjusted Case-Shiller Index (1996 dollars)

Your wealth is stolen via a lack of financial literacy, in this example, calling liabilities, assets.

DOES IT MAKE SENSE to **get out of debt** when the rich are using debt to get richer?

Savers   **Debtors**
                              with Financial Education

Savers, on the left in the illustration on the previous page, save their after-tax dollars. The banking system's *fractional reserve system* reduces the purchasing power of their savings by multiplying the savers' money, lending to debtors with financial education (who will invest it) $10 for every dollar in savings. The fractional reserve system is the way "money is printed." Every bank does it.

Add this fact to the equation: Interest on savings is taxed at the highest tax rates and... debt is tax-free.

The Carry Trade

In the world of large investors, there is a term known as the Carry Trade. It is how extremely large investors use debt to make money. For example, in 2014, Japan lowered its interest rates to near zero. Immediately giant investors, such as hedge funds, rushed to borrow billions in yen, converted the yen to dollars, and with those dollars purchased U.S. Treasury bonds that paid a higher interest rate.

In an overly simplified example, let's say a hedge fund, from anywhere in the world, borrows the equivalent of $1 billion U.S. dollars in Japanese yen at 0% interest, converts the yen to $1 billion in U.S. dollars, and buys a billion dollars worth of U.S. bonds that pay 2%. The net result is that the hedge fund earns $20 million on the $1 billion in borrowed money.

This is known as the Carry Trade, symbolized by the wheelbarrow in the illustration on the previous page.

Borrowing yen to buy U.S. bonds causes:

- the U.S. dollar to grow stronger because people are buying dollars to invest in bonds;

- bond prices to go up;

- interest rates to fall;

- U.S. exports to become more expensive causing people to buy more Japanese products because Japanese products are cheaper;

- unemployment to rise in America;

- gold and silver prices to come down

... and life becomes more difficult for the poor and middle class everywhere.

Obviously, if Japan raises its interest rates, the world would go into chaos, as it did in 2007.

Keeping It Simple

In an even more overly-simplified example, it would be like you borrowing $1 million from one bank, paying 0% interest on the loan, and then "carrying" the money across town where you deposited that $1 million in a bank that paid you 5% interest. You would earn $50,000 on the interest-free loan (on the $1 million you borrowed.)

If the bank that was charging you 0% interest suddenly raised its interest rate to 10% on the $1 million you borrowed, you would be in serious financial trouble. You would have to pay $100,000 in interest, eating up the $50,000 you earned in interest (at 5%) AND costing you $50,000 loss. This is what causes economic panics and crashes.

The biggest banks don't care if they lose billions because the government always seems to step in to "bail them out" if they make mistakes. They use the excuse that "The big banks are too big to fail."

You and I would probably have to declare bankruptcy.

The rich have the power to "bailout" their banks. In today's world, if the banks make money, they win. If the banks lose money, you and I lose.

This is why Bucky Fuller said, "They're playing games with our money." This is one example of how our wealth is stolen via our money, via what Fuller called GRUNCH, "The **Gr**oss **Un**iversal **C**ash **H**eist."

Your wealth is stolen via your savings.

DOES IT MAKE SENSE to **save money** when the government is printing money?

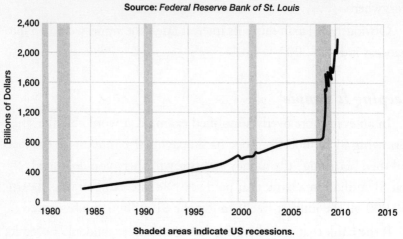

When banks print money, inflation goes up.

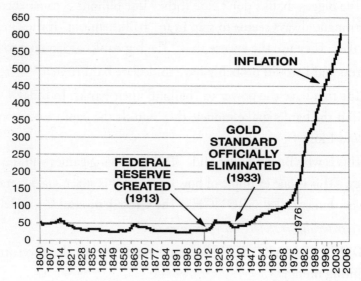

Keep in mind: Governments do include food and fuel prices in the inflation numbers.

In 1929, after the "Great Crash" the United States did not print money, so it went into the "Great Depression."

In 1918, the German Weimar government *did* print money and Germany went into the "Great Inflation."

The chart below shows what happened in Germany.

GERMANY WEIMAR HYPERINFLATION
Value of One Gold Mark in Paper Marks

Paper Marks

"However enormous may be the appearant rise in the circulation in 1922, actually the real figures show a decline." –Prof. Karl Eister

"In proportion to the need, less money circulates in Germany now than before the war," –Prof. Julius Wolfe

1918 1919 1920 1921 1922 1923

dollarvigilante.com

Today, America appears to be following the 1918-1923 Germans into hyperinflation.

Today, America appears to be following the 1918-1923 Germans into hyperinflation. The chart below is proof how the Fed, Wall Street and President Reagan's Plunge Protection Team, keeps "goosing" the Dow, preventing it from crashing.

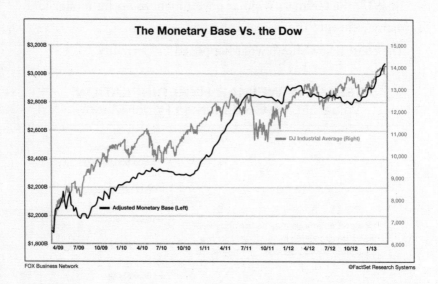

DOES IT MAKE SENSE to **invest for the long term**, when the stock markets are at all-time highs and professional investors are using HFT, high frequency trading, to invest for "the short term" using computers to buy and sell stocks thousands of times every second?

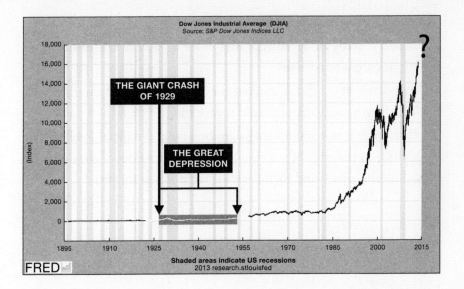

In *Rich Dad's Prophecy*, published in 2002, rich dad predicted that a giant crash would occur around 2016. That book also predicted an earlier crash that would occur prior to 2016, and that was the crash of 2007.

When you look at the chart above it seems likely that *Rich Dad's Prophecy* might come true. Let's hope not. And, as everyone knows, things go up and things come down. So why would you invest for the long term when the stock market is at all-time highs?

If rich dad and Bucky Fuller are correct, those in the stock market could be hit the hardest. It's what Chris Martenson, in his book *Crash Course*, calls tertiary wealth.

Your wealth is being stolen by investing for the long term in tertiary wealth, paper assets like stocks, bonds, mutual funds, and savings. During this economic era, I'd be very suspicious of anything that's printed on paper.

For those of you who invest in tertiary assets, I encourage you to research Bert Dohmen and his *Wellington Letter*. I have found that his is the most accurate forecaster of the markets—and has been for more than 30 years.

What is Financial Education?

If cash is trash, financial education is *the opposite* of traditional education taught in schools.

Part Three of this book is about the other side of the coin, the duality, the yin and yang of financial education.

Part Three is not about being right or wrong. Financial intelligence is standing on the edge of a coin—looking at both sides of the coin, the heads and the tails—and then deciding what is best for you.

Chapter Nine

THE **OPPOSITE** OF "GO TO SCHOOL"

"Integrity is the essence of everything successful."
— R. Buckminster Fuller

In 1973, I returned to Hawaii from Vietnam. I was stationed at the Marine Corps Air Station at Kaneohe, Hawaii. At the time I had another year and a half left on my contract with the Marine Corp.

I went to both dads, asking for ideas on what I should do next. I loved flying, I loved the Marines, but the war was over and it was time for me to move on.

My poor dad suggested I go back to school, get my MBA and, possibly, a doctorate degree.

My rich dad suggested I take seminars on real estate investing.

This is an example of opposites in education. Pictured on the following page is a financial statement to illustrate the differences.

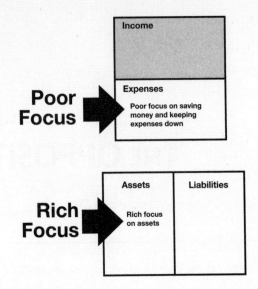

My poor dad recommended that I go back to school so I could get a high-paying job and a steady paycheck in corporate America. He was recommending that I work for money in the income column.

My rich dad was recommending I learn to use debt to acquire tax-free cash flow from assets.

Taking the suggestions of both dads, I signed up for the MBA program at the University of Hawaii and a 3-day real estate investment seminar. After completing my real estate seminar and buying my first cash-flow-producing "asset," I dropped out of the MBA program. I was 26 years old and beginning to understand the differences between a paycheck and cash flow, debt and taxes.

Q: *What are the differences between:*

1. Being an employee, with a MBA climbing a corporate ladder, working for paychecks, bonuses, and a retirement portfolio filled with paper assets.

2. Being an entrepreneur, building businesses and investing in the real estate, working to create assets that produce cash flow.

A: There are many differences. A few are:

1. **Retire Young**

   Kim was 37 and I was 47 when we achieved financial freedom. As stated earlier, I was over $800,000 in debt from losses from my nylon wallet business when Kim and I took our leap of faith in 1984. Yet we were financially free by 1994. I doubt if we would have achieved what we did, if not for what I learned from a 3-day real estate seminar.

   In 10 years, we had built a financial education business as entrepreneurs, paid off most of my past debt, and acquired enough cash flow from real estate investments to be financially free.

   My book *Retire Young Retire Rich* is an account of our 10-year process.

2. **Debt and Taxes**

   The primary advantages of real estate over paper assets—tertiary wealth such as stocks, bonds, mutual funds, and savings—is the power of debt and taxes. Simply put, debt and taxes make you poorer if you invest in paper assets. Debt and taxes can make you richer, if you are a professional investor in real estate.

3. **Financial Stability**

   Whenever I talk to groups about the coming stock market crash, I can tell immediately who is in the stock market. I can see whose financial future is dependent upon the health of the stock market.

   If someone in the group asks me why I am not worried, I remind them that much of my wealth is in real estate.

   When I am asked why my real estate will not go down in a crash, I remind them that my real estate holdings are always near jobs, jobs that are not affected by stock market crashes. For example, most of our apartment complexes are in major oil industrial cities like Houston and Oklahoma City, or next to hospitals, colleges, and large insurance companies. The price of oil may go up and down, but cash flow from renters keeps flowing.

I remind them of what happened to real estate in cities like Detroit, when the auto-industry collapsed. Detroit real estate crashed with the auto industry. Today in Detroit, vacant homes are being torn down. So much for the flawed assumption that a house is an asset.

The lesson is real estate is only as good as the jobs near the property.

If the financial services industry collapses, high-priced real estate in cities like New York, London, Shanghai, and Tokyo, will suffer.

Most people need a roof over their heads. If they cannot afford the money for rent, the government often subsidizes the rent money.

These are some of the reasons why some real estate is less affected by market crashes. And only some of the things I learned in my 3-day real estate investment seminar in 1973.

If I had continued on with my MBA, and found a high-paying corporate job, I would probably be a struggling, middle-management executive today, worried about losing my job to younger and more tech-savvy workers who are willing to work for less, and living in fear of a stock market crash that would wipe out my retirement.

Instead, every time the stock and real estate markets crash, as they did in 2007, I grow richer buying more real estate assets with debt, increasing my cash flow, and paying less in taxes.

Those are some of the advantages of seeing *the opposite side to education.*

Lesson from Fuller

During one of his talks, Fuller spoke on the word *integrity*. His definition was that things with integrity "held their shape." He then said, a triangle was the minimum shape that had integrity.

As he spoke, I better understood why my rich dad was richer than my poor dad, even though my poor dad held a PhD.

The following is my interpretation of Fuller's talk on integrity applied to education.

College Kids: Many students leave school unprepared for the real world due to a lack of professional education.

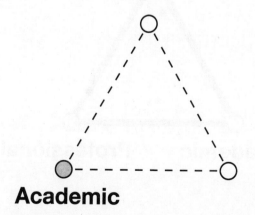

Academic

Many have to go back to school to gain professional education.

Poor Dad: My poor dad had only two of the three points of the triangle.

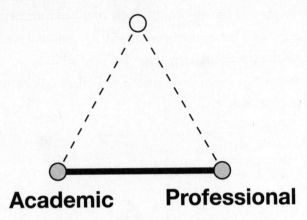

My poor dad was academically gifted and trained professionally as a teacher.

But without financial education, money literally slipped through his hands.

Rich Dad: My rich dad had all three types of education.

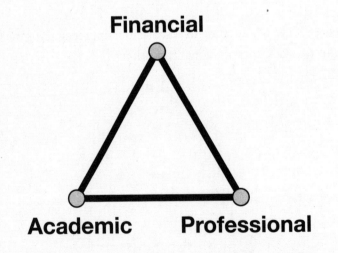

Professional Investor

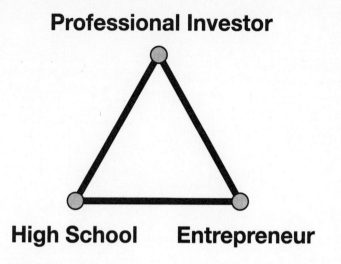

High School   Entrepreneur

Rather than go to college, rich dad attended two to four business and investment, weekend seminars a year.

Rather than go on for my MBA, in 1973, I followed in my rich dad's educational path. In 1996, after Kim and I were financially free, The Rich Dad Company was founded to provide seminars, educational products, coaching, and mentorship programs on entrepreneurship and investing for people who want financial freedom more than job security.

Lesson for Your Second Chance

If you go back to school, know the difference between a paycheck and cash flow. They are opposites when it comes to education.

Financial education is...

The Opposite Side of the Coin

When you go to school you learn to work for money.

Financial education teaches you to acquire assets that produce cash flow.

Chapter Ten

THE **OPPOSITE** OF
"DON'T MAKE MISTAKES"

"Mistakes are sins, only when not admitted."
— R. Buckminster Fuller

At the end of my 3-day real estate seminar, in 1973, the instructor said, "Now your education begins." This puzzled the class. We thought the 3 days in the *seminar* was our education.

As the seminar ended, the instructor—who was a real, real estate investor with passive income, not a teacher working for a paycheck—broke the class of 30 or 40 people into groups. Our assignment was to look at, evaluate, and write a short report on 100 investment properties in the next 90 days.

I was in a group of four. All four of us agreed to get together for 90 days to complete the assignment. As you might have guessed, by the end of the 90 days only two of us were left. The other two were too busy working for a paycheck to complete the assignment. They did not have time to look for assets.

This 90-day process was the most important 90 days in my financial life. Those 90 days transformed me from a poor person into a rich person.

Pictured on the next page is a diagram called the Cone of Learning, developed by educational psychologist Edgar Dale. Please take a moment to study it.

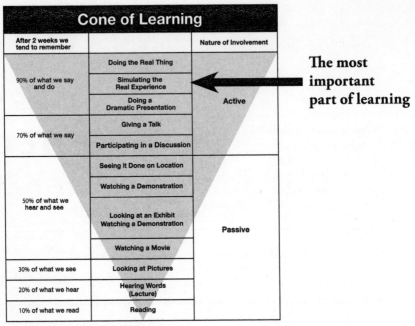

The most important part of learning

Source: Cone of Learning adapted from Dale, (1969)

For 90 days, the instructor had us focused on the second section of the Cone of Learning: simulating the real experience.

For 90 days we did not buy anything. Initially our little group of four would meet in the afternoon, go through property listings, looking for properties that met the criteria we learned in class. Then we'd make calls to real estate agents, setting up appointments to see the properties, often three to five a day. At the end of the day, we would write up our summaries on a single page in a spiral notebook—our findings, the pros and cons… the good, the bad, and the opportunity.

It was a painful, tedious, and slow process at first. We felt like babies learning to walk. By the end of the first month, two of our team had dropped out. They grew tired of not finding anything worth buying.

One of the things that discouraged us was real estate brokers who continually said, "What you're looking for doesn't exist in Hawaii." They'd often follow that statement with: "Real estate in Hawaii is expensive. You cannot find low-priced properties that produce positive cash flow here."

As rich dad often said, "The reason they are real estate *brokers* is because they are *broker* than you." What he meant is that most employees and self-employed individuals work for money. In the case of real estate agents, they work for commissions. As real estate investors, on the business owner and professional investor side of the quadrant, we were looking for assets that produced cash flow.

Knowing the difference in mindsets, between Es and Ss, and Bs and Is, kept me going. By the end of the second month, we were flying. We were still not finding anything, but our minds could see slight distinctions, subtle differences, things we had not seen before. We were beginning to see the "invisible."

At the end of 90 days, I thanked my partner and we went our separate ways.

Of the 100 properties we evaluated, we had identified only five properties that had potential. He knew which ones he was going to pursue and so did I. Just as our instructor said, "Out of one hundred properties, you might be lucky to find one 'hot' property." He said, "The purpose of the 3-day course and the 90-day process was to teach us how to go through the 99 bad properties faster and faster, to find that one great property."

My first investment property was a 1-bedroom/1-bath condo, across the street from a beautiful white sand beach in a small village near Lahaina, Maui, which is some of the most expensive real estate in Hawaii. It was not luxury real estate; it was housing for employees who worked in the luxury hotels in Lahaina.

The price of the property was $18,000, an incredibly low price. It was one of those properties the real estate agents said did not exist. Comparable units in the area were going for $26,000. The seller was the developer of the condo project and did not want to pay real estate agents a commission. Consequently, the agents, who work for those commissions, had no incentive to tell me about the project. I stumbled across it by accident.

The seller had 12 condos he wanted to sell quickly. He asked that I put 10% down and told me that he would finance the rest. I did not have to go to a bank for a mortgage—which was good because my credit was bad and I did not earn much money. I used my credit card to finance my down payment of $1,800. After all expenses were paid, I netted $25 a month in positive cash flow.

Now I can hear some of you saying, "Those deals don't exist anymore. Real estate prices are much higher today."

That is exactly what our instructor, in 1973, said people would say. He said, "Most people are so busy working for a paycheck they do not have time to get rich." He said, "It is easier to say these deals don't exist than go out and look at 100 properties in 90 days to find one."

He also said, "The deal of a lifetime comes along everyday."

And I know that to be a true statement. Some of the best investments Kim and I have found were sitting right in front of us. We never would have found them if we weren't looking for them. Kim found her best investment right across the street from where we live in Phoenix. It was the investment that transformed her into a rich woman. She would never have 'seen' it—the good deal—if she had not looked at thousands of 'bad deals.'

In Chapter 7 of this book, I wrote about my friend Graeme, in Scotland, who found a 150-year-old church that the government gave him the money to purchase and refurbish. For over four years, people in the neighborhood walked right by the giant For Sale sign in front of the church on their way to work, never stopping to look for an asset. They were too busy looking for a paycheck.

In 1973, that first real estate deal blew my mind, I had acquired an asset that produced $25 per month and didn't use a dime of my own money to do it. I had just experienced how to use debt to become richer. I went back and purchased two more of those same units. I was crossing over to the other side of the coin.

I had crossed the line from poor and middle class into the world of the rich. Just as the instructor had said, "I would never have to say, 'I can't afford it' ever again. Today, Kim and I own several thousand cash-flowing apartment properties, commercial properties, a luxury hotel, a boutique hotel, five golf courses, and oil wells. Every year we add more assets like those to our financial statement and pay less in taxes. If the stock, real estate, and oil markets crash again, which they will because all markets crash, we will acquire more assets at even lower prices, using the power of debt and taxes to increase our cash flow.

Q: *Don't you feel sorry for people who cannot see what you see?*

A: Yes and no. Because we all have equal opportunity. Anyone can do what the rich do, if they want to do it. The same tax laws the rich use are available for everyone to use, but only if they have financial education and real life financial experience.

The real problem is our choices in education, choices which blind us from seeing *the opposite side of money.* The reason I write, create games, and teach is to give others the same opportunities my rich dad gave me.

Everywhere I go in the world, people always say, "You can't do that here." Even when I speak in cities like Phoenix, cities where I am *doing* what they say cannot be done. The reason they can't do what I do where they live is because they were taught to work for money, job security, and a paycheck. Those words blind them and prevent them from seeing *the opposite side of the coin.*

The Power of Mistakes

Another reason why so few people see the other side, or other points of view, is because our schools punish students for making mistakes. The question is: How can anyone learn anything if they're afraid of making mistakes?

When you watch a baby learning to walk, you'll see them stand and fall and cry. After a while, they'll try again… standing, falling, and crying. They repeat the process until they stand, walk, then run. Their next challenge is to learn to ride a bicycle. The process of learning continues. Again, the child falls off the bicycle until they learn to ride. Their world expands with the more mistakes they make.

Then they go to school.

In school they learn that students who memorize the right answers are smart. Students who make mistakes are stupid. Then they get a job, where they are fired if they make mistakes. In other words, once a child goes to school, their learning process becomes retarded. At the age of five, they begin to learn to fear—and avoid—making mistakes.

When I talk about becoming an entrepreneur and starting a business, or investing in real estate, the first thoughts that cross the mind of most employees are: "What if I make a mistake? What if I lose money? What if I fail?" This is why most people are not rich. They have learned to fear making mistakes. They are taught that only stupid people make mistakes. They are taught not to *make* mistakes, rather than how to learn from their mistakes.

Failing to Succeed

If you look at the real world, the world outside the school system, you'll see that the biggest failures are the biggest winners. For example, Thomas Edison failed over a thousand times, before inventing the electric light bulb and going on to found General Electric.

In his book *Outliers*, Malcolm Gladwell writes that few rock bands have ever failed more than the Beatles. He writes that as teenagers, they performed up to 12 hours a day, everyday, for free beer an and audience of pretty women.

Tiger Woods started playing golf at the age of three. After school, he would practice at a local golf course until it was too dark to see the balls he was hitting.

If you'll look again at the Cone of Learning you will understand why failure leads to success.

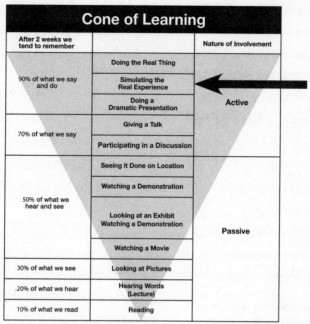

After 2 weeks we tend to remember		Nature of Involvement	
	Doing the Real Thing		
90% of what we say and do	**Simulating the Real Experience**	**Active**	
	Doing a Dramatic Presentation		
70% of what we say	**Giving a Talk**		
	Participating in a Discussion		
	Seeing it Done on Location		
	Watching a Demonstration		
50% of what we hear and see	**Looking at an Exhibit Watching a Demonstration**	**Passive**	
	Watching a Movie		
30% of what we see	**Looking at Pictures**		
20% of what we hear	**Hearing Words (Lecture)**		
10% of what we read	**Reading**		

Source: Cone of Learning adapted from Dale, (1969)

The line just below *doing the real thing* is the most important line on the Cone of Learning. The learning through *simulation* separates winners from losers.

Opposite: Mistakes

The difference between my MBA program and the 3-day real estate seminar was that second line—simulating the real experience.

The entire time I was in night school, working toward my MBA, there was always an underlying theme of "Do not make mistakes." The reason to study hard in school was so that I would not make mistakes once I got a job.

This was in sharp contrast to my instructor for my 3-day real estate course. He encouraged us, emphatically pleading with us, to immediately begin making mistakes. That's why he said that our education began when we left his class.

After making 100 mistakes in 90 days, then (and only then) did he recommend moving up to the top line on the Cone of Leaning— *Doing the Real Thing*. That meant buying something.

After doing the real thing, making $25 a month in cash flow using 100% debt, I dropped out of the MBA program. I did not want to work for job security and a paycheck… and I did not want to live my life in fear of losing my job if I made a mistake.

Playing CASHFLOW

Many people think I am giving them a sales pitch when I suggest that they play the *CASHFLOW* game at least 100 times and then teach 100 people how to play the game. Many think that I only want their money.

While sales are important to The Rich Dad Company, my primary reason for recommending that people play our *CASHFLOW* game at least 100 times—and teach 100 people—is because that is how my rich dad taught his son and me. Starting at the age of nine, while playing *Monopoly*® over and over again, he passed on words of wisdom as his son and I made mistake after mistake playing the game.

Topic:
**Educational Entrepreneurs:
Teaching the Game**

Guest:
Darren Weeks

The Rich Dad Radio Show
download the free app
www.richdad.com/radio

Like my rich dad and my real estate instructor, I too encourage people to make as many mistakes as they can before doing the real thing, and using real money.

Rich Dad Advisor Darren Weeks followed my advice and began teaching people to play *CASHFLOW*. So far, he has taught over 100,000 people, across Canada, the United States, and Europe to play the *CASHFLOW* game and has become a multi-millionaire in the process. He simply did—in real life—what he learned from playing and teaching the game, which is to acquire assets that produce cash flow.

Q: *So making mistakes and learning from our mistakes is the key to success?*

A: It is. In the real world it is call *practice*. For example, professional football teams practice five days a week, then play only one day.

This is why doctors and lawyers called their business a 'practice,' rather than a business.

In music and the theater, practice is called a 'rehearsal.'

Q: *So practices and rehearsals are where professionals make mistakes and learn from their mistakes, before doing the real thing?*

A: Yes. In 2014, I was at the Ryder Cup in Scotland, watching some of the best golfers in the world play for the United States and European teams. They spent the day before the matches practicing, on the practice tee and playing practice rounds, and before they hit at the ball off the tee, they always took two or three practice swings… before doing the real thing. That's why they are winners in the game of golf. Winners make more mistakes than amateurs.

Bucky Fuller on Mistakes

Fuller had this to say about mistakes:

"Human beings were given a left foot and a right foot to make a mistake first to the left then to the right again, and repeat."

My sketch on the following page puts Bucky's words into a picture.

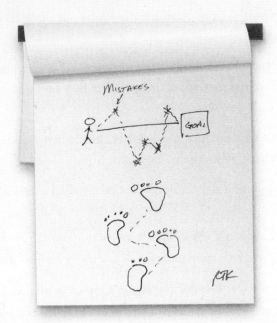

In an article entitled "Mistake Mystique" Fuller writes:

> *"It is only at the moment of human's realistic admission*
> *to selves of having made a mistake that they are closest to*
> *that mysterious integrity governing the universe."*

In other words, the moment a person admits to making a mistake, they come closer to god.

Fuller states:

> *"Mistakes are sins only when not admitted."*

In other words we sin when we *omit* something and are closer to god when we *admit* something.

And when we admit to making a mistake, Fuller says, *"Only then are humans able to free themselves from the misconceptions that brought about their mistakes."*

In other words, god designed humans to learn by making mistakes.

In "Mistake Mystique," Fuller states:

"At present, teachers, professors, and their helpers go over the student's examination, looking for errors. They usually ratio the percentage of error to the percentage of correctly remembered concepts to which students have been exposed.

"I suggest that the teaching world alter this practice and adopt the requirements that all student periodically submit a written account of all the mistakes they have made, not only regarding the course subject but in their self-discipline, during the term, which also recording what they have learned from the recognition that they have made the mistakes; the report should summarize what it is they have really learned, not only in their courses, out on their own intuition, and initiative.

"I suggest then that the faculty be marked as well as the students on a basis of their effectiveness in helping students learn about any subject— doing so by nature's prescribed trial and error leverage. The more mistakes the students discover, the higher their grade."

This is exactly the process my real estate instructor had us go through. We wrote down what we learned from our mistakes, not our successes. I am convinced this is one reason why I have made so much money, with minimal losses, from my real estate investments.

Again, learning in the real world is opposite from learning in school.

Lesson for Your Second Chance

In school, the person who makes the fewest mistakes wins. In real life, the person who makes the most mistakes wins.

Financial education is…

The Opposite Side of the Coin

Find a place you can practice, practice, and practice, making mistake after mistake.

Remember, the most successful people make the most mistakes.

Chapter Eleven

THE **OPPOSITE** OF "GET GOOD GRADES"

"I would say, then, that you are faced with a future in which
education is going to be number one amongst the great world industries."
— R. Buckminster Fuller

Education is a very big word.

Education is more important today than ever before.

For billions of people, the answer to today's economic crisis is, "Go back to school." The question is: Is that the best answer for you? Will traditional education give you your second chance in life?

As Fuller predicted, education is going to be number one among the great world industries. But the question is, What kind of education? Will it be the same education you went experienced in school? Will it be students sitting in a room listening to a teacher, memorizing answers, and taking tests? Will it be online learning? Or will it be a radically different educational process?

I believe it will be the latter. If education is going to be the world's great industry, it cannot remain in its present state, controlled by the government and labor unions. Someday soon, a new educational process will emerge, and we will look back at children sitting in classrooms, listening to teachers, memorizing answers, taking tests, and say, "How barbaric. How did anyone learn anything?"

The chart below speaks to a disturbing trend. It shows that unemployment is rising for jobless workers with some college education.

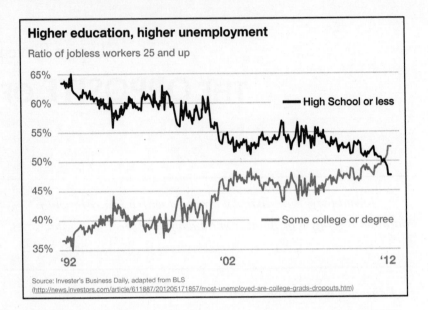

Higher education, higher unemployment

Ratio of jobless workers 25 and up

Source: Invester's Business Daily, adapted from BLS
(http://news.investors.com/article/611887/201205171857/most-unemployed-are-college-grads-dropouts.htm)

Will going back to school change their lives for the better?

Threat to National Security

Retired Four-Star Admiral Mike Mullen, former chairman of the Joint Chiefs of Staff, states that the top two biggest threats to national security are:

1. The national debt

2. K-12 education

Admiral Mullen's concern for the national debt is reflected in the following chart:

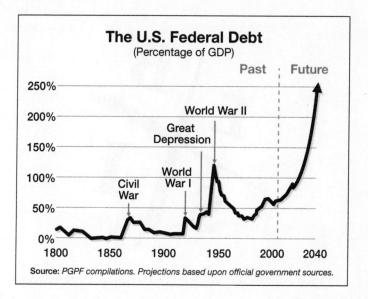

The U.S. Federal Debt
(Percentage of GDP)

The Admiral's concern for K-12 education is reflected in the following are statistics.

1. After World War II, the United States had the #1 high school graduation rate in the world. Today, the United States has dropped to #22 among the 27 industrialized nations.

2. Less than half—46%—finish college. This ranks the United States dead last, at 18 out of 18 industrialized countries.

3. Two-thirds of college professors report that what is taught in high school does not prepare students for college.

Q: *Does college prepare you for the real world?*

A: It depends upon how you define the real world… and what you want in life.

Again, the CASHFLOW Quadrant below shows the four different worlds in the world of money.

Traditional education—high school, trade schools, colleges, and graduate schools—prepare students for the E-and-S side of the quadrant, my poor dad's side. Those on the left side of the quadrant work for money. Traditional education does not prepare students for the B and I quadrants, my rich dad's side where people work to acquire assets and cash flow.

For your second chance in the world of money, you will need to decide which quadrants are best for you.

The good news is that on the right side, the B and I side of the quadrant, you can learn by using your stronger intelligence.

Q: *There are different intelligences?*

A: Yes, there are many different types of intelligences. Unfortunately, our educational system emphasizes and focuses primarily on two intelligences: verbal-linguistic intelligence and logical-mathematical.

Simply put, if you are good at reading and writing and enjoy math, you will do well in school. If you are not blessed with these two intelligences, good luck.

Q: *Who discovered the different intelligences?*

A: Professor Howard Gardner of Harvard University, and he wrote about them in his 1983 book, *Frames of Mind*. In that book, he identified seven different intelligences. They are:

1. **Verbal-linguistic intelligence:** They learn by reading and listening. They think in words. They enjoy word games, word puzzles, writing poetry and stories.

2. **Logical-mathematical intelligence:** They think conceptually, abstractly, and are able to explore patterns and relationships.

3. **Body-kinesthetic intelligence:** These people often become athletes, dancers, and surgeons. They learn by body activity.

4. **Visual-Spatial intelligence:** They think in terms of physical space, as do architects, artists, and sailors. Very aware of their environments. They like to draw and daydream.

5. **Musical intelligence:** Person shows sensitivity to rhythm and sound. They love music. Often study better with music in background.

6. **Interpersonal intelligence:** Ability to interact with others. Great communicators, who learn through interaction with others. They have many friends, empathy for others, and are street smart.

7. **Intrapersonal intelligence:** Communicate with self, understanding one's own interests and goals. They tend to shy away from others. They're in tune with their own feelings, have wisdom, intuition, motivation, and a strong will. Very independent learners.

Gardner has gone on to identify many more intelligences. He recognizes that these different intelligences make it difficult for our one-size-fits-all education to support different students. This is why so many students learn to hate school, even though they love learning.

For example, I did not like reading, writing, or math, but I loved surfing and playing football, which I practiced for hours. I went to the military academy because learning was first physical. I was graded on how well I could design and sail large ships. I did well in flight school, again because learning to fly was physical. You cannot learn to fly a plane by reading a book. The math and science was extremely difficult for me and, if not for physical learning, I would never have received a college degree.

As an adult, I love real estate investing because it is investing in things I can see, touch, and feel. I do not care for stocks, bonds, and mutual funds because paper-asset investing is primarily for those who are good at reading and math. Entrepreneurs must be strong in interpersonal intelligence, communicating with many different people from different professions. The most important intelligence for entrepreneurs is intrapersonal intelligence, the ability to handle risk, financial losses, going without a paycheck for long periods of time, being responsible for personal mistakes and mistakes of employees, and constant emotional stress.

The question is, what is your strongest intelligence? What are your second and third strongest intelligences?

The differences in intelligences is what causes us to be different people. And those differences account for why some people are better suited to operate in certain quadrants. For example, if you are not strong with intrapersonal intelligence, it is best you stay in the E quadrant.

Education for Human Beings

One problem with our current educational system is that it is Industrial Age education. Students are treated like robots being assembled on an assembly line by other robots. All robots learn on a schedule designed by other robots. If a robot cannot keep up with the assembly-line curriculum, it's sent back to the start of the line and labeled retarded, slow, or with a disease created by teachers, a disease called ADD or Attention Deficit Disorder. In reality: extreme boredom.

The problem is we are human beings. We are not robots. All human beings are different. In a family of four kids, all four children will be very different. Even identical twins are different.

Before you find your second chance, it is important for you to respect your unique intelligence, your strengths and your weaknesses. Just because you were not born rich, did not do well in school, or do not do well climbing the corporate ladder for bigger paychecks, does not mean you cannot find wealth, freedom, and happiness. This is why the following section on education for human beings, not robots, is important for your second chance in life.

The Tetrahedron

Fuller taught us that the tetrahedron, pictured below, was the minimum structure in the universe. The tetrahedron was different from a triangle because a tetrahedron defined a *volume* and a triangle defined an *area*.

Since humans have *volume*, I will use the tetrahedron to represent human intelligence and what makes us human beings.

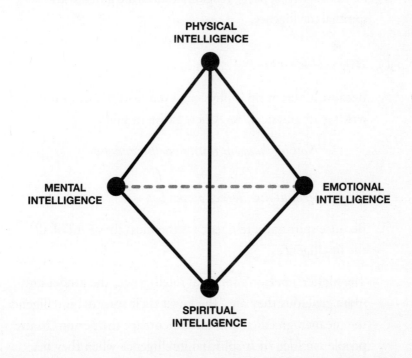

Different Intelligences

I have been teaching professionally since 1984. The more I taught, the more I realized humans had four different intelligences. The four intelligences of a human being are:

1. **Physical Intelligence:** Great athletes are gifted physical learners. Physical intelligence is found in the muscles. "Golfers will say you need to develop *muscle memory.*"

2. **Mental Intelligence:** Most people who do well in school are gifted mental learners. *Mental intelligence is found in the brain.* People will say, "Let me think about it."

3. **Emotional Intelligence:** Emotional intelligence is known as the "success" intelligence. That means the higher a person's emotional intelligence, the better they are at handling life's challenges. Challenges such as fear, loss, anger, and boredom. *Emotional intelligence is located in the stomach… in our gut.*

4. **Spiritual Intelligence:** *Spiritual intelligence is found in the heart.* Artists, poets, religious leaders, are gifted with spiritual intelligence.

Q: *Why is physical intelligence on top?*

A: Because all learning is physical, even reading, thinking, and writing are physical. As Albert Einstein said,

> *"Nothing happens until something moves."*

Q: *Why is spiritual intelligence on the bottom?*

A: Because spiritual intelligence is the most powerful of all the intelligences.

The higher a person's spiritual intelligence, the kinder and more generous they are. The lower their spiritual intelligence, the meaner, greedier, and (often) corrupt the person. Many people sacrifice their spiritual intelligence when they lie, cheat, and steal. As you know, there are people who will sell their souls for money. Many people sell their soul working in a business that kills their spirit. A few people will even kill a family member for money.

I believe this financial crisis is a primarily spiritual crisis. There is too much greed, crime, and corruption running the world.

This is why strengthening the four intelligences that make you a human being, is important, especially if you want a second chance in life.

Q: *How do I strengthen my different intelligences?*

A: You can strengthen your intelligences by changing your environments. For example, going to the gym can strengthen your physical intelligence. Your physical intelligence is also strengthened when you learn new business skills such as learning to sell or taking a painting class.

Going to a library, sitting quietly to read, and study can strengthen your mental intelligence. Taking an investment class, which is especially important if you are afraid of losing money, can strengthen your mental intelligence.

Q: *Even emotional intelligence?*

A: Yes, emotional intelligence may be the most important intelligence for those serious about a second chance.

Gardner called emotional intelligence intrapersonal intelligence. Some people call it the success intelligence. If a person cannot learn to control their emotions they may never achieve their dreams in life.

Q: *Can you give me some examples?*

A: Sure. There are many people who are very smart mentally, but are weak emotionally. For example, many schoolteachers are gifted with mental intelligence, but emotions, such as the fear of failing, often hold them back financially.

Another example of emotional intelligence is called delayed gratification. Many people want to get rich quick. Working to get rich quick is a sign of low emotional intelligence. Those people cannot delay gratification. I have a friend who invests in real estate. His problem is that, rather than be happy with steady cash flow, he sells his property (for capital gains—and pays taxes on those gains) the moment real estate prices go up. Selling for capital gains is killing the goose that is laying golden eggs.

Q: *How do I strengthen my emotional intelligence?*

A: Hire a coach. All professional athletes have coaches. Most successful people have coaches. I have met many great coaches and they have enhanced my life greatly. The job of a coach is to bring out the best in you.

If you cannot afford a coach, find a friend who will be your coach, holding you accountable for doing what you know you need to do.

I also have emotional coaches, often called 'therapists,' someone you can talk to about your deepest and darkest doubts and fears.

Many people stuff or suppress their emotions. For example, a friend of mine lost their son. Rather than seek professional help, she "toughed it out." She "buried their emotions." The problem with stuffing down emotions is that it takes energy to keep emotions down, to hold them in. If the emotion is released, a person has more energy for productive things. Stuffed emotions often lead to "dis-ease." This friend of mine was later diagnosed with cancer. I do not know if there is a relationship between emotions and disease, but I suspect there is.

Rich Dad Advisors Josh and Lisa Lannon, are social entrepreneurs. They build clinics that work with people who have drug and alcohol addictions. Their new venture is working with veterans, service men and women who return with emotional damage from serving in war zones. They state that most addictions and mental problems stem from emotional problems.

Topic:
Social Entrepreneurship
Guests:
Josh and Lisa Lannon

The Rich Dad Radio Show
download the free app
www.richdad.com/radio

What Is Faith?

Emotional and spiritual intelligence is essential to faith. Faith is vital for your second chance. Bucky Fuller said:

> *"Faith is much better than belief.*
> *Belief is when someone else does the thinking."*

When Kim and I set off on our journey, our leap of faith in 1984, all we had was our faith in ourselves and faith that if we did the right things, things would work out. One facet to our faith was that we would get smarter along the way. We had faith that our intelligences would grow, even though neither Kim nor I were not rocket scientists in school. We both have our college degrees, but what we learned along the way we did not learn in school.

What kept us going was faith and emotional intelligence, not academic intelligence. We delayed gratification by going for long periods without paychecks. And even though cash was tight, we kept investing with debt and creative financing, never 'flipping' our properties, even though we could have used the money. Rather than flip our properties for quick cash (and higher taxes), we worked harder in our business to produce more cash flow. By delaying gratification, we became better entrepreneurs and investors because we did not have very much money. In other words, adversity made us smarter.

Lesson from Bucky Fuller

One of my favorite quotes from Fuller is:

"God is a verb, not a noun."

That is why I put physical intelligence at the top of the tetrahedron and spiritual intelligence at the base. For you to find your genius—especially if you did not do well in school—you have to do something… make mistakes, and learn. That is the way you find the faith to discover your true, god-given intelligence, your unique genius.

Fuller's suggestion for your second chance is:

"The things to do are: the things that need doing, that you see need to be done, and that no one else seems to see need to be done. Then you will conceive your own way of doing that which needs to be done—that no one else has told you to do or how to do it. This will bring out the real you that often gets buried inside a character that has acquired a superficial array of behaviors induced or imposed by others on the individual."

Your unique intelligence, your true genius, will emerge when you start doing things, because you are doing what you believe needs to be done, without anyone telling you how to do it.

That is what Kim and I did in 1984. We had no qualifications to be teachers. We were only doing what we saw needed to be done, which was to provide financial education for everyone and anyone who wants to learn.

Lesson for Your Second Chance

Evaluate the four intelligences of your tetrahedron. Use a rating system of one to 10, with 10 being the highest.

1. How strong is your physical intelligence?

2. How strong is your mental intelligence?

3. How strong is your emotional intelligence?

4. How strong is your spiritual intelligence?

If you score yourself over 30, you have a pretty good chance for a second chance in your financial life. If you score yourself below 30, find a friend you trust and talk over your strengths and weaknesses.

Your second chance will require that you develop and use all four of your intelligences.

Financial education is...

The Opposite Side of the Coin

Talking over your intelligences could be the best thing you can do. Admitting your weaknesses is the first step in gaining strengths.

Again, everything is opposite.

Chapter Twelve

THE **OPPOSITE** OF
"GET A GOOD JOB"

"Over specialization leads to extinction."
                              – R. Buckminster Fuller

When I was in school, everyone wanted to climb the corporate ladder. My classmates wanted to be VPs of XYZ Corp or Sales Managers at ABC Corp. They wanted to be high-paid employees.

Today, everyone wants to be an entrepreneur.

With high unemployment, technology replacing people in the workforce, global competition, and less job security, people dream of being their own boss, starting their own business, and enjoying a life of financial freedom.

Today we have high school kids and college dropouts who are billionaires—and it's because they're entrepreneurs, not employees.

Today, we live in a Start-Up World. Many colleges and universities have 'incubators' nurtured with the hope of launching the next Google or Facebook.

The fact that millions of people are becoming entrepreneurs is a good thing. Entrepreneurs have the power to save the economy. Unfortunately, statistics show that nine out of 10 new businesses will be out of business in five years.

The reason most new businesses fail is because traditional education trains students to be specialists. And entrepreneurs are generalists.

Nine out of 10 new businesses fail because the entrepreneur is too specialized. They do not have the generalized business skills to survive.

Q: *What are the differences between specialists and generalists?*

A: A specialist knows a lot about a little. A generalist knows a little about a lot.

Q: *So why do specialists fail?*

A: They lack the business skills required to be entrepreneurs, skills that are usually not taught in school.

Q: *Name a skill not taught in school.*

A: Entrepreneurs must be able to sell. If an entrepreneur cannot sell, they don't eat.

The reason so many people do not quit their jobs is because they cannot out-sell their paycheck.

Q: *What do you mean by that? What do you mean they cannot* out-sell their paycheck?

A: Let's say a person earns $10,000 a month via paycheck. If they become an entrepreneur, they have to bring in at least $50,000 in sales.

Q: *Why $50,000 in sales?*

A: It's just a rule of thumb, an approximate 5-to-1 ratio. For every dollar you earned as an employee, you have to bring in at least five times that as an entrepreneur to feed yourself *and* feed the business.

When you become an entrepreneur, you have expenses employees don't have. You have product costs, equipment costs, costs of doing business, taxes, professional services, and on and on. When you hire your first employee, your costs, risks, and headaches go up.

Studies show that most entrepreneurs earn less than their employees when the number of hours they actually work are calculated. For example, many entrepreneurs go to work after the business is closed for the day. The paperwork—from compliance with government regulations, bookkeeping, taxes, payroll, and marketing and sales support is staggering. The employee goes home and enjoys life, but for the entrepreneur the day is just beginning. This is one reason why the vast majority of businesses fail in the first five years.

Q: *So what can I do?*

A: Keep your full time job and start a part-time business. Every employee at Rich Dad is encouraged to have a part-time, 'incubator' business. We do not want them to leave, yet we want them to one day be a financially free human being. Many are close to replacing their paychecks with cash flow from their part-time business or their investments. Hopefully they will stay and work with the Rich Dad Company, even if they're financially free, just because they like working there and enjoy the opportunities to learn and study together.

Topic:
How to Increase Your Income

Guest:
Blair Singer

The Rich Dad Radio Show
download the free app
www.richdad.com/radio

Q: *So your employees are specialists, learning to be generalists in their spare time. Is that what you're saying?*

A: Yes. When people go back to school, they become more specialized. They learn computer programming, auto repair, a foreign language, or get their Masters degree. They learn a lot about a little, meaning a very narrow and specialized education.

Q: *So how does a person become a generalist? What do they study?*

A: The B-I Triangle sums it up… It illustrates the 8 Integrities of a business—and their relationship to each other.

Q: *What is the B-I Triangle? What does it represent?*

A: The B-I Triangle is what an asset looks like.

Q: *The B-I triangle is a diagram of an asset?*

A: Yes. As you can see the B-I Triangle is made up of the 8 components that I call integrities—because they're essential to success. Collectively, they keep a business, the asset, whole, complete, functioning, and producing cash flow. That's the bottom line.

Q: *So, if one of the 8 Integrities is weak or missing, the business will fail or struggle financially?*

A: Exactly. Whenever I talk with a struggling entrepreneur, the 8 Integrities of the B-I Triangle serve as a checklist—a simple diagnostic guide to discover what is missing or what is out of integrity.

Q: *So schools train students to be specialists working within one of the integrities of the B-I Triangle?*

A: Yes. And to be an entrepreneur, you need to be a generalist, knowing a little about each of them. And knowing when and where you need specialists.

Q: *But the product, or P is the smallest section. Does that mean the product is least important?*

A: It does. Product alone is of little value. So many people rush around saying, "I have a great idea for a new product." Another reason that nine out of 10 new businesses fail is because they focus on the product, not the whole business.

Q: *When a new entrepreneur starts a business, are they the entire B-I Triangle?*

A: Yes. They are responsible for all 8 Integrities. They start as specialists in the S quadrant. Very few make it to the B quadrant.

Q: *Why is that?*

A: Each quadrant represents a different mindset. Very few small entrepreneurs have the mindset of giant entrepreneurs such as Steve Jobs.

Q: *So for an S-quadrant entrepreneur to grow he or she must hire employees who are smarter and more specialized than they are—for every one of the integrities?*

A: Yes, the entrepreneur hires *specialists*. For example, the first specialist an entrepreneur must hire is a bookkeeper, someone who will keep accurate records of income and expenses. Many entrepreneurs find themselves in serious trouble in less than a year because they did not keep good records. For the entrepreneur to grow into a B-quadrant business, it's often necessary to hire a CEO to run the company.

Q: *What about entrepreneurs who do their own books?*

A: It keeps them small. If you do your own books, you will probably never grow big enough to hire a CEO.

Q: *Is that why you say the entrepreneur must out-sell their paycheck? The entrepreneur must be able to afford specialists if they want to grow?*

A: Exactly. When you look at the CASHFLOW Quadrant below, you can see the bigger picture.

S-quadrant entrepreneurs are entrepreneurs who work for money. For example, a person who owns a restaurant that sells hamburgers operates from the S-quadrant.

B-quadrant entrepreneurs work to build assets that produce cash flow.

Ray Kroc built a B-quadrant hamburger business known as McDonald's.

Q: *So how do I learn to build a B-quadrant business?*

A: You must build the framework, the outer triangle, of the B-I Triangle. You must have a strong mission, a great team, and be a leader who can inspire a team to follow you.

Q: *How do I learn those integrities?*

A: Military schools focus on these integrities. For example, my first day at the military academy I attended in New York we focused was the mission. At the Academy, like in the Marine Corps, mission is everything.

This is why I wrote *8 Lessons in Military Leadership for Entrepreneurs.* This book explains how and why those with military training have the basics for becoming great entrepreneurs.

Q: *How does a person learn mission, team, and leadership skills without going to military school?*

A: Joining a network marketing company is a great way to build leadership skills, lead a team, and support a shared mission.

The best thing about network marketing is that you learn to lead people without having to issue them paychecks.

Most corporate leaders have the power of a paycheck. If you do not do what your boss tells you to do, there's a good chance you'll be fired.

In network marketing, you have to learn to be an inspirational, mission-driven leader, some who can train people to be successful—even without the short-term gratification of a paycheck. You are training people who can operate without a paycheck. If you can do that, you can do almost anything.

Missionaries also step up to the challenges of mission, leadership, and team. My best friend was a Mormon missionary in Northern Ireland. His job was to convert Catholics to the Mormon religion. Today, he is an incredibly successful entrepreneur.

You can also strengthen your integrities as a volunteer working in your church or for a charity, leading volunteers (people who work for free...) and helping to grow your church or favorite charity.

There are many ways you can gain real-life experience in mission, team, and leadership. I gained mine in military school and in the Marine Corps. For your second chance, you'll want to find the ways that works for you, so you can gain real-life leadership experience.

Q: *What happens if I am an entrepreneur, but don't really have a mission... or the leadership skills to build and inspire a team?*

A: Then odds are you will remain an entrepreneur in the S quadrant. There is nothing wrong with that, as long as you are happiest there.

Just remember, S-quadrant entrepreneurs often pay a higher tax rate than their employees. The entrepreneurs who pay the lowest tax rates are entrepreneurs in the B and I quadrants.

The King of the Jungle

In the world of 'big cats' there are leopards and lions. Leopards are similar to entrepreneurs in the S quadrant. Leopards are loners. They hunt by themselves—and if they don't kill, they don't eat.

The male lion has a *pride*. In the business world, that *pride* is a B-quadrant business, a team of specialists. The male lion does not hunt. The pride hunts. Once the pride has made a kill, the male lion walks over and enjoys the feast.

This is not the most elegant example of the differences between an S-quadrant entrepreneur and a B-quadrant entrepreneur, but I believe you get the picture.

If you want to learn more about what types of specialists make up a B-quadrant business, you may want to read my Rich Dad Advisors' books or listen to them on the Rich Dad Radio Show. Their wisdom will guide you into your future, if you want to be a generalist who leads specialists.

Q: *Why are people skills so important?*

A: People are like icebergs. When we first meet a person, we meet only the part of the iceberg that is above water. We do not see the 99% that is below the water line. People skills are required to deal effectively with the entire person.

Q: *How do I guide my children to the B and I quadrants?*

A: Donald Trump's two sons, Don Jr. and Eric, are good friends of mine. They were on Rich Dad Radio talking about how their dad is developing them to be leaders in the B and I quadrants. They are not two spoiled brats, as many children (rich and poor) are.

And they are not specialists. They are generalists—bright young men and strong leaders with great people skills. They are being groomed to be leaders in the B and I quadrants.

Lessons from Bucky Fuller

I have heard Bucky say:

*"What usually happens in the educational process
is that the faculties are dulled, overloaded, stuffed and
paralyzed so that by the time most people are mature
they have lost their innate capabilities."*

During his talks he emphasized this point: *"over specialization leads to extinction."* One reason why so many people are going back to school is because technology has rendered them obsolete. Unfortunately, they go to school and learn to be specialists, rather than generalists.

Fuller often used the example of the mighty dinosaur becoming extinct because dinosaurs were too specialized. They were not able to adapt to the changing environment.

Today, book publishers, many of whom are my friends and business associates, are the dinosaurs. Amazon is the new publishing giant that is changing the environment for books.

In October of last year I was with my Marine Corps squad in Pensacola. According to a few of the guys, rumor has it that all branches of the service are cutting back on the training of jet pilots. The prediction is that pilotless drones will replace human pilots… just as the Google self-driving car may replace taxi drivers and Uber drivers. More real-world example of the huge changes to skills, training, and jobs… and how technology continues to change our world.

The Smartest Thing to Do

What is considered "smart" is changing. As I've said, when I was in school, all of my classmates wanted to climb the corporate ladder.

Today, everyone wants to become an entrepreneur. Everyone has a million-dollar idea in their head. The problem is, schools do not teach people to be entrepreneurs.

For your second chance, you need to decide what is best for you. Which *quadrant* is best for you?

For many people, the smart thing to do is get a good job, save money, live debt free, invest in the stock market and hope that money will be there when they need it. For some, clinging to financial security in the E and S quadrants is smart.

For other people, the smart thing to do is become an entrepreneur. That often means being millions of dollars in debt—debt used to acquire businesses and real estate that create a life of financial freedom in the B and I quadrants.

Q: *What is the difference between the E and S side of the quadrant and the B and I side of the quadrant?*

A: The difference lies in your choice of education and advisors.

Q: *What determines what's "smart" for me? What I should do...*

A: Your spirit tells you which path to follow. What inspires you? What challenges you? What path is best suited for your unique gifts and talents?

Every time I thought about going to work in corporate America, my stomach turned. I became nauseous. There are people who feel that way every day when they think about their job or work day.

When I think about being an entrepreneur, my spirit soars. I get happy—even though I know being an entrepreneur is often a much harder road than working for a paycheck in corporate America.

I did not want to be a specialist, a small entrepreneur in the S quadrant.

Q: *So S-quadrant entrepreneurs have to be the smartest ones on their team? And B-quadrant entrepreneurs don't have to be the smartest person, they just need the smartest team?*

A: You got it. I've never been the smartest person on my team, and I never want to be. Rich dad said, "If you're the smartest person on your team, your team's in trouble." And if rich dad were alive today he would say, "Specialists always work for generalists." For example: I don't work for doctors; they work for me. That's one of the reasons why I wrote the book *Why "A" Students Work for "C" Students*.

So what is smart for you? Your spirit knows your answer.

Lesson for Your Second Chance

The opposite of job security is financial freedom.

Job security requires specialized education.

Financial freedom requires generalized education.

Your task is to decide which is best for you, security or freedom. They are very different. In fact, they are opposites. The more security you seek, the less freedom you have. That's why all prisons have *maximum security* cells.

Financial education is...

The Opposite Side of the Coin

Employees and the self-employed are specialists.

Entrepreneurs are generalists.

Chapter Thirteen
THE **OPPOSITE** OF
"GET OUT OF DEBT"

---

*"The Generalized Principle of epheralization
is the ability to do more with less."*
— R. Buckminster Fuller

Most financial experts say, "Get out of debt. Live debt free." Don't they know that after 1971, when President Richard Nixon took the U.S. dollar off the gold standard, the U.S. dollar became debt?

While living debt free may be good advice for people without financial education, it is not smart financial advice.

There are two kinds of debt in the world of money. They are:

1. Good debt.

2. Bad debt.

Simply put, good debt makes you richer and bad debt makes you poorer. Without financial education, it isn't surprising that millions of people (and the United States government) are buried under mountains of bad debt.

The Big Spenders

Many people believe it was the Democrats that increased the national debt.

But that isn't the story the charts tell.

As I've stated in the opening pages of this book, I am not a Republican or a Democrat. And the research behind the Cone of Learning indicates, looking at a picture is better than listening to words, especially political speeches.

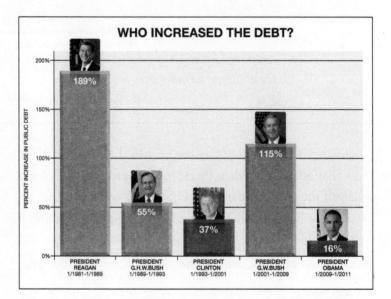

The problem with this debt is that it's bad debt... debt the taxpayers and their children must pay.

Much of the debt incurred by Republicans goes to the rich who control the military-industrial complex, banks, pharmaceutical companies, and other corporations.

Much of the debt accrued by Democrats goes to entitlement programs and corporations that profit from entitlement programs.

Social Security and Medicare are generally not included in the national debt numbers, although they represent debt obligations much, much larger than the national debt. These two debts—Social

Security and Medicare—are considered off-balance-sheet debt. That would be like you owing a million dollars, but not reporting it on a credit application when you applied for a loan. If you and I did what our government does, we could be sent to jail.

Nobody knows the exact number for Social Security and Medicare debt. Educated guesses put Social Security debt at $23 trillion and Medicare at $87 trillion. That's trillion… with a *t*. I have seen other estimates as high as $125 trillion. The U.S. national debt is a mere $17 trillion.

Q: *Are you saying the United States is bankrupt?*

A: I could make a case to support that position. It wouldn't be hard.

What Is Good Debt?

Good debt is simply debt that makes you richer. For example, when I buy an apartment complex, I use debt to finance the property. If the apartments puts money in my pocket every month, then my debt is good debt. If, on the other hand, my apartments lose money every month and I have to make the mortgage payment, that same debt becomes bad debt. Once again, it is cash flow that determines if something is good or bad debt.

Q: *Is that why you say, "Your house is not an asset?" For most homeowners, their house is taking money out of their pockets.*

A: Yes. Even if your house is debt free, cash is still flowing out of your pocket for taxes, maintenance, insurance, and utilities.

Leverage

A very important word in the world of money is the word *leverage*. Leverage is similar to Fuller's word *ephemeralization*, which means the ability to do more with less.

One of the primary reasons why the poor grow poorer and the middle class shrinks, is because they have little to no leverage. When the poor and middle class think about how to make more money, they think about working harder and longer. Unfortunately, when you work harder and longer, you may make more money but move into higher tax brackets.

Financial Education is Leverage

One purpose of financial education is to give you leverage, the ability to ephemeralize, and be able to do more with less.

Let me give you some examples of financial leverage, ways to do more with less.

1. **Debt**

   As a professional, active investor in the I quadrant, I want to use as much debt as possible to acquire assets. The reason Kim and I own thousands of properties is not because we've been able to save money to buy them. We *use debt* to buy them. That is why that 3-day real estate program was priceless for me. It taught me how to leverage debt.

2. **Licensing**

   If you will take a look at the photo of the Rich Dad employees at the front of this book, you may notice that we are a very small company. Yet, via licensing, we are a very, very, large international business. When I write a book, that book is *licensed* to over 50 publishers throughout the world. These publishers pay The Rich Dad Company a *royalty* for the right to publish my books and games.

3. **Social media**

   Today's social media world offers huge leverage, if used properly. Today, at the Rich Dad offices, we have a tiny television and radio studio through which we stay in touch with millions of people all over the world.

4. **Brand**

   Rich Dad is an international brand. Being a brand is huge leverage. A brand speaks louder than words. And communicates two things: trust and differentiation. Examples of differentiation are found in our positioning. We don't say "save money"… our position is the opposite side of that coin.

We do not recommend investing for the long term in stocks, bonds, and mutual funds. We believe the opposite: keep your money moving. And we do not place high value on job security. Instead, the Rich Dad brand stands for financial freedom.

5. **People**

   Employees have almost zero leverage because they are their *employer's* leverage. Entrepreneurship offers you the ability to leverage the time and efforts of others—*your* employees—to grow your business and your asset column.

6. **More with Less**

   Delivering higher quality products or services for a lower price is another form of ephemeralization. When a person asks for a raise, charges more per hour, raises prices, or lowers quality to save money, they are working against the Generalized Principle of ephemeralization. They are doing less for more. The opposite of doing more with less.

Debt as Leverage

When financial experts advise, "Get out of debt," they handicap people because they take away a lot of leverage. This type of advice is not financial education. Because without debt, a person is unable to do more with less.

The following is a real-life example of using debt as leverage. I will keep the numbers simple.

In the 1980s, I purchased a 2-bedroom/1-bath house for $50,000. It was a cute house, in a good neighborhood, next to a park with a pond. The problem was the house was in need of repair.

I put $5,000 down and the seller financed the balance, $45,000, at 10% interest. *Seller-financing* means I didn't need a bank loan. My total monthly payments, PITI, (Principle, Interest, Taxes, and Insurance), were about $450. Rents in the area were running at around $750 a month.

Once I had tied the property up, I went to my banker and asked to borrow $5,000 for a "home-improvement loan."

With that $5,000 loan, I added a large master bedroom with an adjoining bath, and fixed the rest of the house. I now had an almost-new, 3-bedroom/2-bath house. The new rent was $1,000 a month.

When interest rates started to go back down, I went back to the banker who loaned me the $5,000 and asked for a new loan—this time on the entire house.

The appraisal came in at $95,000. My banker gave me an 80% loan: $76,000 at 9.0% fixed for 10 years. I paid back the seller's $45,000 loan, the banker's $5,000 home improvement loan, and put approximately $25,000 in my pocket tax-free.

My total PITI was approximately $700.00 a month. I set aside $100 a month for repairs and unexpected expenses. My tenant's payment of $1000 a month put approximately $200 a month in net cash flow into my pocket each month.

Q: *So you had none of your own money in this investment?*

A: Correct. That means my return was infinite.

Q: *Infinite? Why is it infinite?*

A: Because when ROI, or return on investment, is calculated the return is based upon how much equity or how much of the investor's money is in the investment. Since I had no money in equity—none of my own money in the investment after the re-finance—the ROI was infinite.

Q: *So your real return is a result of your knowledge, your financial education? Without that you probably couldn't do these things, right? Find and finance investments that give you an infinite return?*

A: That's right. That is why one of our positioning statements for The Rich Dad Company is knowledge: the new money.

Q: *So you put $25,000, tax-free, into your pocket because the $25,000 is debt?*

A: Yes. But if I had sold the property, the $25,000 would have been subject to capital gains tax, which for me, in my income tax bracket, would be 20%.

Q: *OK… if you had sold the property, your net gain after taxes would have been $20,000?*

A: Even less. Here's why: as long as I still owned the property I was earning approximately $200 a month in cash flow, an additional $2,400 a year in passive income, the lowest-taxed of all incomes.

Q: *How many types of income are there?*

A: There are three basic types.

1. Ordinary

2. Portfolio

3. Passive

Ordinary income is income from wages, interest on savings, and 401(k) savings programs. Ordinary income is taxed at the highest tax rates. Working for ordinary income is another reason the poor get poorer and middle class is shrinking.

Portfolio income is also called capital gains, or income from selling something. People who flip houses, trade stocks, or sell businesses pay capital gains taxes, taxed at the second-highest tax rate.

Passive income is cash flow from assets. Since I do not sell the real estate properties I own—choosing, instead, to 'borrow-out' my gains—I realize and receive my capital gains via debt and passive income from rental income, the lowest-taxed of all incomes.

Now I can hear some of you saying, "You can't do that. You cannot get seller financing." And you are right: If you say you can't, you can't.

Q: *So what about people who live outside the United States? Can they do this, too?*

A: Sure they can. The terms and rules may be a little different, but the basic concepts are true all over the world.

When I was first starting out, in 1973, my real estate instructor said everyone would say, "You can't do that here." He said, "People without financial education always say, 'You can't do that here'—even though people are doing it."

Q: *So why do people say, "You can't do that here?"*

A: Because it's easy to say, "You can't do that here." Lazy people always find it easier to say "You can't do... " something rather than take classes, study, practice, make mistakes, fail a few times, and learn how you can do something... something others say you can't.

Q: *Does this strategy only apply to real estate? Or can I do this with anything?*

A: You can do this with anything. Stocks and stock options are a particularly easy way to make money with nothing. The advantage real estate has over stocks is the power of long-term debt.

Q: *So debt is leverage. And if I don't know how to use debt I work harder and harder for less and less?*

A: Yes. Let me give you one more example of how debt makes me richer.

When the stock and real estate markets crashed in 2007, we did not buy stocks at low prices. Instead we bought hundreds of millions of dollars worth of real estate using debt. We could buy much more real estate than stocks, because we were using our banker's money. Besides, bankers aren't likely to lend hundreds of millions of dollars to anyone who plans to buy stocks.

In 2014, Ken McElroy, his partner Ross, Kim, and I refinanced nearly $100 million in debt, debt on our apartment houses purchased after the 2007 crash. The average interest rate on our apartment houses was 5.0%. The new debt on that $100 million is at approximately 3.0%.

That means we received millions of dollars in capital gains back and an additional $2 million in cash flow due to the lowered interest rates.

Q: *Where does the additional $2 million come from?*

A: The $2 million in cash flow comes from the savings, the difference between paying 5% interest on $100 million of debt and 3% interest.

Q: *And that is what Fuller calls the Generalized Principle of ephemeralization, the ability to do more with less?*

A: Yes.

Q: *And this doesn't apply only to real estate?*

A: Correct. There are examples of ephemeralization everywhere. It's safe to say that everyone who is rich has used some form of leverage to get rich. For example, when a musician cuts a record and sells a million records, that is epehmeralization. When someone develops an app and sells a million copies of their app, that's ephemeralization, that's another way of doing more with less. The advantage of real estate is the power of both debt and taxes.

Q: *So when a financial advisor advises me to get out of debt, they are taking away one way for me to leverage, to ephemeralize? To do more with less?*

A: Yes. And while they may mean well, they do not provide financial education. Financial education should show you the other side of the coin, and teach you to use debt to become richer, not poorer.

The Law of Compensation

Q: *But what if I make mistakes with debt?*

A: That is why you take real estate classes and practice, practice, practice. I've taken many classes and I love to practice. I'd rather practice than buy impulsively and lose money.

In the world of money, there is a law known as the Law of Compensation.

Q: *What is the Law of Compensation?*

A: Simply put it means that the more you learn (and practice and slowly take on bigger challenges) the more your intelligence and experience grows—and the more your compensation will grow.

For example, when Kim was first learning to invest, her financial plan was to purchase two small houses a year, 20 houses in 10 years. In less than 18 months, she had bought her 20 houses. Today, she has thousands of properties, earning millions of dollars in cash flow each year. She is also hundreds of millions of dollars in debt. That is an example of The Law of Compensation.

A Word of Caution

I have gone to a number of real estate seminars where the instructor makes the process of finding a great property sound tough, risky, and time consuming.

At the end of the class they often say, "Rather than spending your time looking for properties, making mistakes, and being frustrated with tenants and repairs, just give us your money and we'll find, finance, purchase, and manage the property for you."

I suggest you stay away from these types of instructors and organizations. They are not teachers. They are promoters. They are not any different from a mutual fund salesperson, a person who invites you to a free financial-planning seminar, and then tells you the smart thing to do is for you to give them your money.

Q: *What's wrong with giving someone else your money? Why not let them do all the work?*

A: Great question. And the answer may surprise you. When you turn your money over to someone else, the Law of Compensation does not work for you.

You may remember from studying the Cone of Learning that the two most important lines—the two most effective ways to learn—are simulations and doing the real thing. If you truly want to be financially free, you must practice and do the real thing. Yourself.

Q: *But if I get my cash flow and tax advantages, what is wrong with someone else doing the investing for me?*

A: The problem is real estate. Real estate is not liquid. To be liquid means, you can buy or sell it quickly. Stocks and mutual funds are extremely liquid. You can buy and sell in seconds. With real estate, the opposite is true. If you make a mistake, it is a long, slow, expensive process to get rid of a bad property. Millions of homeowners and "flippers" have found out just how illiquid real estate can be.

So if you are not willing to practice, practice, practice, I suggest that you not invest in investment real estate. Remember that when a real estate instructor says, "I will invest for you," you are still the person responsible for the monthly mortgage payments, problems with tenants, the expenses for maintenance and upkeep, and insurance—not the instructor. Worst of all, you learn little to nothing. The Law of Compensation and leverage work against you.

The reason you want to learn to use debt is because debt is today's money. Debt is the most powerful force in the world of money. The reason you want to take classes and practice is to learn to harness this most powerful of forces.

If you are not willing to start small, learning how to use debt to invest in real estate, it is best you save money, live debt free, and invest for the long term in mutual funds. At least savings and mutual funds are liquid.

Lesson from Bucky Fuller

Bucky Fuller said:

> *"Don't fight forces, use them."*

The reason I included the chart on the U.S. Presidents and debt at the beginning of this chapter is because if things do not change, debt will bring down the United States, a country that was once the richest country in the world. Debt will enslave our children and their children's children.

Traditional education teaches people to live debt free. And while you may choose to be personally debt free, our leaders are putting the future of our world in debt.

If you do not want to be a slave to government debt, fight fire with fire. Learn to use the forces of personal debt to counter the incompetence of our leaders.

Lesson for Your Second Chance

If you plan to live a debt-free life, what other type of leverage do you plan to use? How will you ephemeralize your life? How do you plan on doing more with less?

The board game *CASHFLOW* is the only game in the world that teaches you how to use debt to get rich.
It's a simulation using play money.

If you fail to learn to use some type of leverage, you will work hard all your life and still end up poor.

If you want to learn to harness the power of debt, play *CASHFLOW* and use every opportunity to get into debt, rather than get out of debt. When you play games, you can lose the game but still learn a lot.

Financial education is...

The Opposite Side of the Coin

Bad debt makes the poor and middle class poorer.

Bad debt is debt you pay for yourself.

Good debt makes the rich richer.

Good debt is debt someone else pays off for you.

Financial education is learning how to harness the power of debt, because today... debt is money.

Chapter Fourteen

THE OPPOSITE OF "LIVE BELOW YOUR MEANS"

"God wants all of us to be rich."

– R. Buckminster Fuller

Most financial experts recommend that you "live below your means." The question is: Do you *want* to live below your means?

Obviously, most people do not like living below their means. That is why so many people are in credit card debt, living paycheck to paycheck, living in houses and driving cars they cannot afford, and going on vacations just to get away from their jobs, bills, fears, and financial problems.

The irony is that most of the people that look rich are poorer than most poor people. Many poor people do not carry the consumer debt the middle class can afford. The middle class is deep in consumer debt—just to keep up with the Joneses. I can't tell you how often I meet people who drive a Mercedes and live in nice neighborhoods, have kids in private schools, but are two paychecks away from bankruptcy.

Since most people do not *want* to live below their means, that advice often falls on deaf ears.

Instead, I recommend the opposite. Rather than *live below your means*, a person should learn to *expand their means*, so they can enjoy a richer life.

Q: *How does a person expand their means?*

A: A person expands their means by taking control of their asset column. Currently, GRUNCH is in control of most people's asset columns. This is why most people are taught to save money, buy a house, and invest for the long term in the stock market.

The Game of Money

I've said it before; a picture is worth a thousand words. Pictured below are the differences between the rich, poor, and middle class. As you can tell, each of the three groups is playing a completely different game of money.

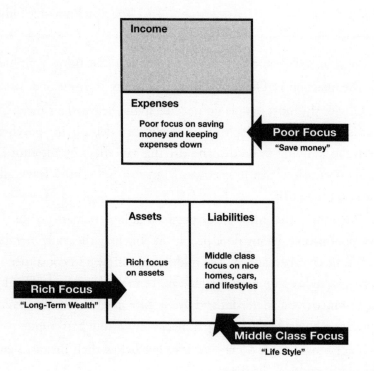

Change Your Game

Your second chance begins when you change your game. Rather than work hard to save money, or work hard to look rich, simply change your focus from your income column to your asset column. Why let GRUNCH control your asset column? Why follow the advice of financial 'experts' and mindlessly turn your money over to GRUNCH?

The asset column is where the rich play their game of money. Why not you?

How to Pay Less in Taxes

The first thing that happens when you focus on your asset column is that your taxes start to go down.

For example, when you start your own home-based business many expenses that were personal, after-tax expenses immediately become pre-tax business expenses.

If you have a business, many expenses—such as some travel, hotel, and meals—can be tax-deductible business expenses. Obviously you need to check with a qualified tax advisor or your CPA before claiming any deductions.

The lesson is: By shifting focus to the asset column, the focal point of the rich, you begin to enjoy some of the tax benefits they enjoy.

I Wish I Had a Ferrari

Recently, I drove up to a property Kim and I own, and parked my Ferrari. Three young construction workers, sweating in the hot Arizona sun, stopped working to admire my car. One smiled and said, "I wish I could afford a Ferrari."

"You can," I replied.

"No, we can't," another young man replied. "We did not go to college. We came from poor families, so we could not afford to go to college. That is why we are laborers."

I asked if I could show them how they could afford a Ferrari, even if they didn't go to college. All three said, "yes."

To explain, I drew the following diagram on a piece of paper.

BALANCE SHEET

Assets	Liabilities
Property	Ferrari

Pointing to my apartment building where they were working, I said, "This property is paying for my Ferrari. This property is also paying for you and the work you do to improve my property."

As they began to understand the difference between assets and liabilities, I explained rich dad's lesson—the rich don't work for money—and how the rich work, instead, for assets that produce cash flow.

"Didn't you go to college to learn to do that?" one of them asked.

"No," I replied, and explained that I learned how to do what I do by taking a 3-day seminar for $385 when I was about their age. When they understood I was only playing *Monopoly* in real life, and that the apartment complex where they were working was a red hotel, the lights in their heads went on.

"So we can do the same thing?" they asked.

"Why not?" I asked. "If I can do it, so can you. It is not rocket science."

I then went on to explain that my assets buy my liabilities. I also explained that most people struggle financially because they buy liabilities that they believe are assets.

"So you expand your means… rather than live below your means?" one man asked.

"Correct," I replied. "Inside each of you is a rich person, a poor person, and a middle class person. By choosing to focus on your asset column, then learning more and more about assets, the rich person in you comes out."

I went on to explain that the word education is derived from the Greek word educe, which means to draw out. Traditional education is designed to draw out the middle class person in people. It takes financial education to draw out the rich person in them.

"And financial education is opposite from traditional education?"

"Yes," I replied.

"Is real estate the only kind of asset?"

"No," I replied, and went on to explain that JK Rowling was on welfare when she wrote the Harry Potter books. Her books and movies made her a billionaire.

I told them about an acquaintance of mine who never finished high school, but is a millionaire today, selling eggs. In high school, his grandmother gave him a few chickens. He was soon breeding chickens and selling their eggs. Today, at the age of 50, he sells over a million eggs a day.

I reminded them of Colonel Sanders, who had only a chicken recipe, which he turned into the Kentucky Fried Chicken empire.

And they'd all heard of Mark Zuckerberg, a guy their age who never finished school, but who created Facebook.

I stressed that I was making this sound simple, but that it isn't easy.

"So if we focus on our asset column, we can expand our means, make more money from cash flow rather than a paycheck, and pay less in taxes? Is that what you're saying?"

"Correct," I replied. "And on top of that you will be able to drive any car you want and let your assets pay for the car."

As I drove off, I could see them talking excitedly. I haven't seen them since so I do not know what happened after our discussion.

At least I knew they understood that they did not have to live below their means. Not if they didn't want to. All they had to do was take control of their asset column.

Lesson from Bucky Fuller

People often ask, "How did Fuller survive after he stopped working for money in 1927?"

I explain that Bucky did the same things rich dad taught his son and me to do. Rather than work for money, Fuller began creating assets in his asset column. Rather than real property, most of his assets were *intellectual* property. Intellectual property is invisible assets such as patents, books, licenses, and trademarks.

I own many of the same kinds of assets. This book is one of them. As soon as it was completed, it was licensed to book publishers all over the world.

Lesson for Your Second Chance

First: Make a list of all the good things in life you want. Call it your Wish List.

For years, Kim and I would drive by the house we now live in and say, "Someday that house will be ours." Today, it is.

The difference is, first we bought rental properties that, today, pay the monthly mortgage on our dream house.

Second: Make a list of the different assets you want to acquire, assets that will pay for the dreams of your life.

Do not worry if you do not yet know how to acquire those assets. Admitting you don't know something is how learning begins. People who know everything, learn nothing.

Third: Look at this list—everyday.

Financial education is...

The Opposite Side of the Coin

Expanding your means and living below your means are two sides of the same coin, two points of view on how you approach life. Conventional wisdom most often supports living below your means, but we all have the choice—the chance—to live a richer life and that starts with focusing on your asset column and expanding your means.

Chapter Fifteen
THE **OPPOSITE** OF
"DON'T CHEAT"

"Above all co-operate and don't hold back on one another or try to gain at the expense of another. Any success is such lopsidedness will be increasingly short-lived."

– R. Buckminster Fuller

In school, if you ask for help it's considered cheating—especially at test time. In fact, when I was in high school, I looked at my poor dad's teacher's manual and it defined cheating as "giving aid to someone in need." To me, that sounded like being a human being.

When I was still in high school, my rich dad would include his son and me in on his Saturday morning meetings with his team. The first thing I noticed was that my rich dad did not have to be the smartest person on his team. In fact, he may have been the least-educated person on his team.

Surrounding him were his attorneys, accountants, banker, managers, real estate broker, and stockbroker. Rather than tell people what to do, he would discuss problems he was facing and allow his advisors to offer suggestions on how to solve those problems.

At home, I would see my poor dad, sitting with a stack of bills, struggling to figure out how he as going to pay them all.

What I am saying is that my rich dad solved his financial problems by asking for help from people smarter than he was. My rich dad was cooperative.

My poor dad did the opposite. He solved his financial problems on his own. He wouldn't cheat.

In the real world of business, the opposite of cheating is cooperation.

Q: *So what should my team look like? Who should be on it?*

A: Take a look at my advisors. They are my team.

1. Tom Wheelwright is a CPA and my advisor on taxes. As you know, taxes can be your largest expense.

2. Ken McElroy is my advisor on debt. As you know, President Richard Nixon took the dollar off the gold standard in 1971. When that happed, debt became the new money.

3. Blair Singer, who has been my friend and advisor since 1981, is my go-to guy for sales. If one of my businesses is having trouble with sales, Blair is the person that goes in to teach everyone in the business how to be better at selling. As he says, "Sales = Income." If your income is low, it is because you or your business is not selling. If you are an entrepreneur, your number-one skill must be the ability to sell others, as well as yourself.

4. Andy Tanner is my advisor on paper assets and the stock market. He is the best teacher I know when it comes to teaching people how to gain cash flow from stocks.

5. Darren Weeks is my advisor on being an entrepreneur in education. He has become very rich teaching hundreds of thousands of people to play *CASHFLOW.*

6. Garrett Sutton is my advisor on legal matters. He has saved my wealth many times over by protecting my assets from predatory law suits and onerous taxes.

7. Lisa and Josh Lannon are my experts on social capitalism. As you might expect, if you are perceived as a business without a heart, you are soon out of business.

And, of course, there's Kim... Her passion is to teach women. She speaks with a compassion and understanding most men do not have.

Q: *Are you saying I should have all the same types of advisors?*

A: No, not at all. I offer my list of advisors only as an example. Each advisor has written a book in which they share their knowledge and experience.

Also, each Advisor is a frequent guest on the Rich Dad Radio Show. All of our radio programs are archived so you can go to richdadradio.com/radio and listen to each Advisor whenever it's convenient for you.

Topic:
Cover Your Assets
Guest:
Garrett Sutton, Esq.

The Rich Dad Radio Show
download the free app
www.richdad.com/radio

Q: *Why do you encourage us to listen to your Advisors?*

A: There are many reasons.

One reason is that listening to an Advisor on Rich Dad Radio delivers a key component of the Cone of Learning.

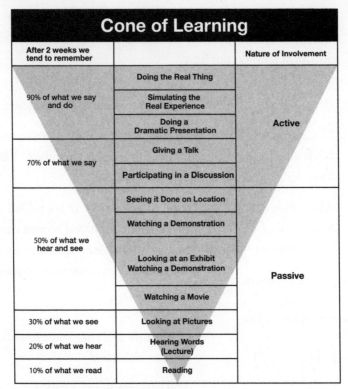

Source: Cone of Learning adapted from Dale, (1969)

The primary reason I share my Advisors with you is so you can gain insights into how to tell good advisors from bad advisors.

Remember, the opposite of cheating is cooperation. And cooperation means you don't have to be the smartest person to be rich. It's better to have a smart team.

Lesson from Bucky Fuller

This is one of my favorite Fuller quotes:

"Of course, our failures are a consequence of many factors, but possibly one of the most important is the fact that society operates on the theory that specialization is the key to success, not realizing that specialization precludes comprehensive thinking."

Fuller is talking about that fact the our schools train us to be specialists—accountants, engineers, or lawyers. The problem is: Problem-solving requires many different types of specialists.

Fuller would have called my rich dad a generalist, not a specialist. Rich dad was an entrepreneur, a generalist who knew a lot about many different things.

A specialist, such as an attorney or accountant, knows a lot, but a little.

This is why rich dad had a team of specialists to help solve his financial problems, and so should you.

Are you beginning to understand that when it comes to true financial education we focus on opposites? And when it comes to a team you need both specialists and generalists to solve any problem.

Lesson for Your Second Chance

Here are a few steps you may want to follow:

1. Make a list of your team of advisors.

2. If you do not have any, listen to my advisors on Rich Dad Radio so you have a better idea of what you want for your advisors.

3. If you have advisors, but you are not happy with them, listen to Rich Dad Radio so you can choose better advisors.

4. Know the difference between advisors and brokers. Too many people take advice from sales people, not advisors.

5. As Warren Buffett says:

   "Never ask an insurance salesman if you need more insurance."

Financial education is...

The Opposite Side of the Coin

Remember three things:

First: The only place where asking for help is called cheating, is in school. It is OK to be stupid. It is not OK to pretend to be smart. It's hard to get smarter if you think you already know all you need to know.

Second: As you grow smarter, your team should, too. If a member of your team is not constantly learning and improving, replace them.

Third: The opposite of stupid is smart. The best way to get smart is to be humble enough to admit that you do not know everything. If you have an advisor who knows everything, find a new advisor. It is difficult to get smarter if you already know all the answers.

Chapter Sixteen

THE **OPPOSITE** OF
"THE RICH ARE GREEDY"

---

*"Are you spontaneously enthusiastic
about everyone having everything you can have?"*
— R. Buckminster Fuller

Many people believe the rich are greedy.

And some are.

Many people believe the only way a person can become rich is by being greedy.

And many rich people do get rich by being greedy.

Rich dad often said: "It is not how much money a person makes that disturbs people. It is how they make their money."

For example, when a star football player makes millions, most people are OK with the fact that they're rich. They have worked hard for years—starting as kids with a dream, practicing for years for free, then turning pro and making millions of dollars by making millions of sports fans happy. Few people think they are greedy. Millions of adoring fans are happy they are rich.

The same is true with movie stars who make millions. Most people are not upset that they make lots of money. Tom Hanks and Sandra Bullock make millions because millions of people love watching them.

And when I was a kid, I was happy the Beatles made millions selling millions of records. Their music made me very happy.

But when a rich employer, intentionally, pays their employees peanuts, most people get upset.

My point is that when people get rich by being cheap, cruel, dishonest, criminal, unethical, or immoral, honest people become upset.

High Blood Pressure

My blood pressure goes up every time I think about:

… the bankers that caused the crash of 2007 being paid bonuses, even though millions lost their jobs, their homes, and their futures.

… corrupt politicians who use their power to make themselves and their friends richer.

… CEOs who are paid millions running their companies into the ground. Their incompetence costs their employees their jobs and their shareholders their money.

… the Fed, Wall Street, and the U.S. government, pumping trillions of counterfeit dollars into the big banks, protecting their rich friends at the expense of the poor, the middle class, and future generations to come.

… government public servant unions, stealing from the people they are supposed to be serving, via bonuses and pensions. Many public servants retire earning much more than military veterans who risked their lives serving their country.

Recent examples that I am aware of include:

- a city of Phoenix librarian who retired at age 58 and was paid a bonus of $286,000 and an annual pension over $102,000 for the rest of her life.

- three Phoenix firefighters who, in 2011, received over $1 million each—plus their pensions—when they retired.

A report that the top 50 government retirees in Phoenix will receive, collectively, $183 million (from taxpayer dollars) by the time they reach age 75.

Many people in Phoenix are upset. They think these government employees are greedy. Millions of dollars are going to a few people, rather a more broad distribution.

Consider, for a moment, another point of view: The public servants think they are generous. They've dedicated their lives to public service.

What do you think? These same payouts are going on in most states and cities in America.

All of the examples above are symptoms of extreme greed and corruption. The great cash heist is on. Greed seems to be taking over the world.

Get Rich by Being Generous

On the opposite side of the coin, many people become rich by being generous.

Walt Disney became very rich by making millions of people happy. And Henry Ford became very rich by making the automobile affordable for the working class.

Sergey Brin of Google is a billionaire because he made access to information easier than going to the local library.

Learning to be Rich and Generous

If you read *Rich Dad Poor Dad*, you may recall that my poor dad became very angry with my rich dad because my rich dad did not pay his son and me. He wanted us to work for free.

In exchange for our time, rich dad taught his son and me to be rich by being generous. Our lessons began by playing *Monopoly* for hours.

Most of us know the formula for wealth from the game of *Monopoly*. Very simply, the formula is four green houses, converted to one red hotel.

Today, Kim and I play *Monopoly* in real life. We have thousands of little green houses, also known as apartments, two hotels, five golf courses, commercial buildings, several businesses, and many oil wells.

We also share our knowledge by writing our books and creating financial-education games.

Some people would say we are greedy. We think we are generous.

Many of the people who accuse the rich of being greedy often have only one house. Their balance sheet looks like this:

BALANCE SHEET

Assets	Liabilities
0 houses	1 house

Who do you think is greedy? Employee or Entrepreneur?

Kim and I are responsible, both directly and indirectly, for thousands of jobs via our worldwide businesses and investments. For example, our red hotel—a large Phoenix resort—employs more than 800 people. Think about the millions in tax dollars generated by those 800 employees. Think about all the other businesses, stores, restaurants, doctors, dentists, and families that the income from those 800 employees touch.

This is why I become testy when I hear people categorically say, "The rich are greedy."

I believe that it's the lack of financial education in our schools that causes people to become greedy. When people have money but no assets, they become greedy, desperate, and needy.

Q: *Are you saying the people who call the rich greedy, are themselves even greedier than the rich?*

A: Yes and no. I am saying your point of view depends on which side of the coin you're on.

My poor dad saw my rich dad as greedy. My rich dad saw my poor dad as greedy. In my eyes, both were very generous men.

Your job is to stand on the edge of the coin to determine what is true for you. Your second chance begins with your definition of what is generous and what is greedy.

Q: *Why did your rich dad see your poor dad as greedy?*

A: My poor dad believed in taking from the rich and giving to the poor. My poor dad thought the rich should pay higher wages and be subject to higher taxes rates.

Q: *Your poor dad was a socialist?*

A: You could say that. He was a good man who believed in helping people.

Q: *And your rich dad was a capitalist?*

A: That's a fair assessment. He, too, was a good man who believed in helping people.

Q: *How can you say the same thing about both men?*

A: Because it's true. Both were good men who believed in helping people. Their views on how to help people were opposite.

Lesson from Bucky Fuller

Bucky Fuller made many predictions and many have come true. His predictions that have not yet come true require more time and advances in technology.

Two predictions that have haunted me are:

1. He predicted that humans born after 1945, and who did not smoke, had a life expectancy of 140 years. He made his prediction based upon the accelerating acceleration in medical technology.

2. He predicted unemployment would increase as computers replaced humans. He said: "Man is going to be displaced altogether as a specialist by the computer. Man himself is being forced to reestablish, employ, and enjoy his innate 'comprehensivity.'"

Decades ago, in the '60s and '70s, he was predicting that unemployment would increase with advances in technology.

He said the idea of "earning a living" would become an obsolete idea.

"We must do away with the absolutely specious notion that everybody has to earn a living."

Fuller also said:

> *"We find all the no-life-support-wealth-producing people going*
> *to their 1980 jobs in their cars or buses, spending trillions*
> *of dollar's worth of petroleum daily to get to their no-wealth-*
> *producing jobs. It doesn't take a computer to tell you that it*
> *will save both Universe and humanity trillions of dollars a day*
> *to pay them handsomely to stay at home."*

In 2014, as entitlement programs grow and young graduates are unable to find jobs, I can hear Fuller saying to our class in 1983, "In the future, it will make more sense to pay people to stay at home."

In 1983, that idea was outside my reality.

Q: *So what's your concern?*

A: Fuller's predictions are coming true. Today, even low-wage countries such as China, are realizing the challenges of mass unemployment. Today in China there are thousands of factories sitting idle.

My concern is: What will happen if billions of people are unemployed and live past 100?

Q: *That could never happen, could it?*

A: That is exactly what I thought back in 1983. Today, I am less certain. What would happen to China, the United States, and the world, if hundreds of millions were out of work and governments went bust, attempting to pay them to stay at home? That thought disturbs me.

In 1983, Fuller told our class that it would be our generation that would be faced with those problems in the future. My concern is that the future is here today.

Q: *What did he mean when he said: "Man himself is being forced to reestablish, employ, and enjoy his innate "comprehensivity."*

A: He believed most people would be happy to be paid to stay at home. It would be good for our environment if fewer people were stuck in traffic driving to and from work, only to do jobs that did not make our world a better place.

By comprehensivity, he meant a few humans, paid to stay at home, would be inspired to do their "spirit's work" and fulfill their god-given life's purpose. He said millions would do things that he referred to as "spontaneously arousable" and people would begin to solve our planet's problems, not for a paycheck, but because they wanted to solve the problem.

Q: *Is that what you did?*

A: Yes. After reading *Grunch* in 1983, I knew what I had to do.

Q: *And what was that?*

A: I knew I had to do what George Orwell stated in his book, *1984*: "In a time of universal deceit, telling the truth is a revolutionary act."

And, coincidently, in 1984 Kim and I took our leap of faith.

Q: *And what are your solutions?*

A: Education needs to change. We can no longer say to people, "Go to school and get a job."

We must train people to be entrepreneurs, not employees. The world needs entrepreneurs who will create jobs and work to solve world problems, rather than work just to make money.

The good news is, today, millions of people are becoming entrepreneurs. The problem is most are becoming entrepreneurs in the S quadrant, continuing to work for money.

The world needs more B-quadrant entrepreneurs who create assets that produce cash flow. Assets that don't just make money, but assets that change the world.

Q: *So are you asking me to ask myself, "What would I do if I did not have to earn a living? What gift would I give if I never needed a paycheck again?" Is that what you are asking me?*

A: Yes. Those are the questions I asked myself in 1983.

Lesson for Your Second Chance

Ask yourself that question: "If I never had to work for money again, what would I do?" Then ask yourself: "Would I be greedy or generous with my knowledge and my life?" They're two sides of the same coin.

Financial education is...

The Opposite Side of the Coin

You can choose to hoard your knowledge, be greedy with what you have and what you know. Or share it. Financial education is about generosity, not greed.

Chapter Seventeen

THE **OPPOSITE** OF "INVESTING IS RISKY"

---

*"I have spent most of my life
unlearning things that were proved not to be true."*
– R. Buckminster Fuller

Most people believe investing is risky.

And for most people investing *is* risky.

GRUNCH wants you to believe that investing is risky.

Q: *Why would GRUNCH want you to believe that?*

A: So you'll turn your money over to them.

Q: *That's why you think there's no financial education in schools, isn't it?*

A: It seems that way to me. That's why most teachers advise students to save money and invest for the long term in the stock market. That advice sends your money directly into the pockets of GRUNCH.

Q: *Are you saying that's bad?*

A: No. Because, again, there are always at least two sides to everything. Some people believe investing is risky and others do not. The question is: What do you believe? What do you *want* to believe?

As Fuller said:

> *"I have spent most of my life unlearning things that were proved not to be true."*

Q: *But isn't what you do risky?*

A: Yes, there is risk, but there is risk in everything.
Did you fall down learning to walk?

Q: *Sure.*

A: Today, can you now walk without falling?

Q: *Of course.*

A: Well the same is true with investing.
Do you drive a car?

Q: *Yes, I drive a car.*

A: How did you learn to drive a car?

Q: *My father taught me.*

A: Did his guidance decrease or increase your risks in driving a car?

Q: *It decreased the risk. OK… I get your point.*

A: Do you understand why I invested in a 3-day seminar on real estate investing and spent 90 days practicing—looking for investments—before I invested my money?

Q: *So you could reduce your risk?*

A: And increase my rewards. Today, that 3-day course and the 90 days of practice have made me a multimillionaire. But more importantly, it reduced my financial risks and increased my rewards… rewards such as never needing a job, never worrying about the ups and downs of the stock market. Education and practice have given me the freedom to make as much money as I want without working—and I've been able enjoy life more without the fear and worry of keeping my boss happy and not getting fired.

Q: *So the opposite of risk is reward?*

A: That is one opposite. For me, the opposite side to risk is *control*. Risk + Control = Rewards.

Learning to Fly

In 1969, I reported to Pensacola, Florida to learn to fly. It was an exhilarating, exciting, and expanding educational process. I walked in a caterpillar and two years later flew out as a butterfly. It was beyond educational. It was transformational.

The same thing happened for me years later when I sat down in the 3-day real estate seminar. I walked in a poor man… and two years later I was a rich man. I never needed a job or paycheck again.

Examples of Controls

I learned a lot about risk, reward, and controls flying in Vietnam. Many of those controls I still use today as an investor. Some of those controls are:

1. **Control over my education**

   As pilots we were always in school. We never stopped learning. Learning and living went hand in hand. The more we learned the more our chances of survival increased.

2. **Control over my advisors**

   My teachers in flight school were real pilots. Most people are in financial trouble because they take financial advice from sales people—not rich people.

3. Control over my time

Most people are so busy working they have no time to get rich.

Q: *Can you give me an example of how taking control of education, advisors, and time can reduce my risks and increase my rewards?*

A: Sure. Let's say I invest $10,000 in shares of Exxon. I receive no guarantee of a return. But if I invest $10,000 in an oil well, the government guarantees me a $3,200 return via a tax deduction.

Q: *A guaranteed 32% return? Can anyone do that? Get that tax credit?*

A: Sure. Anyone can invest in the same kinds of investments. Again, it all comes back to the three controls. You must control your education, your advisors, and your time.

If you would like to learn more about how this 32% tax deduction works, listen to the Rich Dad Radio Show on the subject with special guest Mike Mauceli. As you listen to the program, notice how the three controls—education, advisors, and time—can reduce your risks and increase your returns.

Topic:
Government-Guaranteed ROIs… with Gas and Oil

Guests:
Mike Mauceli and Tom Wheelwright, CPA

The Rich Dad Radio Show
download the free app
www.richdad.com/radio

The Power of Trust

On every U.S. dollar are the words "In God We Trust." In my opinion, these words are fraudulent. I doubt that god trusts the U.S. dollar.

Wall Street bankers who work for GRUNCH often say, "Gold is a barbaric relic of the past." Of course they would say that. Gold is their competition. They do not like gold… because they cannot print gold.

On the other side of the coin, there is some truth to gold being a barbaric metal. Other than ornamental jewelry, gold has very little value. Silver, on the other hand, has much more value than gold. Silver is a precious metal as well as an industrial metal. Gold is hoarded and silver is consumed. To me, this makes silver more valuable than gold.

Q: *If gold has very little value, why did god create gold? Why have humans covet, hoard, kill, and conquer entire nations… for gold?*

Topic:
**The Gold Standard…
Revisited**

Guest:
Steve Forbes

The Rich Dad Radio Show
download the free app
www.richdad.com/radio

A: The answer is found in the word *trust*. Gold is trustworthy. Gold is rare, an element that cannot be counterfeited.

In his latest book, *Money*, released in 2014, Steve Forbes, CEO of the Forbes Media empire, is calling for a return to the gold standard. In his book, Steve states three important reasons why the world needs to go back on the gold standard.

They are:

1. Paper money is not wealth.

2. If the United States had remained on the gold standard, incomes today would be 50% higher.

3. The gold standard will increase trust. Gold allows strangers to trade, to do business with one another with confidence. When people do not trust the 'money' they are using, trade decreases and economies contract.

In other words, when governments print money, trust amongst people and nations goes down, trade goes down, and when trade goes down, economies contract. When economies contract, honest people suffer, and often become desperate people. That desperation can lead to increases in crime, violence, immorality, and terrorism.

Reducing the Risk

When trust is low, risk goes up.

The more money the government prints, the more our trust in it will go down and risk goes up. Today, billions of people are nervous about the future.

The way you begin to reduce your risks is by increasing the trust in yourself… via your education, advisors and your time.

Q: *How do I start building trust in myself?*

A: Again: It begins with words. You build trust in yourself by learning the language of money, a language that's not taught in schools.

The Language of Money

In 2009, the former First Vice President of Peru, Raul Diez-Canseco Terry invited Kim and me to visit his spectacular country, the private educational system he founded, and his home in Lima. Raul is an educational entrepreneur. The school system he founded begins with kindergarten and goes through college. It is an innovative system, preparing students for the real world of commerce.

Obviously, Machu Picchu was on our itinerary. While looking over this magnificent civilization on top of the Andes, I asked Romero, one of the Inca scholars, in our party, "What separated those that lived at the highest levels from those that lived at the lower levels." Without hesitation, he replied, "Language. Those who lived at the highest levels spoke 'Quechua,' the language of commerce." Romero explained it was Quechua that empowered the Inca Empire to dominate the west coast of South America.

Today, in the modern world, not much has changed. The richest people speak the language of commerce, *the language of money*, a language not taught in schools. The difference between my rich dad and my poor dad were the words they spoke. While both spoke English they did not speak the same language.

If you learn a few new words every month, your trust in yourself will go up, risks will go down, and rewards will go up.

Q: *Would you give me an example of words that will make me richer?*

A: Sure. You already know that *assets* put money in your pocket and *liabilities* take money from your pocket.

Other words that are important are *cash flow* versus *capital gains*. The poor and middle class invest for capital gains. They buy, hold, and pray that prices will go up. Real estate 'flippers' invest for capital gains. That is why they think investing is risky. They have no control over whether the price goes or down. They see very little cash flow. And when they sell and make a profit, they pay capital-gains taxes, the second highest of all taxes.

Q: *So the rich invest for cash flow?*

A: The rich on the B-and I-side of the quadrant invest for many things. They invest for cash flow, capital gains, control, and tax advantages.

Q: *How do I learn to do that?*

A: Change your education, your advisors, and what you do with your time. If you do that, you'll find that the words you use will change.

You'll learn more about how the rich on the B-and I-side of the quadrant invest—capital gains, cash flow, and reduced taxes—in the next chapter.

Q: *And what are some of the differences between S-quadrant entrepreneurs and B-quadrant entrepreneurs?*

A: S-quadrant entrepreneurs work for money by providing products or services.

Q: *Aren't they assets?*

A: No, not in most cases. A true asset produces cash flow. Products and services produce money.

Q: *Can you explain that in more detail… in simpler terms?*

A: Sure. And I want you to notice the differences in words.

Let's say that an entrepreneur opens a restaurant. The entrepreneur provides great food and great service. The food is the *product* and the employees provide the *service*. The next day, the process starts all over again. Everyone is working for ordinary income, *paychecks* and *tips*. *Ordinary income* is the highest-taxed income. When you work for money, save money, and invest in a 401(k), your income is taxed at *ordinary income* tax rates.

If I am a B-quadrant real estate entrepreneur, an investor who owns the building the restaurant is in, I have provided an *asset*. I have used *debt* to acquire the building, and I receive *passive* income, the least-taxed income. On top of this, I pay less and less in taxes due to *depreciation, amortization,* and *appreciation,* all different types of income.

Q: *Depreciation, amortization, and appreciation are different types of income?*

A: Yes. If you do not understand the differences in the words, talk to a tax accountant or tax attorney, or read Tom Wheelwright's book *Tax-Free Wealth.* The lesson in this chapter is about risk, the importance of words, and how words can reduce risk. You may want to listen to shows with Tom on Rich Dad Radio.

Q: *So the S-quadrant entrepreneur works harder and harder, takes all the risks, and pays more in taxes. The B-quadrant entrepreneur works less, makes more money, and pays less in taxes?*

A: Yes. The point is the differences in words and that individuals in different quadrants use different words.

I'll share this story again, but in a different context. In *Rich Dad Poor Dad* I wrote about Ray Kroc, founder of McDonald's saying, "I am not in the hamburger business. I am in the real estate business." In other words, McDonald's hamburgers and French fries, their *products* and *services*, pay for the real estate, the *real asset*. This is why McDonald's is one of the biggest real estate companies in the world.

Simply said, the poor and middle class use the words of the E and S quadrants. The rich use the words of the B and I quadrants, the language of money, the language the Incas called *Quechua*.

Rich dad often said, "Words have the power to make you rich or poor. If you want to be rich, learn the words that will make you rich. The best news is… words are free."

Lesson from Bucky Fuller

In *Grunch of Giants*, Fuller wrote:

> *"Corporations are neither physical nor metaphysical phenomena.*
> *They are socioeconomic ploys—legally enacted game-playing—*
> *agreed upon only between overwhelmingly powerful socioeconomic*
> *individuals and by them imposed upon human society*
> *and its all unwitting members."*

Q: *What does he mean?*

A: I believe he was saying that it's risky to trust GRUNCH, the invisible power behind our world's biggest banks and corporations.

To me he is saying it is risky to trust your personal asset column to GRUNCH. If you insist on investing in paper assets, do not invest for the long term. Instead, take classes on how to invest in stock options, and learn how to make money when markets are going up or down.

On the other side of the coin, if you want to reduce your risks and be rich, you may want to learn the language of GRUNCH, the language of the B and I quadrants.

Reducing Risk in the Stock Market

If your investments are in the stock market, you may want to listen to Rich Dad Advisor Andy Tanner on Rich Dad Radio.

Andy has a gift for using humor to make his points. For example, in a radio segment when he was our guest for the hour, he said, "If you are taking a cruise on the Titanic, the first thing you want to do is count the number of life boats."

Investing one hour of your time, listening to Andy Tanner is a great way to start your second chance.

Topic:
Paper Assets and the Stock Market

Guest:
Andy Tanner

The Rich Dad Radio Show
download the free app
www.richdad.com/radio

Lesson for Your Second Chance

Many financial experts say, "To achieve higher returns requires higher risk."

Q: *Why do they say that if it's not true?*

A: Who knows? That person could be a liar, a con man, or just an idiot.

Most probably, he is just repeating what he has been told to say. He has not done what Fuller recommends:

> *"I have spent most of my life unlearning things that were proved not to be true."*

Today, millions of Americans, through their 401(k)s and IRAs, blindly turn their money over to people they do not know or trust. They follow the instructions of parrots, repeating what *they* have been told to say. That's a risky proposition.

Financial education is...

The Opposite Side of the Coin

The opposite of risk is control. For your second chance in life, take back control of your education, your advisors, and your time.

Chapter Eighteen

THE **OPPOSITE** OF "SAVE MONEY"

Our wealth is stolen via our money. Why save it?"

– R. Buckminster Fuller

Many financial experts say, "Save, save, save—'til it hurts."

A sane person would ask, "Why save money when governments are printing money?"

Why Savers Are Losers

Our wealth is lost when we save money. When a person saves money, their wealth is stolen via the Fractional Reserve System. If, for example, the fractional reserve is 10, that means the banks are allowed to lend $10 for every $1 on deposit. During the Bill Clinton presidency, a few of the megabanks such as Bank of America and Citibank operated at a fractional reserve limit of 34. For every dollar in savings, $34 was loaned to borrowers. This means the purchasing power of a dollar held in savings was diluted by a multiple of 34.

The fractional reserve system of banking is one of the ways 'money is printed' and why savers are losers. Simply put, money is created when money is borrowed, not when it's saved.

Another way savers are losers is by saving in mutual funds. Mutual fund companies make their money via hidden fees.

As John Bogle, founder of The Vanguard Group, Inc., has asked: "Do you really want to invest in a system where you put up 100 percent of the capital, you the mutual fund shareholder, you take 100 percent of the risk and you get 30 percent of the return?" The flip side of which is that the fund itself puts up no money, takes no risk, but reaps 70 percent of the return.

During the days of the German Weimar Republic, savers were the biggest losers. Between 1918 and 1923, millionaires became paupers within five years.

Q: *So what is the opposite of saving money? Is it getting into debt?*

A: Yes and no. Debt alone is not the answer. Debt is only part of the answer.

The opposite of saving is known as the "velocity of money." Most people "park" their money where they save or invest for retirement. Smart people keep their money moving.

Simply put, when you park your money, your money loses value. When you keep your money moving, your money increases in value.

Think of a person sitting around all day watching TV. Then think of a person running, riding a bicycle, and climbing mountains. Which person will be healthier in 10 years?

Q: *So the faster I move my money the better?"*

A: Yes—if you know how to do it. The Germans who did well during the German hyperinflation were those who moved their money out of Germany, into other currencies such as U.S. dollars, British pounds, and French francs. Germans who saved their money in German marks, in Germany, were the biggest losers.

Q: *Are you saying I should buy other currencies?*

A: No. Today, things are different. Today, the world is involved in a global currency war. Most governments are doing the same things the Germans did in 1918.

Q: *Why?*

A: Today, most governments are afraid that their currency will become stronger, healthier. For example, if the U.S. dollar is strong, then United States exports become expensive and U.S. unemployment rises.

As I've said, all world leaders live in fear of rising unemployment. So they will do almost anything to keep people employed, even if it means destroying their currency.

Q: *So the United States will print money to weaken the dollar?*

A: That is one option.

Q: *So what should I do?*

A: I will tell you what *I* do—but that doesn't mean I recommend that you do what I do.

Q: *Why not? And* if *not, why tell me about it?*

A: Because what I do is rather sophisticated. It has taken me years to learn how to do it. In fact, I am still learning.

And I tell you about it so you can see the other side of the coin. If you see what most people never see, you will better understand how the real game of money is played. The really rich do not park their money—they keep their money moving.

Q: *And what if I want to do what you do?*

A: Then I say, "Good luck—and welcome to the game." You will play a game with some big winners, but few survivors.

After you see the diagram and understand how the game is played, then you can decide if you want to play the game known as The Velocity of Money. Only you can decide if this game is for you.

The Velocity of Money

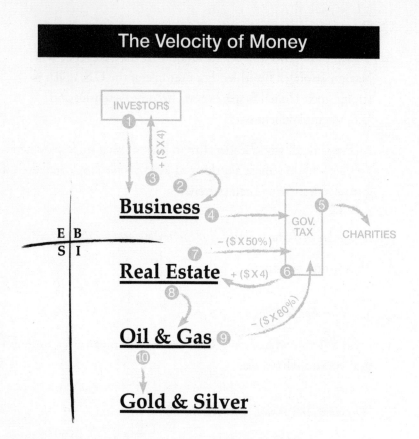

Follow the numbered arrows to track the flow of money...

1. Arrow number 1 shows where the game began for Kim and me when we raised $250,000 from investors to fund The Rich Dad Company.

2. The second arrow represents reinvesting money into the business. The reason the arrow loops around and back to the business is to illustrate that the reinvested money is tax-free.

   This tax-free income is used to hire more people, buy more equipment, and grow the business.

3. The third arrow represents repaying our investors ($ X 4). That means they received a 400% return on their money in two years, or $1 million.

4. The fourth arrow represents the point at which Kim and I finally took our money out of the company, via paychecks and bonuses—money that is taxed by the government. It was nearly three years before we pulled any money out of the business.

5. The fifth arrow represents tithing, which means we gave 10% of our gross income to registered charitable organizations. Although we receive tax deductions from the government for this money, the primary reason for tithing is spiritual. The tax deductions are only an added advantage.

    We tithe because we believe god is our partner. If we do not pay our partner, our partner stops working.

    Always remember, if you want a smile, give a smile. If you want a punch, throw a punch. And if you want more money, give money.

    I always chuckle when I hear a person say, "I'll give money, when I have money." From my point of view, the reason they do not have money is because they do not *give* money.

6. Arrow 6 indicates our investments in real estate. Beside the arrow is ($ X 4). The $ represents our equity, our down payment into a real estate investment. The 4 represents the bank debt secured to acquire the property. The debt makes up for the tax liability.

7. Arrow 7 represents the tax deduction we received from the government—so ($ X 50%) means we get money back from the government by paying less in taxes. It is called *phantom cash flow*.

    For example, let's say I owe $1,200 in taxes on my personal income.

    Because I have investment property, the government allows me to deduct "losses." One type of "loss" is called *depreciation*.

Keeping things simple, let's say my *depreciation* is $500.

This means, rather than pay $1,200 in taxes to the government, my tax bill is reduced to $700. The $500 in depreciation is called *phantom cash flow* because it is money that stayed in my pocket. I did not have to pay that $500 to the government.

8. Arrow 8 represents cash flowing into oil wells and gas investments.

9. Arrow 9 represents the reduction in taxes—($ X 80%)—which is the money the government allows me to deduct from my tax bill for investments in gas and oil.

I wrote about investing in oil and gas, and receiving a 32% return on my money, in a previous chapter.

I receive a 32% return by assuming I am in the 40% tax bracket. If I invest $1,000 into an oil or gas well, the government allows me an 80% deduction. $800 X 40% = $320, a 32% return in reduced taxes. Again, rather than pay the government, that $320 stays in my pocket.

Notice my tax bill coming down:

$ 1,200
< 500 >
< 320 >
$ 380

On the B- and I-side of the quadrant, the more I invest, the less I pay in taxes.

10. Arrow 10 points to gold and silver.

Rather than save money, I would rather save gold and silver.
I do not consider gold and silver a good investment, per se, because gold and silver are subject to very high taxes.

I suspect taxes are high on the sale of gold and silver because the U.S. government does not want citizens to own gold and silver.

I only keep gold and silver as a *hedge*, as insurance against the possible collapse of the dollar, just as the German Reischmark collapsed in 1923.

And that is my personal playbook for the game known as The Velocity of Money.

Remember, this is an overly simplified explanation of a very complex process and that the numbers are all approximate and will vary with market conditions and tax brackets. Before doing anything, always consult an attorney and an accountant who specializes in this type of process.

If your advisors do not understand this process, get them Tom Wheelwright's book *Tax-Free Wealth* to use as a guide.

Topic:
**How to Use Taxes
to Make You Rich**

Guest:
Tom Wheelwright, CPA

The Rich Dad Radio Show
download the free app
www.richdad.com/radio

If your advisor says, "You can't do this here," get a new advisor. Versions of this process are used all over the world. It is the game of money the rich play.

Q: *How do I better understand the 10 steps in the game?*

A: The Cone of Learning suggests a proven path: *participate in a discussion* with a group of friends. If you and your friends follow the 10 steps in the diagram at least

10 times, your mind will see the 'invisible' world of money, a world very few people ever see.

Q: *Let me get this straight. You started with investor money. You have absolutely no money in the game, as you call it. And today, you make millions without risking any of your own money?*

A: Yes.

Q: *And the more money you make, the more you have to invest. The more you invest, the more money you make… and you do it in a way that allows you to pay less in taxes?*

A: Yes.

Q: *And if your money slows down, your income goes down and your taxes go up?*

A: Yes.

Q: *And you get your money from people who 'park' their money in banks as savings and retirement accounts?*

A: Yes.

Q: *You take savers' money and give it speed. Your job is to keep savers' money moving?*

A: Yes.

Q: *So that's why the rich get richer. Money has to keep moving? Cash has to keep flowing. Cash has to be used to acquire more assets that produce cash flow? Is that correct? Is that the game?*

A: That's correct.

Q: *And if cash stops flowing, the economy stops?*

A: Yes.

Q: *And that's why the government gives you tax breaks. Because you create jobs and use debt to produce housing, food, and energy?*

A: Yes. Cash flow keeps the economy moving. If everyone just saved money, the economy would crash. So taxes are incentives from the government. Taxes are a government's way of saying, "This is what the government needs done." When homeowners receive a tax deduction for interest paid on a mortgage, that's the government saying, "Thank you, you're doing what we want you to do."

Q: *When the poor and middle class save their money, cash stops flowing, so the government taxes their money. They're punished for not moving their money?*

A: Yes.

Q: *I noticed you don't invest in paper assets, stocks, bonds, or mutual funds... or saving money. Why not?*

A: Because paper assets are tertiary wealth.

Q: *Your investments are primary and secondary wealth, resources or production? Is that right?*

A: Yes.

Q: *Why primary and secondary wealth?*

A: Because that's what the government wants done. That is what entrepreneurs do. Entrepreneurs don't have jobs. Entrepreneurs create jobs. Entrepreneurs don't buy stocks. Entrepreneurs build companies and *sell* stock, sell shares in their company.

Q: *Is this what real financial education is? Financial education must disclose both sides of the coin?*

A: Yes. Most quasi-"financial education" is about only one side— investing in paper assets, or tertiary wealth that's sold to Es and Ss. The B and I side is where real wealth comes from.

Q: *Can Es and Ss enjoy the same tax benefits?*

A: Yes and no. It depends on what you mean by tax benefits. For most Es and Ss, the best they can do is to invest through a Roth IRA.

Q: *What is wrong with that?*

A: It's tertiary wealth… with high risks and returns that are dependent upon capital gains rather than cash flow. There are no controls, and only long-term tax benefits. But the main reason is that I'd have to "park" my money in that Roth IRA.

Q: *So the rich create money out of nothing. The rest of us work for them… and pay taxes?*

A: Congratulations. You've got it. You can now see that unity is plurality, the opposite side of the coin, the yin and the yang. You now know more about money than 99% of the people in the world. You can now see the invisible. When you see the other side, you understand how assets are created.

Q: *So money is created in my brain?*

A: Yes. True assets don't exist. True assets are created. I told you the story of my friend in Scotland who took a 150-year-old church and turned it into an asset. The *asset* did not exist until he put the pieces together. For nearly five years, people walked past the For Sale sign in front of that church every day… on their way to work to earn and collect a paycheck. They saw only an old, run-down church. Graeme saw an asset.

That asset first took shape in his mind, then in his heart and his emotions. And then he took action. That is what true financial education is. True financial education is not working for a paycheck, paying taxes, saving money, and investing for the long term in the stock market. That's slavery.

True financial education empowers you to create assets out of nothing. Remember, Google did not exist a few years ago, neither did Amazon… and neither did The Rich Dad Company.

Q: *So there is a fortune in my head?*

A: That's for you to decide. Your reality—your life—starts in your head. So do the ideas of looking for a job, saving money, getting out of debt, and investing for the long term in the stock market. You can look at it either way.

Each quadrant of the CASHFLOW Quadrant, offers a different perspective from which to view the world. Those in one quadrant learn differently than those in another quadrant because each quadrant has different values.

For example, employees in the E quadrant value job security and a steady paycheck. Self-employed entrepreneurs value independence and doing things on their own. The B-quadrant entrepreneur works with a team and focuses the team to create assets that produce cash flow. And the I-quadrant person invests in B-quadrant entrepreneurs, because they produce assets that produce more assets. Rarely do they invest in S-quadrant entrepreneurs.

Q: *So those in each quadrant value different types of education?*

A: Yes.

Q: *So, for my second chance, I need to decide what I want to learn. And it's possible that I'll need to unlearn what I've learned.*

A: Yes. Here's a good way to look at it: Two cars cannot fit in a one-car garage. The same is true with education. If you want to increase the size of your world, you may need to increase the size of your garage. When you see both sides of money, you increase the size of your world to a world of greater possibilities.

   I'll repeat a quote from Fuller:

   > *"I have spent most of my life unlearning things that were proved not to be true."*

Q: *So what do I do now?*

A: Decide what's best for you. We are all human beings, which means we are all different. We have different gifts, different intelligences, and different dreams.

In 1973 I had to decide what life was best for me. Would I be better off on the E and S side of life, or the B and I side? Then I had to decide what type of education would take me where I wanted to go. An MBA and a life of working in the E or S quadrants, or life as an entrepreneur in the B and I quadrants?

In 1973, I knew neither choice was going to be easy. I had to decide which choice inspired me to be the best I could be.

And now it is time for you to decide what's best for you.

Lesson from Bucky Fuller

This is what Fuller said about the importance of choice in education:

*"There will come a time when the proper education of children,
by a glorified system of spontaneous education of choice, similar
to the Montessori System, will be made possible."*

Translation: "Why not allow children to decide what they want to learn?"

That is what Steve Jobs did when he dropped out of Reed College. He dropped out of Reed College so that he could *drop back in*, and he dropped in so he could study the subjects *he wanted to study.*

GRUNCH controls the subjects we study. That is why billions of people are in financial crisis today.

When I was nine years old, I asked my teacher,

"When will we learn about money?"

When her answer was "We don't teach you about money in school," I went in search of a teacher who *would* teach me what I wanted to learn, and that is how I found my rich dad.

Fuller also said:

*"Education by choice, with its marvelous motivating
psychology of desire for truth, will make life ever cleaner
and happier, more rhythmical and artistic."*

In other words, true education is our spiritual desire to know the truth.

Lesson for Your Second Chance

Always remember, the rich do not save money. The rich keep their money moving.

Financial education is…

The Opposite Side of the Coin

Life is about choices. And when you position yourself on the edge of the coin, in a spot where you can see both sides, you give yourself the advantage of being able to see how traditional thinking and traditional education are exactly opposite of the path to a rich life.

Keeping your money moving—at high velocity—is the opposite of "parking" your money for the long term.

Chapter Nineteen

THE OPPOSITE OF
"AN EMERGENCY IS BAD"

"The things to do are: the things that need doing, that you see need to be done, and that no one else seems to see need to be done."
— R. Buckminster Fuller

As you know, our world faces many challenges, many much bigger than a financial crisis.

Many people ask, "What is our government going to do about it?"

And I believe that is a major part of our crisis: Too many people expecting our government to solve our problems. Too many people are dependent upon the government for a paycheck.

Fuller did not care much for politics. He said:

"My ideas have undergone a process of emergence by emergency. When they are needed badly enough, they are accepted."

He also said that we had a choice of creating heaven—or hell—on earth. He warned that our generation, not his, would face the biggest crisis of all—a crisis marking the end of the Industrial Age and the beginning of the Information Age.

His forecast was accurate. Today we are all in a giant, global state of emergency.

The good news is that Fuller often spoke on the Generalized Principle of *emergence through emergency*. He explained that out of all *emergencies*, something new and better *emerges*.

He used the example of an unborn chick, still in its shell, panicking as it grows larger, trapped in a tight little shell, with food, air, space, and life support running out. Just when things look the darkest, the chick breaks through its shell and emerges into a whole new world.

Fuller was concerned about whether or not humans would choose to create heaven on earth—or choose oblivion—as we evolved into the future.

He warned us not to be complacent, not to let our politicians determine humanity's future. He warned that the old guard that controlled power would fight to hold on to that power.

Our challenge as we enter this global emergency is: Who determines our future?

I will leave you with these thoughts for your second chance and your future.

Steve Jobs said:

> *"You can't connect the dots looking forward;*
> *you can only connect them looking backwards.*
> *So you have to trust that the dots will somehow connect*
> *in your future."*

To begin your second chance, take some time and look backwards. Then connect the dots and ask yourself, *What in my past is pointing to my future?*

When I asked myself that question, I realized my future began when I raised my hand, in the fourth grade, and asked, "When are we going to learn about money?"

In that same speech, Steve Jobs offered the best advice for these times:

> *"Stay hungry. Stay foolish."*

In 1984, Kim and I did something really *foolish*. We took a leap into the unknown, looking for answers to the same question I had asked decades earlier: Why don't we learn about money in school?

In 1984, Kim and I were very hungry and very foolish.

And Steve Jobs is correct. Being hungry and foolish has been a good thing. If we had not taken our leap of faith into the unknown, we would never have become friends with John Denver, spent an hour with Oprah Winfrey on her television show, co-authored books with Donald Trump, gotten to know Steve Forbes, been granted audiences with world leaders like Shimon Peres, President of Israel, and, most importantly, traveled the world to meet millions of great people like you.

It's been great being hungry and foolish and I have no plans to change the way I operate.

There are a number of questions I would like you to ask yourself:

1. If I connect the dots of my past, where is my future going?

2. When I was a kid, what questions did I want answered?

3. What do I see that needs to be done—and that no one else is doing?

   This is a very important question. Because if you do what needs to be done, without being told how to do it, your true genius will emerge.

4. What cause am I willing to be hungry and foolish for?

5. How much good is my work doing for the world?

That question pushed me over the edge. When I stepped back and looked at my rock-and-roll business, the answer to that question was, "Not much." I was working hard, making money, but not doing much for the world.

When I realized that I was working hard—providing jobs, making money, but not doing much for the world—I knew my days in the rock-and-roll business were numbered. I loved my work, but I knew that working only because I loved what I was doing was greedy.

Not long after I committed to my leap of faith and resigned from my company, I met Kim.

I doubt I would have met her if I were wishy-washy and indecisive about my future. In my heart, I believe god sent her to me, because god knew I as going to need help.

Do the Opposite

Here are a few ideas as you consider your second chance and what that could mean to your life, your spirit, your family, and your future:

1. Rather than look for a job, look for problems that need solving.

2. Rather than work hard for money, work hard to serve more people.

3. Rather than ask god for help, find ways you can help god.

I believe the answers to these questions will guide your second chance.

In closing, I leave you with these words of wisdom from Margaret Mead:

> *"Never doubt that a small group of thoughtful,*
> *committed citizens can change the world;*
> *indeed, it's the only thing that ever has."*

And from Albert Einstein:

> *"We can't solve problems by using the same kind of thinking we used*
> *when we created them.*

And, lastly, from Bucky Fuller:

> *"We are called to be architects of the future, not its victims."*

Lesson for Your Second Chance

How will you emerge from the crises we face? Will the life you create be heaven on earth? Or the opposite? The future is determined by the choices you make.

Financial education is…

The Opposite Side of the Coin

Most people see only the chaos or crisis in an emergency. The opposite side of the coin is the opportunity that lies within every emergency. The opportunity that you can leverage in creating your second chance.

Thank you for reading this book.

— RTK

FINAL THOUGHTS

"What can I do?" Bucky Fuller would ask. "I'm just a little guy..."

Three years after this photo was taken I started to work on what *I* could do.

I believe we need financial education in our schools and available to everyone, rich and poor alike.

We need an educational system that teaches people to learn from their mistakes, rather than be punished for making them.

We need to teach that there are three sides to every coin— heads, tails, and the edge. Three points of view... with the 'edge' representing intelligence and the point where you can see both sides.

In a small way, I believe these three changes to the way we think and act will change our world.

Robert with Bucky Fuller
The Future of Business Event • Kirkwood, California • 1981

AFTERWORD

I know your spirit has incredible power.

I know because if I held your head underwater, your spirit would take over.

This book was written to inspire your spirit, for your spirit to be the driving force of your second chance... a second chance to take control of your money, your life, and our world.

"We are not human beings having a spiritual experience. We are spiritual beings having a human experience."

– Pierre Tielhard de Chardin,
French philosopher

About the Author
Robert Kiyosaki

Best known as the author of *Rich Dad Poor Dad*—the #1 personal finance book of all time—Robert Kiyosaki has challenged and changed the way tens of millions of people around the world think about money. He is an entrepreneur, educator, and investor who believes the world needs more entrepreneurs who will create jobs.

With perspectives on money and investing that often contradict conventional wisdom, Robert has earned an international reputation for straight talk, irreverence, and courage and has become a passionate and outspoken advocate for financial education.

Robert and Kim Kiyosaki are founders of The Rich Dad Company, a financial education company, and creators of the *CASHFLOW*® games. In 2014, the company will leverage the global success of the Rich Dad games in the launch of a new and breakthrough offering in mobile and online gaming.

Robert has been heralded as a visionary who has a gift for simplifying complex concepts—ideas related to money, investing, finance, and economics—and has shared his personal journey to financial freedom in ways that resonate with audiences of all ages and backgrounds. His core principles and messages—like "your house is not an asset" and "invest for cash flow" and "savers are losers"—have ignited a firestorm of criticism and ridicule... only to have played out on the world economic stage over the past decade in ways that were both unsettling and prophetic.

His point of view is that "old" advice—go to college, get a good job, save money, get out of debt, invest for the long term, and diversify—has become obsolete advice in today's fast-paced Information Age. His Rich Dad philosophies and messages challenge the status quo. His teachings encourage people to become financially educated and to take an active role in investing for their future.

The author of 19 books, including the international blockbuster *Rich Dad Poor Dad*, Robert has been a featured guest with media outlets in every corner of the world— from CNN, the BBC, Fox News, Al Jazeera, GBTV and PBS, to *Larry King Live*, *Oprah*, *Peoples Daily*, *Sydney Morning Herald*, *The Doctors*, *Straits Times*, *Bloomberg*, *NPR*, *USA TODAY*, and hundreds of others—and his books have topped international bestsellers lists for more than a decade. He continues to teach and inspire audiences around the world.

His most recent books include *Unfair Advantage: The Power of Financial Education*, *Midas Touch*, the second book he has co-authored with Donald Trump, and *Why "A" Students Work for "C" Students*.

To learn more, visit RichDad.com

The Rich Dad Company's
SECOND CHANCE

Let the Games Begin!

The Rich Dad Company has been around since 1997. We've had amazing successes and have changed millions of lives. We have focused on our mission—to elevate the financial well being of humanity—and done so through every vehicle possible. We offered books to read, board games to play, seminars to attend, and even coaches to guide you through the process.

And while the world-wide success was great, we realized that the world was changing.

Robert likes to cite a quote from Joel Barker: "Your past success guarantees nothing in your future." We had started to focus on our past successes and stopped looking to the future. We knew we had to change that. And, whenever you look to the future, reviewing Buckminster Fuller is always a great place to start.

One of Bucky Fuller's Generalized Principles is, "The more people I serve, the more effective I become."

The key to the future had become very clear. We needed to serve more people. We have always focused on serving more people first. It is why Robert and Kim created the *CASHFLOW* board game in the first place. It's why they wrote books, instead of focusing only on seminars.

To serve more people we needed to put another of Bucky's Generalized Principles into action: ephemeralization.

Ephemeralizarion is doing more with less. How could we get the Rich Dad messages to more people? How could we do it better—and do it for less? If we could figure a way to do it for less, then we knew we would be able to reach more people.

In 2011, The Rich Dad Company solved the ephemeralization riddle and entered a new creative arena.

Rich Dad President Shane Caniglia saw the future of the company, the future of personal interaction, and a future of spreading the message of financial independence. His vision: Digital Gaming.

Evolving technology and the explosion of mobile apps is an opportunity that could give The Rich Dad Company a "second chance," a way to revitalize and re-energize our ability to engage a new, younger and more tech-savvy audience, while making sure we continued to serve our loyal, existing community.

What made this exciting is that what he saw as the future was actually our past. It's a bit of little-known Rich Dad trivia that the company's first product was our board game *CASHFLOW*. The book—*Rich Dad Poor Dad*, a 1997 release that has become an international bestseller and the #1 Personal Finance book of all time—was actually written as a 'brochure' to market and sell the *CASHFLOW* game.

The questions were: How do you enter the digital gaming world? With the mobile space awash with thousands upon thousands of apps, how can you set yourself apart?

The first step was to remember our mission and keep it at the forefront of our efforts in app development. We knew we had to further the mission of educating the world and elevating the financial well-being of people everywhere. There will always be those who have the potential to break out of their Rat-Race lives, lives ruled by 9-to-5 jobs and living paycheck-to-paycheck as someone else's asset. Lives where their dreams are something that only happens in their sleep.

As we began the development process we focused on two foundational beliefs:

- Mission should guide us

- Produce a quality product and success will follow

The core development team headed to the GDC (Game Developer's Conference) to take stock of the industry's direction, gain new insights, and search for contacts that might become allies in delivering our message.

As with many searches, what you find isn't always what you need. The team met a contact at the GDC who claimed to understand the Rich Dad messages. They made promises about delivery, messaging, and respecting the spirit of the brand.

We spent many hours exchanging emails and having conference calls to determine if it was a fit. We took multiple trips to visit their studio and meet their team and had them fly out to Phoenix for meetings with our entire team at Rich Dad. This company's founder had a great reputation within the gaming industry—as a consultant. The company touted its expertise in making games more fun and capitalizing on the psychology of the casual gamer.

We were excited about starting out on this endeavor with our new partner. We started conceptualizing: What game mechanics were we looking for? Did we want to create an iteration of the *CASHFLOW* board game, or come up with something entirely new? Was a hybrid the answer? Ideas and plans began to take shape.

We saw some cracks began to start. Once the "courtship" stage was over, we got a better look at the company we had engaged for this project. As milestones were missed, or only half-met, the reasons and excuses began to pile up. We quickly became concerned. We were in a pinch. Do we stop now… or press on, since we'd already started? We had already chosen and charted our path with this partner and we didn't have the in-house expertise to challenge our partner or even validate our concerns.

To alleviate our concerns, we put out feelers to those close to Rich Dad and we were able to find someone with the right experience in the game industry—and someone who embraced the Rich Dad ideals. He had worked his way up through some top-tier game development companies, founded gaming companies of his own, and then sold them. Best of all, he was an associate of someone close to The Rich Dad Company and we were very confident in his experience and his ability to mesh with our team.

With our new in-house expert onboard, he quickly assessed our partner's strengths and capabilities. Our fears were legitimized. Instead of continuing to see if the stone could swim, we cut ties with that partner and moved on.

As with many "second chances," this new journey wasn't quite as easy or hassle-free as we had anticipated. It stretched us beyond what was comfortable. But we knew we had an incredible opportunity and knew we couldn't quit. We acknowledged our mistakes, found the lessons in them and made the necessary changes. It happens. It was expensive. But we learned a lot.

While this initial setback would discourage many teams, the Rich Dad philosophy once again created an opportunity when most would see a failure. We now knew what to be aware of in future developer partnerships. The first partner had been given too much latitude and too much autonomy. They had claimed to understand our message, but it became clear that they were just paying us lip service.

The Rich Dad dev team began its search again, from the ground up. They understood that they couldn't simply step into the marketplace and trust the first smiling "friend" to step up. This new search led to the relationship with a game developer agency. Like most industries, there are those who have inside knowledge and, if you can leverage that knowledge, you can avoid the pitfalls that others are forced to navigate. This dev agency knew the industry. The agency knew all the best development studios and they knew who would be a good fit for the vision the Rich Dad game.

The search began with a list of 25 studios we thought could bring our concept into the world. From those 25, 14 submitted proposals we found acceptable. Only seven were a fit with the culture and mindset of Rich Dad.

We could have simply reviewed the proposals, made some conference calls, and picked the first studio that "worked" and met our requirements. But we had learned from our past mistakes; we knew we had to dig deeper. We crisscrossed the country, met personally with each studio, toured their facilities, reviewed their past games and apps, interviewed their teams and got to know them on a ground level. Only when we knew in our bones that we had the right team did we make a selection.

This does not mean it was easy or even smooth. We created six different versions of our game. Every time we'd make one we'd ask ourselves, "How can we make it better?" We never asked how we could make it "the best." The best means you've stopped. It means you're finished. Making it better is an ongoing task that goes past the initial release and into the updates, refinements, communication improvements, and enhanced learning. It's a process that never ends.

And we needed to make sure we stayed true to the brand. When you are making a game with tanks and hovercrafts and futuristic buildings, it can be a challenge to make it teach our core principles of passive income and assets. The hardest part of all was learning how to balance fun with learning. This created much debate and strife within the team. Where was that perfect balance?

As we continued in the process of game development, "make it better" became our mantra. We vowed to never settle. And "making it better" didn't just apply to the game. It applied to everything in our app and game world. We found contacts at Apple and asked ourselves: How could we make that relationship better? We brought in consultants and advisors and challenged ourselves: How could we make this larger team better? How could we make our partners better? And, most importantly, we wanted to make sure that the game continued to get better and better with every iteration. In today's world, financial literacy is a serious and growing problem and we were committed to addressing that need in a new way with a new game.

On June 15, 2014, the *Capital City* game launched on iOS and Android. It was an important milestone for The Rich Dad Company that reflected a major achievement that resulted from a challenging two-year project. Through the lessons we learned and the team we assembled, we developed a few other new apps along the way—all created to spread our message and our mission.

We produced an app that is a direct replica of the *CASHFLOW* board game called: *CASHFLOW–The Investing* Game. This game entered the Apple Store's Finance category at #1. It still holds that ranking to this day.

Through the journey of creating *Capital City*, we also created *Rich Dad Poor Dad* powered by Clutch Learning. This app condensed all of the lessons from Robert's international best-selling book and turned them into mini-games, animations, videos, and interactive exercises—all in an attempt to "gamify" learning. We also created a financial statement to accompany our board game and a radio show app (for The Rich Dad Radio Show) so you can listen to the Rich Dad Radio Show anytime, anywhere.

All of these apps were a result of the process and learning that took place making *Capital City*. They are a direct result of seizing opportunities for a "second chance" and creating a future in which we could serve more people.

Creating these apps taught us lessons that we applied in the production of *Capital City* and gave us a chance to show Apple the high-quality work we were committed to producing. The result? Apple, a leader known for its high industry standards that often led to apps being rejected, trusted our relationship and the strength of the Rich Dad brand and approved *Capital City* at record speed. It debuted at #3 in the Games/Educational category—a major feat in a marketplace made up of millions of apps.

And we're not done.

While we feel these apps are good, maybe even great, we are committed to continuously making them better and applying the lessons we've learned for future apps. Robert often tells us that our job is to do more with less and serve more people around the world. The Rich Dad Company is committed to financial education and believes that learning should be fun… and that games and apps are the future of learning for generations to come.

References
&
Resources

Books by Kim Kiyosaki

Rich Woman
Because I Hate Being Told What to Do

It's Rising Time!
What It Really Takes for the Reward of Financial Freedom

Books by Robert Kiyosaki and Donald Trump

Why We Want You To Be Rich
Two Men • One Message

Midas Touch
Why Some Entrepreneurs Get Rich—and Why Most Don't

Rich Dad's Advisor Books

Blair Singer
SalesDogs
You Don't Have to Be an Attack
Dog to Explode Your Income

Team Code of Honor
The Secrets of Champions in Business and in Life

Ken McElroy
The ABCs of Real Estate Investing
The Secrets of Finding Hidden Profits
Most Investors Miss

Advanced Guide to Real Estate Investing
How to Identify the Hottest Markets
and Secure the Best Deals

Tom Wheelwright, CPA
Tax-Free Wealth
How to Build Massive Wealth by
Permanently Lowering Your Taxes

Andy Tanner
Stock Market Cash Flow
Four Pillars of Investing for
Thriving in Today's Markets

Josh and Lisa Lannon
The Social Capitalist
Passion and Profits—An Entrepreneurial Journey

Rich Dad's Advisor Books

Garrett Sutton, Esq.

Start Your Own Corporation
Why the Rich Own their Own Companies
and Everyone Else Works for Them

Writing Winning Business Plans
How to Prepare a Business Plan that Investors will
Want to Read – and Invest In

Buying & Selling a Business
How You Can Win in the Business Quadrant

The ABCs of Getting Out of Debt
Turn Bad Debt into Good Debt and
Bad Credit into Good Credit

Run Your Own Corporation
How to Legally Operate and
Properly Maintain Your Company into the Future

Loopholes of Real Estate
Secrets of Successful Real Estate Investing

INCOME STATEMENT

Income
Expenses

BALANCE SHEET

Assets	Liabilities

INCOME STATEMENT

1 Income

Description	Cash Flow
Salary:	
Interest/Dividends:	
Real Estate/Business:	

Profession

Dream

Auditor
(Person on your right)

$	Salary

+

$	Passive Income

(Cash Flow from Interest/Dividends
and Real Estate/Business)

= | $ | Total Income |

If **Passive Income** is greater than **Total Expenses**, you're out of the Rat Race!

—

$	Total Expenses

= | $ | |

PAYDAY

Monthly Cash Flow

2 Expenses

Taxes:	
Home Mortgage Payment:	
School Loan Payment:	
Car Loan Payment:	
Credit Card Payment:	
Other Expenses:	
Bank Loan Payment: (10% of Bank Loan Total)	
Per Child Expense: ____ **x** (# of Children):	

BALANCE SHEET

3 Assets

Savings:		
Precious Metals, Etc.:		
Stocks/Funds/CDs:	# of Shares:	Cost/Share:
Real Estate/Business:	Down Payment:	Cost:

4 Liabilities

Home Mortgage:	
School Loans:	
Car Loans:	
Credit Card Debt:	
Bank Loan:	
Real Estate/Business:	Mortgage/Liability:

This Financial Statement is used in the *CASHFLOW* game.

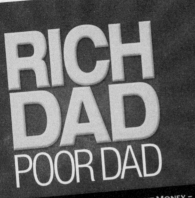

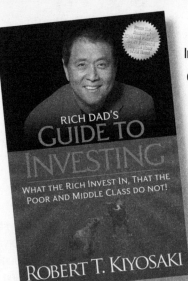

UNFAIR advantage
THE POWER OF FINANCIAL EDUCATION

CAC107
$18.26

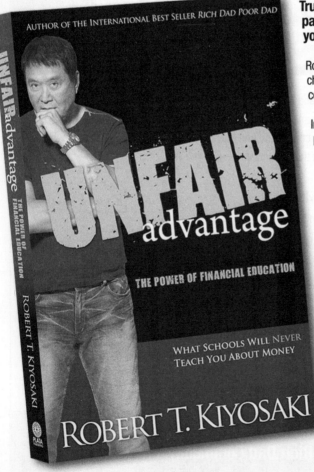

True financial education is the path to creating the life you want for yourself and your family.

Robert encourages and inspires you to change the one thing that is within your control: yourself.

In Unfair Advantage, Robert challenges people around the world to stop blindly accepting that they are destined to struggle financially all their lives.

This book is about the power of financial education and the five Unfair Advantages that real financial education offers:

The Unfair Advantage of Knowledge
The Unfair Advantage of Taxes
The Unfair Advantage of Debt
The Unfair Advantage of Risk
The Unfair Advantage of Compensation

In true Rich Dad style, *Unfair Advantage* challenges readers to appreciate two points of view and experience how the power of real financial education is their unfair advantage.

www.richdad.com